# The project manager as change agent

# The project manager as change agent

Leadership, influence and negotiation

Composed and edited by

## J. Rodney Turner, Kristoffer V. Grude and Lynn Thurloway

THE McGRAW-HILL COMPANIES

**London** · New York · St Louis · San Francisco · Auckland
Bogotá · Caracas · Lisbon · Madrid · Mexico
Milan · Montreal · New Delhi · Panama · Paris · San Juan
São Paulo · Singapore · Sydney · Tokyo · Toronto

Published by
McGRAW-HILL Publishing Company
Shoppenhangers Road, Maidenhead, Berkshire, SL6 2QL, England
Telephone 01628 23432
Fax 01628 770224

---

**British Library Cataloguing in Publication Data**
Turner, Rodney
    The project manager as change agent: leadership, influence and
negotiation
    1. Industrial project management    2. Organizational change
    I. Title   II. Grude, Kristoffer V.    III. Thurloway, Lynn
658.4'04

ISBN 0-07-707741-5

**Library of Congress Cataloging-in-Publication Data**
Turner, J. Rodney (John Rodney),
    The project manager as change agent: leadership, influence and nego-
tiation/composed and edited by J. Rodney Turner, Kristoffer V. Grude
and Lynn Thurloway.
        p.    cm.
    ISBN 0-07-707741-5
    1. Industrial project management.    2. Organization change.
3. Leadership.    I. Grude, Kristoffer V.    II. Thurloway, Lynn.
III. Title.
HD69.P75T853    1996
658.4'04—dc20                                                      96-562
                                                                    CIP

*McGraw-Hill*

A Division of The McGraw-Hill Companies

12345   CUP   99876

Typeset by Alden Bookset Ltd
and printed and bound in Great Britain at the University Press, Cambridge.

Printed on permanent paper in compliance with ISO Standard 9706.

*To Georgina: A baby sister for Edward*

# Contents

# Foreword

Anthony Reid
*Principal Consultant, Management Achievement*
*Co-ordinator, Project Organization and Teamworking Special Interest Group*
*Association of Project Managers*

Project management has become the panacea for resolving all complexities and difficulties in larger organizations, be they the health service, financial institutions, retailing corporations or providers of computer services.

The recognition that a project management approach has a part to play in making goals come to fruition and in helping to resolve problems has highlighted the very special contribution of the project manager in his or her own right.

It gives me great pleasure to introduce *The Project Manager as Change Agent*. It is the first attempt to recognize and to demonstrate the potential scope of this important role and the range of likely skills and attributes that are necessary to fulfil the related responsibilities.

It is a timely presentation and amply put together. The book emphasizes the continual process of change against which we all maintain a perpetual battle – but change goes on relentlessly and gradually undermines all resistance.

The concept of visualizing what you want, facing up to where you are, and deciding what steps are necessary to close the gap, is not new. Adapting a project management approach for each step change is only now coming to be recognized as the 'management process' that will make the intention become reality.

Four needs that come through the book very clearly and which are fundamental for all circumstances of change are:

1. The necessity to identify all of the stakeholders as drivers and often obstacles to change, from both internal and external forces.
2. The need for building strong linkages between project output and organizational strategy – often the most demanding challenge for the project manager.
3. That survival is about versatility and adapting to new circumstances, be it competition, customer desires or new approaches.
4. Project groups or teams are often made up of disparate individuals, frequently all experts in their own fields, who have been pressed into service. Building team performance is one of the key requirements for

implementing change processes – using the project manager as the change agent provides the potential for success.

This book covers the subject well, with references from ancient philosophy 'there is nothing more difficult to arrange, more doubtful of success and more dangerous to carry out, than initiating change in a state's constitution!' to more recent observations from modern gurus, e.g. Handy's criteria for effective managers.

The strongest message is the need for some fundamental requirements if the change process is to happen and the project manager is able to make an effective and useful contribution. There must be:

- an organizational belief and support system
- a project champion who will fight the cause at the boardroom table and maintain the relationship with honour
- the cultural change or evolution which is designed to suit the nature of the business and its desires, and which must be reflected through a system of appropriate values, beliefs and behaviours.

This series of stories encapsulates the potential power of the role as change agent for the project manager. It identifies, develops and illustrates the means to break out of organizational rigidity, fear, submission and weakness, by harnessing the power of vision, commitment, belief and behaviour modelling.

The outcome of such radical change is increasingly evidenced in those new organizations that now experience partnership, mutual endurance and, in consequence, happiness with success for all of the participants.

This book will be successful. Readers will find their commitment well rewarded.

# Preface

The modern view of project management is that it is the management of change. Books arm project managers with quantitative tools to bring projects to a successful conclusion, delivering the required performance on time and within budget. However, they often ignore the role of the project manager as a manager of people. Where books do deal with this, they describe the manager's role as the manager of a team; that is, they deal only with his or her role in managing downwards, leading the team working on the project. The manager must also manage outwards and upwards to win support for the project from a whole raft of people. Without their support, the change being introduced may never happen, or, if it does, it may not achieve its stated purpose and objectives. This book aims to provide project managers with tools to manage the people without whose support their projects will not be successful. Project managers must manage in three fundamental directions (Fig. 0.1):

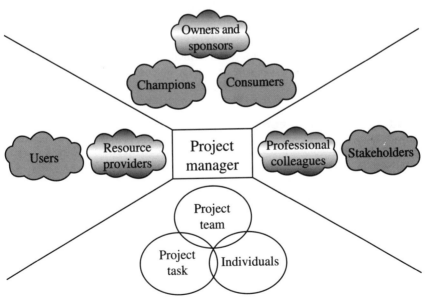

**Figure 0.1** The project manager at the centre of change

1. *Downwards* Providing leadership to their teams, and the individuals in them.
2. *Outwards* Influencing the organization and negotiating support from their peers within the organization, who may include professional colleagues, resource providers, users of the facility produced by the project and other people affected by it.
3. *Upwards* Fulfilling an ambassadorial role for the project, and gaining support from the people occupying positions of power and authority. These people include: owners and sponsors; champions; and consumers of the product produced by the facility.

To fulfil these management roles effectively, project managers must also understand and be able to manage:

- The nature of change
- The culture of projects

## The nature of change

Part 1 deals with the nature of change. Chapter 1 explains the drivers for change, the strategic need that forces change on us. Chapter 2 describes how to diagnose change within an organization, to design the change required and to identify barriers to change. Chapter 3 identifies the role of projects in delivering the required change. Chapter 4 describes how to organize for change. We describe *process management*, a versatile approach to achieving customer requirements, which uses internal procedures as guidelines but which adapts them to meet differing customer requirements, and updates them as the organization learns from experience.

## Leading the organization

Part 2 explains how project managers must provide leadership to the organization, by managing in the three directions described above. Chapter 5 introduces project teams and team roles, and describes how to develop effective teams and how to achieve the best out of the individuals in the team. Chapter 6 describes the role of the manager in greater detail, and considers the styles and traits of effective managers and leaders, decision making and problem solving. Chapter 7 describes *internal marketing*, how to market your project within the organization to win support. Chapter 8 explains the ambassadorial role, influencing the organization, how to develop a stakeholder management strategy, and the role of the *project champion*.

## The culture of projects and project management

Part 3 explains the nature of projects, the way people work on projects and the skills required of them as a project manager. Chapter 9 explains the link between project cultures and project structures. Chapter 10 describes approaches to the management of different cultures on projects. Chapter 11 considers ethics and the project manager. Chapter 12 describes the link between project management and *environmental management*, showing both how good environmental management makes both moral sense and business sense. Chapter 13 explains how you can conduct a project health check to assess your own position.

## Case studies

Part 4 contains several case studies explaining the role of the project manager as change agent. Chapter 14 describes the management of significant strategic change in two insurance companies following changes in the UK insurance industry. Chapter 15 describes changes in the Norwegian defences resulting from the peace dividend.

This book covers these areas by introducing concepts, and illustrating the concepts with case studies. It aims to provide managers with a toolbox of 'soft' management skills, to add to the 'hard' skills they will read about in more traditional books on project management.

The book is aimed at practising managers from a full range of industries and sectors and from all levels:

- Managers of organizational change in a general management environment, as well as managers of traditional engineering or computer projects
- Managers from the public and private sectors
- Managers from government, finance and communications industries, as well as traditional construction and manufacturing industries
- Project managers who need to understand their role at the centre of the organization, team leaders and members who aspire to be project managers and who need to understand the pressures facing their manager, and senior managers who need to understand the pressures facing the managers working for them and the support they must give to the projects they sponsor and champion

The book is also aimed at students on masters courses in management (MBAs and MScs) and students on final-year undergraduate courses who aspire to a career in management.

# Acknowledgements

Our primary thanks go to all the people who have contributed to the text of this book, including: Phil Austin, Wendy Briner, Colin Carnall, Susan Foreman, Eric Gabriel, Alistair Godbold, Bob Graham, Tony Grundy, Colin Hastings, Reza Peymai, Suzanne Pollock, David Rees, Mahen Tampoe, Frank Tyrrell and John Wateridge.

We would also like to thank Patricia Hyde for drawing some of the figures, and Alison Pyper for providing general support, including much faxing of information and some scanning of documents.

We also are forever grateful for the support of our partners, Beverley, Helena and Suleman.

Rodney Turner        Kristoffer Grude        Lynn Thurloway
East Horsley          Droebak            Hammersmith

# Authors' profiles

*Rodney Turner* is Professor and Director of Project Management at Henley Management College, with responsibility for masters degrees, short courses and research in project management. He is also tutor for fellows sponsored by the Engineering Construction Industry Training Board. After graduating from the University of Oxford, he spent several years with ICI working on engineering design, construction and maintenance projects in the petrochemical industry. He worked as a consultant in project management with Coopers & Lybrand before joining Henley Management College in 1989. He still works as a consultant, lectures worldwide, and has published several books and papers on project management. Rodney edits the *International Journal of Project Management*, and is a Council member of the Association of Project Managers with responsibility for international liaison. He is APMs representative on a group working to establish international accreditation of project managers. Previous books by Rodney Turner include: *Goal Directed Project Management*, Kogan Page (1987; reprinted 1988, 1989, 1990, 1991, 1992 (twice) and 1994), with E.S. Andersen, K.V. Grude and T. Haug; *The Handbook of Project-based Management: Improving the processes of achieving your strategic objectives*, McGraw-Hill (1993; reprinted 1993 (twice)); *The Commercial Project Manager: Managing Owners, Sponsors, Partners, Supporters, Stakeholders, Contractors and Consultants*, McGraw-Hill (1995).

*Kristoffer Grude* is a consultant and director of a consultancy providing advice on Business Planning and the Management of Change. Previously he was founding partner and managing director of Coopers & Lybrand's management consultancy in Norway. There he specialized in the management of organizational change projects, advising the Norwegian government and major Norwegian companies, as well as others throughout Europe. He was a member of C&L's European Management Consultancy Services Committee and leader of the Centre of Excellence for project management. Before joining C&L, he was founding partner of PSO Management Consultants, and partner and deputy managing director of Data Logic, a Norwegian software house. He and his fellow partners rescued the company after a management buy-out. Kristoffer has a masters degree from the Norwegian School of Management.

Previous books by Kristoffer Grude include: *Goal Directed Project Management,* Kogan Page (1987; reprinted 1988, 1989, 1990, 1991, 1992 (twice) and 1994), with E.S. Andersen, T. Haug and J.R. Turner. The Norwegian version of this book (by Andersen, Grude and Haug), first published in 1984, has run to three editions, and has been translated into Swedish and Danish. The English version (also written with Professor Turner) has been translated into Dutch and Italian, and is about to appear in a second edition; *Successful Computer Selection,* Norway (1985), with E.S. Andersen and A. Aaroe.

*Lynn Thurloway* joined Henley Management College in 1990. She teaches Project Leadership, Managing Strategic Change and Organizational Behaviour on the MBA/MSc in Project Management, the general MBA and corporate and executive development programmes. Lynn has an MSc in Management from Imperial College and a BA in Applied Social Sciences from Kingston. She is undertaking research for a PhD. Her area of research is the impact of new technology within the office. She is also doing research on project management, and has published papers in the *International Journal of Project Management.*

*Phil Austin* is an independent management consultant, founder of Austin Hall Consulting. He has an MBA from Henley Management College, and is working towards a DBA (Doctor of Business Administration). His interests are in corporate turn-around, especially of engineering companies, industrial marketing, TQM and competitive improvement. He has a BSc in Mechanical Engineering.

*Wendy Briner* is a founding partner of New Organization Consulting, which helps client organizations to use a combination of organizational team working, individual development, and project-based ways of working to help them improve their performance. She is also working with a team of consultants in Berlin who offer training for internal consultants. Wendy works with growing organizations such as Conran Roche and Sun Microsystems, as well as larger organizations in the midst of major transitions, such as BT, Thames Water, and Prudential. Previously she worked for Ashridge Management College, as Business Director for Team-working Services, part of the Ashridge Consulting Group. In this role she became interested in team working across different cultures and national boundaries. Wendy is co-author of Project Leadership with Colin Hastings and Michael Geddes, and has published several articles on project management and organizational change. She has contributed to international conferences, and lectures on the MBA programmes at City University and Henley Management College.

*Colin Carnall* is Director of Programmes and Professor of Management at Henley Management College, where he has been since 1974. He is also Dean of Henley-Nederland and a member of Mid-Downs Health Authority. He is an external examiner on the MBA programmes at Middlesex Business School and Cardiff Business School. Colin trained and worked as an engineer in industry and spent two years at Bradford Management School before joining Henley. He teaches and consults in managing change. His clients include British Airways, Shell, Esso, the National Health Service, the Home Office and many others.

*Susan Foreman* joined the marketing faculty at Henley Management College in 1990 and is now lead tutor in marketing. She teaches on the MBA programmes and executive courses. She has an MSc in Marketing from the Manchester School of Management at UMIST, and has recently completed a PhD. Susan's research and consulting interests are in the area of internal marketing, services marketing and transaction cost approaches to marketing theory. She has written many papers for international conferences, journals and elsewhere. In 1992 and 1993, Susan spent two periods as visiting senior lecturer in Services Marketing at the Graduate School of Business, University of Cape Town.

*Eric Gabriel* is a chartered mechanical engineer. His experience is in managing projects in the power and petrochemical industries. Latterly he has worked in the building industry, and was client's project manager for the Sainsbury Wing of the National Gallery, for new sculpture galleries for the Henry Moore Foundation and for the new Glyndebourne Opera House. He was president of the International Project Management Association from 1985 to 1988, and is a vice-president of the Association of project managers.

*Bob Graham* has been an independent management consultant since the late 1980s. Previously, he was a professor at the Wharton School at the University of Pennsylvania, where he taught operations research. From 1987 to 1988 he was guest professor at the University of the Bundeswehr in Munich, Germany. He has a BS in Systems Analysis, an MBA and PhD in Business Administration, and an MSc in Cultural Anthropology. He is the author of a book, *Project Management as if People Mattered,* and a computer simulation, *The Complete Project Manager.*

*Alistair Godbold* is a project manager with the Scottish Projects Division of the National Air Traffic Service. He has an MBA in project management from Henley Management College and his dissertation was on ethics in project management. He has organized seminars on ethics in business for the Civil Aviation Authority. He is a graduate in computer science.

*Tony Grundy* is a consultant in strategy, change management and marketing development, working with a large number of blue-chip companies. After taking a Behavioural Sciences degree at Cambridge, Tony Grundy became a chartered accountant, qualifying with Ernst and Young in London. He then worked with BP in finance and planning and control of international projects, before becoming UK Finance Director of a European retailer. He then moved to KPMG, where he worked as a consultant in business and financial planning, and restructuring. During this time he took an MBA at City University. Following a spell as a strategy consultant with PA, he became an associate of Cranfield University's School of Management, and he established his own successful consultancy. At Cranfield, he has completed a PhD in Linking Strategic and Financial Management. He is author of *Corporate Strategy and Financial Decision* and *Implementing Strategic Change*. He lectures at Henley Management College, Cambridge University and City Business School.

*Colin Hastings* is a consultant, author, teacher and speaker. He spent ten years in management, and nine years on the faculty of Ashridge Management College, before founding New Organization Consulting in 1987. As a consultant, he focuses on the management of change, project-based ways of working, cross-boundary team working, and new organizational forms. Clients include Rank Xerox, the World Health Organization, BP and Safeway. He is co-author of *Superteams* and *Project Leadership* and author of *The new organization*. He has lectured at many international conferences.

*Reza Peymai* is director of a small business importing specialist food. He has an MBA in project management from Henley Management College, and was for many years quality manager with Kyle Stewart, a medium-sized construction company. The subject of his masters dissertation was the application of process management to the achievement of quality in the construction industry.

*Suzanne Pollock* is Director of Corporate Qualification Programmes and head of the environmental faculty at Henley Management College. She joined the college in 1987, after completing a PhD in Managing Strategic Change and established the certificate and diploma programmes. Her area of interest is in personal skills development, and she has undertaken consultancy assignments for Outward Bound trust, Standard Chartered Bank, Arjo Wiggins Appleton and Rover Group. Recently, she has developed an interest in environmental management. She has developed course materials for the college, written *Improving Environmental Performance* and co-edited *The Environmental Management Handbook*. She has provided environmental management courses for Shell, Grand Metropolitan, John Brown and Rover Group.

*David Rees* is founding director of the Centre for International Communication in Christchurch, Dorset, which offers a range of services including language training, translating and interpreting, cultural briefing, language trainer development, communications training, and international project management. After five years with British Telecom, David worked as a lecturer at the West London Institute and Guildford College of Technology. He obtained a postgraduate Diploma in Economics from Middlesex University and an MBA from Henley Management College. He is now a visiting teaching fellow and member of the Associate Faculty at Henley, where he tutors in Managing People and Managing Strategic Change. David is a member of the British Institute of Management and the Institute of Training and Development. His research interests are in European Management and he is co-author of *Managing People across Europe*.

*Mahen Tampoe* is a consultant in strategic change whose clients include privatized utilities and financial institutions. He trained as an accountant before joining ICL. For eighteen years he was director of ICL's Information Technology Centre in Dublin. He is a member of the Chartered Institute of Management Accountants and has an MBA and PhD from Henley Management College. His research was in the management of knowledge-based organizations. He lectures at Henley, the Civil Service College and London Business School. He has articles published on project management and the management of knowledge workers.

*Frank Tyrrell* is a founding partner of New Organization Consulting, providing consultancy services in the management of change, project-based ways of working, cross-boundary team working, and new organizational forms. Clients include Rank Xerox, the World Health Organization, BP, Safeway and organizations from the financial services sector, including Norwich Union.

*John Wateridge* is a senior lecturer in the Department of Management Systems at Bournemouth University, where he teaches on undergraduate courses, particularly in systems analysis and project management. Before joining Bournemouth University, he worked for ten years as a programmer, systems analyst and project manager on software development projects. He is currently undertaking part-time research at Henley Management College into criteria and associated factors for delivering successful IT projects, and the appropriate methodologies and skills required by IT project managers. He has presented papers at several conferences and published in the *International Journal of Project Management*.

# PART ONE
# CHANGE IN THE
# CONTEXT OF
# ORGANIZATIONS

---

Part One looks at change in the context of organizations and how it is managed.

In Chapter 1, Kristoffer Grude and Rodney Turner identify change as an inherent part of human life and hence an essential part of corporate strategy. They explain why change is inevitable and yet it is in the nature of people to resist it. They consider how the nature of the resistance encountered will vary between normal levels of change and more extreme levels. However, in both cases, the resistance is predictable and should therefore be planned for and managed. This is the role of the *change agent*.

In Chapter 2, Colin Carnall and Rodney Turner describe diagnostic techniques. There are three types conventionally used in the management of change. The first helps diagnose the organization's need to change; identifying strengths and weaknesses of the current operation and opportunities and threats from the competitive environment. These form the basis of strategic analysis, describing how an organization must change to remain competitive in its market place. The second technique helps diagnose the organization's ability to change; identifying pressures reinforcing change and barriers to it. It also helps diagnose the readiness of the people in the organization to change; identifying their expected reaction and their willingness to accept it. The third helps the project manager as change agent identify his or her own effectiveness in that role. In Part 4, we introduce further diagnostic techniques, namely project health checks, to help diagnose the effectiveness of projects and project management to bring the desired change about and to achieve the stated objectives.

In Chapter 3, Tony Grundy, Rodney Turner and Kristoffer Grude describe project-based management as a process for implementing change. They show that the processes used need not be the overly complicated approaches often proposed by traditional project managers (project management as 'rocket science'), but that a simple application of the concepts of project management, based on goal-directed approaches, can provide a powerful vehicle for implementing change. They show how to convert business strategy into the definition of change required, and thence into a project, and how to use the principles of goal-directed project management to plan and manage the change. They illustrate the approach by an example which, though based on an actual project, has been developed for the purpose. Actual examples of change projects in practice are given in Part 5.

In Chapter 4, Rodney Turner and Reza Peymai describe a versatile approach to structuring the work of an organization, with flexible process and project teams managing the routine and novel work respectively. The traditional approach to the management of projects and routine work is a functional approach. The final product moves through different functions of the organization until it is delivered to the customer. Early functions have no contact with the customer; worse, they often have no contact with subsequent functions, in what is dubbed 'over-the-wall' or 'relay-race' management. Customer focus and quality suffer. In process management, the management follows the product through the organization delivering a product the customer wants and needs, and the management approaches are adapted, if necessary, to achieve that. This leads to the proposal of the versatile organization with process teams for managing routine work and project teams, following a process approach, for managing non-routine work.

# 1
# Managing change

Kristoffer Grude and Rodney Turner

## 1.1 Introduction

All is change, nothing is permanent. *Heracleitus* (513BC).[1]

This quotation has become something of a cliché, being alluded to by many modern writers on management such as Rosabeth Moss Kanter, Peter Drucker, Charles Handy, Tom Peters, Michael Porter and others, saying that we should be continually ready to respond to change (and that in the process we should adopt their remedies for identifying and managing change). What is perhaps surprising is that the quotation is about 2500 years old! For nearly three millennia there has been nothing permanent except change itself, so we can fairly predict that it will continue to be so for our lifetimes. Hence the only certainty in our management careers is that we will be involved in change and that we will have to manage change.

In this chapter, we consider what creates the need for organizations to change, but also give a word of caution that organizations should not change for change's sake. We consider the reaction of people to change and in particular their reaction to 'normal' levels of change and to 'extreme', 'life-threatening' levels of change. From this we deduce the need for the change agent to manage the totality of the change process, but in particular, in the context of this book, the reaction of the people within the organization to that process.

## 1.2 The need to change

If you put a frog in water and slowly heat it, the frog will eventually let itself be boiled to death. We, too, will not survive if we do not respond to the way the world is changing.[2]

There are two elements to this quotation:

- The world is changing and if the organization does not respond it will die
- Often we will not notice the change in the outside world occurring and that makes it more difficult to make people respond to changes they have not perceived.

Corporate strategy used to be a simple process, the upper loop in Fig. 1.1. Managers identified the competitive pressures facing their organizations and changed their organizations to respond to those pressures. The changes were usually small compared to the total size of the operation and so could be undertaken as an evolution of the business in what was sometimes called Habitual Incremental Improvement – small adjustments to the sail and the tiller to take advantage of small changes in wind direction. That changed in the late 1970s to early 1980s; the competitive environment became more turbulent and larger, faster, more significant changes were required. Organizations became caught in a triple whammy:

1. Due to internationalization and liberalization of the marketplace, competition became increasingly tougher. In sector after sector profit margins were being squeezed by broadening competition.
2. Yet customers became more demanding, wanting:
   - Better service
   - Shorter delivery times
   - Higher quality
   - Lower prices
   and recognizing their power customers began to make quite unreasonable demands on their suppliers with every expectation of them being fulfilled.
3. At the same time, organizations needed to continue to invest in development, thus developing:
   - Technology
   - New products and markets
   - People
   - Management systems to cope with new legal frameworks and social structures
   - Competitive advantage.

Through all of this organizations had to continue to provide their owners with a return to justify their investment. The water began to boil. Organizations responded by undertaking larger change projects as part of their competitive strategy, the second loop in Fig. 1.1. However, that did not

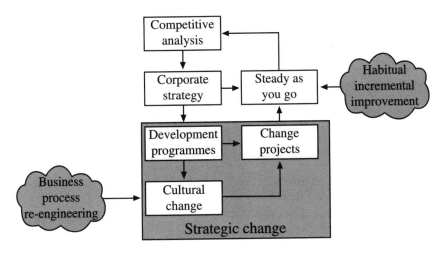

**Figure 1.1**   Change projects as part of competitive strategy

suffice either as the changes introduced required new ways of working and often a new culture in the organization. Managers in the 1990s must now follow the third loop in Fig. 1.1, often changing the organization, its structure and culture as part of their competitive strategy. Johansson *et al.* [3] say that if you are second best in the world, you do not become best by continuous improvement. As the wind direction changes, you sometimes need to tack spontaneously to achieve your ultimate objective of sailing around the buoy upwind of your current position.

## 1.3 The need not to change

However, beware! We appear to be dealing with a subject where mass psychosis is evident. People have become so persuaded by the modern gurus preaching change that they sometimes introduce change for change's sake, without having any clear strategic reason why it is necessary, or if it is necessary, that they have then adopted the right response. Beware the siren voices trying to pull you onto the rocks. Case Study 1.1 is one of Aesop's fables – another story as valid today as it was 2500 years ago. In this story:

– It is not clear that change was ever necessary
– If it was, it is not clear what was the right solution
– By trying to please everybody, the father and his son pleased nobody and lost their donkey (their business).

---

## Case Study 1.1 The miller, his son and their donkey (one of Aesop's fables)

The miller and his son were taking their donkey to town to sell. They were walking alongside it when they passed a group of people who started laughing and said, 'Look at them walking alongside their donkey when they could be riding it.' The father then said to his son, 'You get up on the donkey and I will continue walking alongside.'

Soon they passed a second group of people who began to scorn the son, 'What is the youth of today coming to? Why are you riding, you lazy bones, while your father walks?' The father and son swapped places.

Shortly they came to a third group of people who scorned the father, 'Look at the man riding while his son, a mere child, walks.' The son's legs were getting weary, so the father suggested the son join him on the donkey.

Soon they came to a fourth group of people who asked the miller and his son where they were riding the donkey to. 'We are taking it to market to sell,' said the father. 'Well, you had better not ride it or you will tire it out and nobody will want to buy it. In fact, you had better now carry it the rest of the way,' responded the people. The miller and his son got off and started carrying the donkey.

As they crossed the bridge coming into town, the townpeople started laughing at the sight of the man and his son carrying their donkey. They laughed so loudly that the donkey began to wriggle and the miller and his son dropped it over the edge of the bridge. The donkey was drowned. The miller and his son went home. The miller said, 'I wish I had never left home this morning. Then I had a donkey. I tried to please all those people and now I have nothing.'

---

Before implementing change you must be sure:

1. *It is necessary* You must identify the strategic imperative that is creating the need for change, that is, the need to maintain competitive advantage. However, at times competitive advantage will be maintained by doing nothing, for example in the 100-year-old restaurant, which customers seek precisely because it has remained unchanged for many years.
2. *That the need for change is understood* You must understand what is creating the need for change, what is the problem that is threatening your competitive advantage, not just what the symptoms are.
3. *That you have designed the correct solution* There are many siren voices selling glib solutions, each from their own perspective, all unaware of the full facts of the case. You must design the solution which is the right response to the problem you have identified. This will include not only the right technical solution, but also the right cultural or organizational solution.[4,5] Indeed, we would go further and say that every change project should be viewed as an organizational change project. The technical

change is the facilitator of change, not the primary reason for it. Furthermore, the cultural change must also include a response to overcome the resistance to the change as discussed in the next three sections.

Chapter 2 will help you identify the need for change and the correct response, the organization's readiness for change and your team's skill at managing change.

## 1.4 The ability to change

Human nature is like a stick of Brighton Rock; bite all the way down, it still says Brighton Rock.[6]

Literature and history will both tell you that people do not change fundamentally:

- Heracleitus's quotation and Aesop's fable are as valid 2500 years on
- Reading Plato's description of young people in his day gives you an uncomfortable feeling that it is taken from yesterday's newspaper
- A Roman poet, visiting the seaside in the first century AD, complained about being woken by drunken louts.

So if people are so unchanging, is this at odds with Heracleitus's statement? It is and it is not:

- It is not, because people are so unchanging things are as valid 2500 years on
- But it is, because people prefer things not to change; they prefer their lives to remain stable.

The perceived wisdom is that people resist change. In fact most people are tolerant of some change. Some are more tolerant of change than others, although we would say our experience shows that the majority of people are fairly intolerant of change. (A significant minority positively relish it.) Furthermore, it is not so much change that people resist, as having it imposed on them. However, people put a lot of effort into cementing relationships and reinforcing rituals which give them a feeling of security, continuity and stability.

So, how do we bridge the gap between the radical need for change that we impose on ourselves and our natural reluctance to change? This may seem contradictory. In fact it is more of a dilemma, posing a serious challenge to society and business organizations. Badly handled, change can prove to be a costly and devastating experience. It is made more difficult by the fact that most people will not have noticed that the water is getting hot. Looking on the bright side, history has shown us that people are adaptable, in the right circumstances and with the right coaching. The key to success is understanding the nature of change and managing people's reactions more than the technical elements of the change. There is no doubt that those organizations which master change quicker and better will obtain substantial competitive advantage.

Change agents throughout history have often been vilified. One, Nicolo Machiavelli, was said to be the devil incarnate. It has never been easy to achieve change when in conflict with the establishment. So if you do not have the power to overthrow the establishment (as Lenin suggested you should), then it is essential to get sufficient support from leading individuals (top management), to sponsor and support the change. In today's enlightened and effective organizations, the need for sponsorship is essential. Without the wholehearted support of top management and key employees, you will not succeed as a project manager of change. Equally important is the cooperation and commitment of the people being changed. In order to make the most of people's ability to change, careful planning is needed, but subject to the understanding of human behaviour.

## 1.5 Reactions to change – normal change

Although most people prefer a degree of stability and predictability in their lives, it does not mean they always resist change. Indeed, because change is permanent, a certain level can be said to be 'normal'. Just below this level, people will not notice change; just above, they may resist. However, people resist more having the change imposed on them. If they can participate in the change process and feel a sense of ownership of the ideas, most people will cooperate with change. Most parents know this. Ordering children around results in conflict. Coaching them to do for themselves the things that you want them to do produces better results. Some people grow more flexible with age, others grow more stubborn. Most people remain equally receptive to new learning experience throughout their lives; they just become better at hiding their feelings, less direct in challenging their superiors and more subtle in their ways. Any change process is subject to forces reinforcing the change, and others resisting it, Fig. 1.2. People will block change for different reasons, but they can be turned around to become supporters if the process is well structured. If this is properly understood, the process can be planned. Another way of looking at this is the stakeholder grid, Fig. 1.3. People can be judged against two parameters – whether they view the change positively or negatively and their ability to influence the change. For those people who view the project negatively, we try to find ways of making them view it positively. If that does not work, we try to isolate them so they have no influence on the change. For those who

Performance

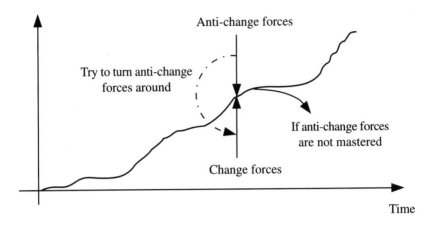

**Figure 1.2**   Forces for and against change

view the change positively, but have no influence, we try to find ways of giving them influence. Case Study 1.2 illustrates this.

## Case Study 1.2  Making a negative viewpoint positive

Rodney Turner was involved in a change project where the main user representative was aged 63. This representative was temporarily promoted from management grade 1 to grade 2. He was due to be made redundant by the project. Under company rules, he would leave on his substantive grade, that is grade 1, and that lower grade would determine his pension for the rest of his life. This man viewed the project extremely negatively and as main user representative had a major influence. The project was not a success. The solution was to find him a role on the project which would make his promotion substantive. At 63 he was unlikely to be promoted anyway, and so his higher pension was also unlikely. Making his promotion substantive would switch his perception of the project.

Planning the change process means:

1. Being able to communicate the change:
   – What is to be changed?
   – Why it is being done?
   – How it is to be done?
2. Understanding how people react to change, either as individuals or as part of an organization or a group within an organization, so that we can plan to handle their reactions and minimize risks.

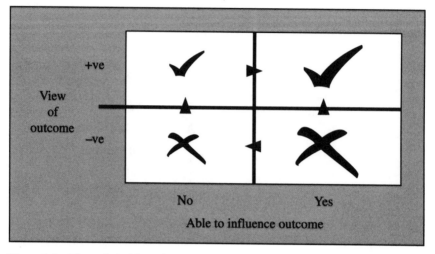

**Figure 1.3** The stakeholder grid

3. Gaining commitment through participation and understanding that this is a many step process (Fig. 1.4.)

How often have we had commitment to a project, only to realize it was superficial and unsustainable, because we did not understand human behaviour sufficiently nor have the patience to plan the project systematically and carry out the necessary steps identified. Technical changes are simple in comparison.[4,5] It is the change agent's role to manage the multi-step process outlined in Fig. 1.4. This person may be the project manager of the technical change. Or he or she may be a manager with wider responsibility for delivering the business benefits of the change project (the competitive advantage), with the technical project manager as a sub-project manager reporting to them. Whoever he or she is, the change agent is project manager of the cultural change.

## 1.6 Reactions to change – extreme change

Organizations, and the people within them, are sometimes faced with a level of change well above normal, such as total reorganization, downsizing or geographical relocation. These cannot be managed just by information, coaching and participation. If radical change is needed, implying a heavy impact on the everyday life of the individual, one cannot expect people to like it. The best you can hope for is an acceptance of the inevitable, so that people are able to adjust themselves to the situation and take their future in their own hands. Research[7] has shown that human beings when confronted

Performance

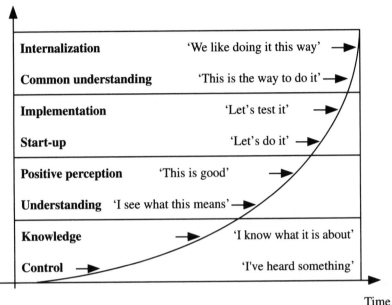

Figure 1.4    The stages of an organization's commitment to change

with major disruption in their lives go through an eight-stage transition process, Table 1.1. This cycle is derived from the observed behaviour of people
told they have a terminal illness. This response cycle is predictable and so
can be planned for. If you fail to do so, you will be ill-equipped to deal
with reactions and problems as they arise – and they will arise. Each individual will react with different intensity and will need a different amount of
time to be taken through the cycle. Hence, it is important that people are
treated individually. Risks and opportunities are rarely self-evident from
the start of the project, but emerge progressively through the stages of the
project. Identifying and managing the factors requires continual diagnosis
and discussion between the parties involved. It is the project manager's
role, as change agent, to plan and facilitate the situation, but he or she will
not succeed without integrating the tasks into the line organization. At the
end of the day, it is the line managers' responsibility to care for their people.

## 1.7 The project manager as change agent

In this chapter, we have seen that change is inevitable; it has been for at
least 2500 years. However, it is probably the case that competitive pressures

**Table 1.1** Emotional response to extreme change

| Stage | Response |
|---|---|
| Stability | Management communicates their vision, the need for change and the consequences |
| Immobilization | People are taken by surprise. Their reaction is anxiety and confusion |
| Denial | People defend themselves against what they see as a threat to their life or livelihood: |
| | – 'They can't mean me!' |
| | – 'Is that what we get for years of loyalty!' |
| | – 'Management is overreacting; it can't be that bad!' |
| Anger | Openly displayed anger towards management emerges. People try to take control, through their power base in the organization, through trade unions, etc. Alliances are formed; efforts to divide management are made; all means to reverse the situation |
| | Management must persistently argue the case, and not indulge in personal warfare |
| Bargaining | People begin to aim for a modified solution. All kinds of remedies will be proposed in order to try to reduce the impact of the change: |
| | – 'If we take a cut in salary?' |
| | – 'If we increase our productivity?' |
| | Management must be steadfast and stick to reality. |
| Depression | Frustration and a feeling of having lost spreads. People find it difficult to work and organizational paralysis sets in |
| | Management must help. They must have plans containing supporting packages and must actively assist individuals in taking responsibility for themselves in the new situation |
| Testing | The individual and the organization start working with alternative exit strategies to try to facilitate the individual's transition: |
| | – 'Did you say I could have six months' pay while looking for a new job?' |
| | – 'Being paid through a year's MBA programme would help the transition.' |
| | Management helps to find realistic alternatives |
| Acceptance | Individuals and the organization deal realistically with the situation. They may not like it but they accept it |
| | Management gives recognition and support towards future plans |
| | New stability is achieved |

for managing change consistently and successfully have never been greater. We identified that, even so, you should not undertake change for its own sake. You should only undertake change for sound strategic reasons, and only after you have identified the actual problem to be solved (rather than the symptoms) and you have identified the change that will bring about your required solution.

We then considered how human nature is unchanging. That is to be expected, given the unchanging nature of the inevitability of change. However, it creates a dilemma for the change agent since it means that people are fundamentally resistant to change. The change agent must plan for and manage the expected resistance. The response will differ depending on the level of change. At near normal levels of change, the resistance can be overcome through education, training, coaching, consultation or coercion. People do not so much resist change, as resist having it imposed on them. At much higher levels of change, especially those that are 'life-threatening' (or at least 'life-style-threatening'), the resistance turns into rejection. People must now be coaxed through a much longer rejection to acceptance cycle.

The change agent must beware that:

- Major change projects fail more often through people problems than technological problems.
- Shock waves from disruptive change can damage the business, as people lose focus. The costs of unnecessary change, too much change and poorly managed change can be enormous.
- Every organization has a finite capacity to change to create competitive advantage. Failure to exploit this capacity effectively will set the business back.

Change is complex; change is risky; change is met with mixed feelings; but change is inevitable. Success requires a carefully planned integration of technology and organizational behaviour. In 1513, Machiavelli[8] said:

... there is nothing more difficult to arrange, nor doubtful of success, and more dangerous to carry through, than initiating changes in a state's constitution, ...

This book describes the role of the project manager as change agent in facilitating the change process, to ensure the organization implements the right changes effectively. This requires the change agent to fulfil several roles:

- Internal consultant
- Team leader
- Ambassador.

In the remainder of this part, we describe the change agent's role as internal consultant. In the next chapter, we consider the use of diagnostic techniques to identify the need for change, the change required and possible resistance to be overcome. We then describe the use of project management as the vehicle for change, and the use and selection of project organizations for change. We end this chapter by explaining process management, by which you define the processes for delivering products, rather than functions for performing roles.

Part Two explains the change agent's role as team leader and ambassador. It describes project managers and their teams, the change agent's role as manager, and the management of task, team and individuals. We also consider internal marketing, winning and maintaining political support for the project, managing the stockholders and the role of the champion.

Part Three returns to the manager's role as internal consultant, considering cultural issues of change management. We explain working in cross-cultural environments, ethical project management and environmentally responsible management. Finally, we return to diagnostic techniques, in particular the use of health checks to maintain a check on the change project during the course of its implementation.

Figure 3.1 illustrates the change process. The first steps are to set the business strategy and define the changes required to achieve it. In the next chapter we describe the use of diagnostic techniques to help in these first two steps.

## 1.8 Summary

1. The world is changing, and organizations which do not respond will die; *but* often people will not notice the change in the outside world, which will make them resistant to change.
2. When introducing change, you must be clear:
   - That change is necessary
   - That change achieves the desired outcome
   - That you are doing what is right for you, not what others want.
3. Although the species inevitably evolves, the individuals do not. People resist change.
4. People are tolerant of some change; different people to different levels. At low levels, people do not so much resist change as resist having it imposed on them. People will often react well if they are actively involved in the change and can be made to see the benefit.
5. However, at extreme levels, change can become life-threatening. Then people respond in a way similar to people with a terminal illness. They must be helped through this response cycle.
6. The project manager has a role to fulfil as change agent to facilitate the change introduced by their projects. This role requires them to be:
   - Internal consultant
   - Team leader
   - Ambassador.

## References

1. Heracleitus, (513BC), quoted in *Oxford Dictionary of Quotations*, 2nd edn., Oxford University Press, Oxford, 1953.

2. Handy, C.B., *The Age of Unreason*, 2nd edition, Business Books, 1991.
3. Johansson, H.J., McHugh, P., Pendlebury, A.J. and Wheeler, W.A., *Business Process Reengineering*, Wiley, 1994.
4. Andersen, E.S., Grude, K.V., Haug, T. and Turner, J.R., *Goal Directed Project Management*, Kogan Page, 1987.
5. Turner, J.R., *The Handbook of Project-Based Management: Improving the processes for achieving strategic objectives*, McGraw-Hill, 1993.
6. Greene, G., *Brighton Rock*, Heinemann, 1938.
7. Hay, J, *Working it out at Work*, Sherwood Publishing, 1993.
8. Machiavelli, N., *The Prince*, translated by G. Bull, Penguin, Harmondsworth, 1981.

# 2
# Diagnosing change

Colin Carnall and Rodney Turner

## 2.1 Introduction

The traditional view of the role of project managers on change projects is that they should manage the change in a structured way and create a project organization to do that. The next two chapters address these two issues. Some people take a narrower view, expecting project managers to inherit an established project organization and needing only to manage the change. Others take a narrower view still, that project managers only manage technical work associated with change, and sometimes only the timescale over which the technical work is delivered. In the mid-1980s, Rodney Turner worked with a project-based organization (since bought by the electrical and electronics giant mentioned in Case Study 2.1) in which the managing director insisted that project managers should not know the budget for their contracts, let alone manage the cost.

The change process starts before the management of the technical work. The first step is to identify the need for change and that need should be to increase the organization's performance, measured by its effectiveness, competitiveness and/or profitability. Having identified the need for change, you then need to identify:

- The drivers for change and the barriers preventing it happen
- The readiness and willingness of the people within the organization to change
- Your own readiness to act as change agent.

If project managers understand the need for change, it will help them to deliver the right change to the organization. If they can identify the drivers for and barriers to change, they can use the drivers to facilitate the change, and include steps in their project plans to overcome the barriers. By being aware of the level of readiness and willingness of the people in

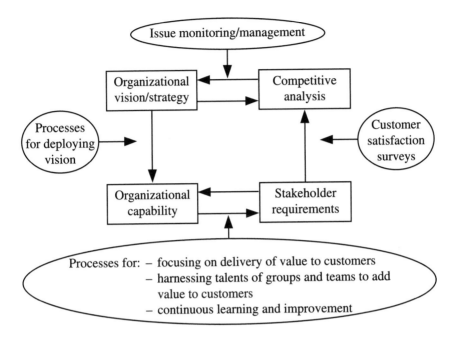

**Figure 2.1**   Change as a learning process

the organization to change, they can include steps in their project plans to increase these where necessary, particularly including educational programmes. And by being aware of your own ability as a change agent, you can reinforce your strengths, compensate for your weaknesses, and seek personal development where necessary. In this chapter we suggest diagnostic tools to help project managers better understand the change process.

## 2.2 Diagnosing the need for change

Achieving change is a learning process, Fig. 2.1. It involves learning about changes in the competitive environment (competition, technology, market demands) and the organization's capability of delivering added value to customers, and then adapting the organization to improve performance in delivering that added value.

### Gap analysis

Gap analysis (Fig. 2.2) is a tool which can help organizations identify where they have a shortfall in performance and what contributes to that shortfall.[1]

Performance

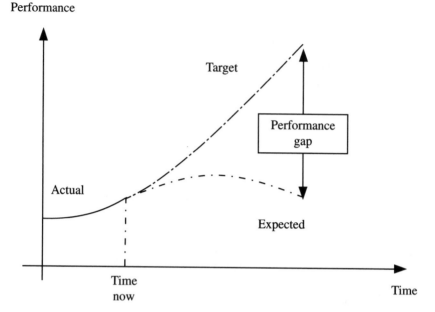

**Figure 2.2** Gap analysis

Against some measure of performance, the organization plots its historical achievement and then projects forward:

– What it would like to achieve
– What it expects to achieve if it continues in its current ways without change.

This will usually identify a shortfall, the gap, in projected performance, which the organization must take action (introduce change) to eliminate. There are many possible measures of performance, depending on what is important to the business, including: quantitative measures such as:

– Sales or turnover
– Profit
– Efficiency or productivity
– Return on capital employed

or more qualitative measures such as:

– Safety performance
– Employee morale
– Ethical behaviour
– Sense of fun from working for the business.

## Causes of the performance gap

The performance gap can be caused by internal or external pressures, or drivers for change:

1. *External pressures* These may be opportunities or threats in the competitive environment, the external marketplace or industry within which the organization operates.
2. *Internal pressures* These are strengths or weaknesses of the organization itself, its products, the technologies it uses to make those products and the culture or management style of the organization.
3. *Comparative benchmarking* This is a way in which an organization can actually measure its performance and help determine the size of the performance gap. The organization compares its performance to similar organizations in the same industry and measures how well it is doing in comparison. This in itself is a driver for change. Remember, if you are second best in the world, you do not become best by continuous improvement.

In Chapter 15, we describe changes brought about in the insurance industry in the late 1980s and early 1990s by severe changes in the environment, and the internal changes insurance companies had to make to respond to these changes. The insurance industry had been relatively stable for almost 200 years, so companies had become fairly rigid and inflexible, changing only very slowly. That had all changed by the late 1980s, some of the change brought about by government legislation, and in Chapter 15 we describe how two companies responded.

## Contributors to performance

Organizations only really have control over their strengths and weaknesses to improve their performance. There are several factors which can be manipulated to contribute to the achievement of higher performance, Fig. 2.3. The more difficult these factors are to achieve, the longer it takes for them to contribute to increased performance, but then the greater their eventual contribution to performance. These factors include the following, in increasing order of ability to influence performance.

OPERATIONAL EFFICIENCY

This is the organization's efficacy at producing its products and may include elements such as speed of working, the efficiency of the workflow and management systems, the ability of the salesforce, the use of automation

Performance

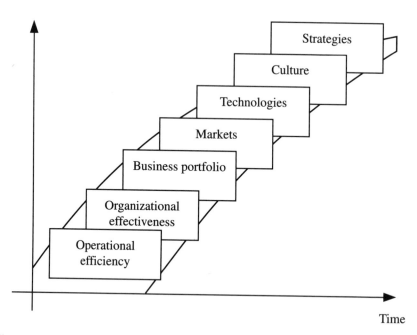

Figure 2.3 Achieving performance improvement

and the continuity of the processes, especially the supply chain from suppliers, through production to customers. In operational efficiency, it is
usually comparatively easy to identify potential improvements, but the
impact on performance is fairly small.

ORGANIZATIONAL EFFECTIVENESS

This goes beyond efficiency and incorporates the organization's capability
in meeting customer requirements and in producing products which add
value for the customer. This covers the organization's adaptability, its
ability to respond to changing requirements, but to continue to deliver to
such requirements efficiently. In Chapter 4, we describe how the implementation of quality procedures can have the reverse effect, making organizations less able to respond. We propose process management as a way of
overcoming this dilemma. Elements which contribute to organizational
effectiveness include management structure and style, use of strategic
information systems, the training of people throughout the organization
and the reward system.

**Quantitative measures**

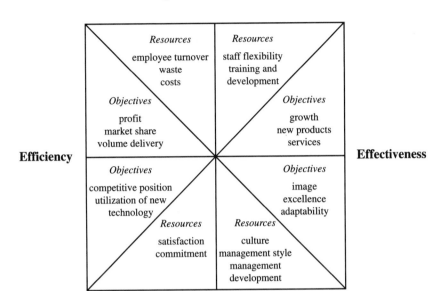

**Qualitative measures**

**Figure 2.4**   Efficiency/effectiveness matrix


Efficiency and effectiveness can be summarized in the effectiveness matrix, Fig. 2.4.[1] This shows how these two factors can contribute to both quantitative and qualitative measures of performance.


BUSINESS PORTFOLIO

This really incorporates all of the following factors. Elements of business performance include the four Ps of classic marketing theory: product, price, promotion and place of sale.[2] These obviously also cover elements such as the customer, the distribution mechanisms (logistics or supply chain management) and profitability. There are also hidden issues such as:

– Quality
– Technology employed, including information systems
– The capability of the management and the supervision
– Product focus.

TECHNOLOGY EMPLOYED

This is a major contributor to performance. We usually assume that 'high tech' means high performance. John Harvey-Jones's television programme on Morgan Cars,[2] however, showed that sometimes the reverse is true (depending on your definition of performance). Good technology can improve the three previous factors – efficiency, effectiveness and product portfolio.

PRODUCT PORTFOLIO AND MARKET

It is the products which provide benefits to customers and so it is ultimately those which provide income. High performance means selling the right products to the right markets. Techniques such as Product Portfolio Analysis and Ansoff Matrix help achieve this.[3]

CULTURE

This also influences performance, but is, in our view, the area which is most susceptible to people (so-called 'gurus') pushing the latest fad. Remember the story of the miller, his son and their donkey from the previous chapter. Essentially with culture you must do what is right for your organization. The current perception is that functional, hierarchical line management leads to poor performance (but see Case Study 2.1). The bureaucratic structure was adopted in the first place because it provided high efficiency, but it works against effectiveness as it makes the organization inflexible and unadaptive. (These ideas are expanded further in Chapter 4.) John Harvey-Jones's television programme on Morgan Cars[2] also showed that different cultures are appropriate in different circumstances.

STRATEGY

Finally, it is through its strategy that the organization tries to respond to the opportunities and threats of the external environment. It is by trying to predict changes to the industry, changing customer needs and enabling technologies, and then developing plans to respond accordingly, that the organization aims to improve its performance. Sometimes it is even possible to change the external environment, at least at the margin, to your benefit.

## Case Study 2.1 Empowerment?

Rodney Turner has a PhD student who is working for a major, UK-based, electronics company. This company is part of an industrial giant in the electrical and electronics industries. It is one of the UK's most successful companies, regularly sitting on a large cash mountain. The student wanted a non-standard company car. It was a Rover, as required, in the right price range, just not one of the standard three models. The decision to allow him to have the non-standard car was taken by the chairman's son. Is that empowerment?

One reason why this company is successful is because accountability for income is delegated to small business units, but control of costs is centrally retained. One assumes that the size of the cash mountain is for the chairman a measure of performance.

---

**Conducting an audit**

To determine future performance of the business, and factors contributing to it, requires detailed analysis of the organization, its products, the industry in which it operates and the context of the business and industry. This analysis is called a diagnostic or audit. Many tools exist to help in this audit. Foreman[3] gives a simplified overview of conducting a strategic marketing audit. Other authors[4,5,6] describe more detailed tools. These are beyond the scope of this book. However, standard questionnaires can help in this process. Figure 2.5 contains a company capability questionnaire developed from that proposed by Rowe, Dickel, Mason and Snyder.[7] Here we find using a scale of 1 to 6 forces you to make a decision to mark items 'average plus' or 'average minus', and avoid the risk of marking everything just average.

## 2.3 Diagnosing barriers to change

We saw in Chapter 1 that not everybody necessarily welcomes change. Turner[8] describes the overt and covert objectives of people involved in a change process. The overt objectives are the changes needed to achieve competitive advantage identified in the previous section. However, the people involved may also have their own objectives (their covert objectives), which can support or hinder the change. Where they hinder the change, they become barriers to change. Case Study 1.2 describes one such example. Barriers to change can also arise because project managers and operations managers operate over different time horizons. This leads to the Projectivity Model, described in Chapter 4. Some barriers to change can arise just from the organization's inability to recognize the performance gap and the problems causing it, and from an inability to find effective solutions to those problems. Adams[9] identifies blocks to problem solving, Fig. 2.6. Some blocks may arise through people deliberately resisting the change, some through them subconsciously resisting it, and some may be completely unintentional, arising because of the culture of the organization or the

Company: ........................................................................................

Date: ........................................................................................

Author: ........................................................................................

| Managerial factors | Poor 0% | Weak 20% | Ave− 40% | Ave+ 60% | Good 80% | Excl 100% |
|---|---|---|---|---|---|---|
| 1. Corporate image and social responsibility | | | | | | |
| 2. Use of strategic plans and strategic analysis | | | | | | |
| 3. Environmental assessment and forecasting | | | | | | |
| 4. Speed of response to changing conditions | | | | | | |
| 5. Flexibility of organizational structure | | | | | | |
| 6. Management communication and control | | | | | | |
| 7. Entrepreneurial orientation | | | | | | |
| 8. Ability to attract and retain highly creative people | | | | | | |
| 9. Ability to meet changing technology | | | | | | |
| 10. Ability to handle inflation | | | | | | |
| 11. Aggressiveness in meeting competition | | | | | | |
| 12. Other | | | | | | |

| Competitive factors | Poor 0% | Weak 20% | Ave− 40% | Ave+ 60% | Good 80% | Excl 100% |
|---|---|---|---|---|---|---|
| 1. Product strength, quality, uniqueness | | | | | | |
| 2. Customer loyalty and satisfaction | | | | | | |
| 3. Market share | | | | | | |
| 4. Low selling and distribution costs | | | | | | |
| 5. Use of experience curve for pricing | | | | | | |
| 6. Use of product life-cycle and replacement cycle | | | | | | |
| 7. Investment in new product development by R&D | | | | | | |
| 8. High barriers to entry in the company's markets | | | | | | |
| 9. Advantage taken of market growth potential | | | | | | |
| 10. Supplier strength and material availability | | | | | | |
| 11. Customer concentration | | | | | | |
| 12. Other | | | | | | |

**Figure 2.5** Diagnostic for organizational capability

| *Financial factors* | *Poor* 0% | *Weak* 20% | *Ave−* 40% | *Ave+* 60% | *Good* 80% | *Excl* 100% |
|---|---|---|---|---|---|---|
| 1. Access to capital when required | | | | | | |
| 2. Degree of capacity utilization | | | | | | |
| 3. Ease of exit from market | | | | | | |
| 4. Profitability, return on investment | | | | | | |
| 5. Liquidity, available internal funds | | | | | | |
| 6. Degree of leverage, financial stability | | | | | | |
| 7. Ability to compete on process | | | | | | |
| 8. Capital investment, capacity to meet demand | | | | | | |
| 9. Stability of costs | | | | | | |
| 10. Ability to sustain effort in cycle demand | | | | | | |
| 11. Elasticity of demand | | | | | | |
| 12. Other | | | | | | |

| *Technical factors* | *Poor* 0% | *Weak* 20% | *Ave−* 40% | *Ave+* 60% | *Good* 80% | *Excl* 100% |
|---|---|---|---|---|---|---|
| 1. Technical and manufacturing skills | | | | | | |
| 2. Resource and personnel utilization | | | | | | |
| 3. Level of technology used in products | | | | | | |
| 4. Strengths of patents and processes | | | | | | |
| 5. Production effectiveness and delivery schedules | | | | | | |
| 6. Value added to product | | | | | | |
| 7. Intensity of labour to produce the product | | | | | | |
| 8. Economies of scale | | | | | | |
| 9. Newness of plant and equipment | | | | | | |
| 10. Application of computer technology | | | | | | |
| 11. Level of coordination and integration | | | | | | |
| 12. Other | | | | | | |

**Figure 2.5**  Diagnostic for organizational capability (cont.)

| Barrier | Comment |
|---|---|
| *Perceptual blocks* | |
| 1. Stereotyping | We see what we expect to see, and construct models to give the solutions we expect |
| 2. Problem isolation | We solve the wrong problem; a different problem gives a more effective solution |
| 3. Tunnel vision | Too narrow a focus prevents an effective solution being found |
| 4. Blinkered vision | People are trained to see problems only in terms of their professional discipline |
| 5. Data overload | We cannot see the wood for the trees |
| 6. Data underload | Our ability to find the best solution is limited by limited data |
| *Emotional blocks* | |
| 1. Risk aversion | Many organizations punish failure. We must be willing to make the occasional mistake (but it must not become a habit, as Oscar Wilde wrote, 'To lose one parent...may be regarded as a misfortune; to lose both looks like carelessness.') |
| 2. Ambiguity aversion | Problems are messy, with solutions based on incomplete and subjective data |
| 3. Urgency | We are often unwilling to sleep on the problem, because of perceived urgency (Dennis Healey said, 'If you find yourself in a hole, stop digging!') |
| 4. Closing options | Radical ideas tend to get rejected early because they involve ambiguity and risk, but they may be the germ of a good idea |
| *Cultural blocks* | |
| 1. Taboos | Some topics cannot be discussed and therefore cannot be faced |
| 2. Lack of fantasy | Our (Anglo-Saxon) culture encourages logical (prescriptive left-brained) behaviour rather than fanciful, intuitive (creative right-brained) behaviour |
| 3. Lack of humour | Problem solving is a serious business! Yet humour, based on juxtaposition of incongruous ideas, encourages lateral thinking |
| 4. Tradition | 'We've always done it this way!' |
| *Environmental blocks* | |
| 1. Lack of support | Change can be stopped by ignoring it, ridiculing it or 'paralysis by analysis' |
| 2. Aversion to criticism | Creative people are often averse to criticism. Acceptance of criticism builds trust and support, and converts imperfect ideas to excellent solutions |
| 3. Boss knows best | Related to the above, senior managers have often got where they are by having effective solutions, and that can lead to them ignoring subordinates |
| *Cognitive blocks* | |
| 1. Incorrect language – Jargon | There are many varieties of the use of incorrect language: Using jargon can often exclude people with ideas to contribute. It is often deliberately used to reinforce demarcations |

**Figure 2.6**  Barriers to effective problem solving

| Barrier | Comment |
|---|---|
| *Cognitive blocks* (cont.) | |
| – Local terminology | We need to be aware of local terminology to get ideas accepted, but equally people sometimes reject good ideas on the spurious grounds that non-standard terminology has been used. The local terminology becomes its own jargon |
| – Cultural diversity | The use of gender, race or other stereotyping is boorish and insensitive, can lead to people feeling isolated and should be avoided. Likewise, excessive Puritanism can be condescending, 'McCarthyistic' and equally make people feel isolated |
| 2. Use of models | Models can aid our thinking, but their overuse can constrain it. Do not let the template be visible in the final solution |
| 3. Use of information | Information is power and makes us experts, but experts can think in narrow lines |

**Figure 2.6**  Barriers to effective problem solving (cont.)

people working in it. Of course you may not necessarily try to be creative all the time:

1. There are people whose 'creativity' can be disrupting to the rest of the group. These people really do need to be frozen out for the greater good.
2. Problem solving goes through divergent and convergent cycles. You are creative in divergent cycles, generating ideas; reflective and analytical in convergent ones, closing options. If you are continually creative, you make no progress. During convergent cycles you may need to challenge people to defend their ideas. That, as we said in Fig. 2.6, can lead to imperfect ideas becoming excellent solutions.

Figure 2.7 contains a diagnostic questionnaire which can help you identify the organization's receptiveness to change and some of the barriers you may encounter. This questionnaire should be completed by all members of the team and the results compared. There are no right or wrong answers, it is only the comparison which is of interest. It is through the comparison that you will identify where barriers and potential areas of conflict lie. Each member of the team should rate the statements in Fig. 2.7 according to the following scale:

1. Disagree strongly
2. Disagree
3. Disagree slightly

4. Agree slightly
5. Agree
6. Agree strongly.

Calculating the average score and spread of scores against each answer will help you to analyse the results.

| No. | Statement | Scores | | | | | | Ave | Spread |
|---|---|---|---|---|---|---|---|---|---|
| 1. | I understand this organization's objectives | 1 | 2 | 3 | 4 | 5 | 6 | | |
| 2. | The organization of work here is effective | 1 | 2 | 3 | 4 | 5 | 6 | | |
| 3. | Managers will always listen to ideas | 1 | 2 | 3 | 4 | 5 | 6 | | |
| 4. | I am encouraged to develop my full potential | 1 | 2 | 3 | 4 | 5 | 6 | | |
| 5. | My line manager is supportive and helps me in my work group | 1 | 2 | 3 | 4 | 5 | 6 | | |
| 6. | My line manager helps me in my work | 1 | 2 | 3 | 4 | 5 | 6 | | |
| 7. | This organization keeps its policies and procedures relevant and up-to-date | 1 | 2 | 3 | 4 | 5 | 6 | | |
| 8. | We regularly achieve our objectives | 1 | 2 | 3 | 4 | 5 | 6 | | |
| 9. | The goals and objectives of this organization are clearly stated | 1 | 2 | 3 | 4 | 5 | 6 | | |
| 10. | Jobs and lines of authority are flexible | 1 | 2 | 3 | 4 | 5 | 6 | | |
| 11. | I can always talk to someone at work if I have a work-related problem | 1 | 2 | 3 | 4 | 5 | 6 | | |
| 12. | The salary that I receive is commensurate with the job that I perform | 1 | 2 | 3 | 4 | 5 | 6 | | |
| 13. | I have all the information and resources I need to do a good job | 1 | 2 | 3 | 4 | 5 | 6 | | |
| 14. | The management style adopted by senior management is helpful and effective | 1 | 2 | 3 | 4 | 5 | 6 | | |
| 15. | We constantly review our methods and introduce improvements | 1 | 2 | 3 | 4 | 5 | 6 | | |
| 16. | Results are attained because people are committed to them | 1 | 2 | 3 | 4 | 5 | 6 | | |
| 17. | The priorities of this organization are understood by its employees | 1 | 2 | 3 | 4 | 5 | 6 | | |
| 18. | The way in which work tasks are divided is sensible and clear | 1 | 2 | 3 | 4 | 5 | 6 | | |
| 19. | My relationships with other members of my work group are good | 1 | 2 | 3 | 4 | 5 | 6 | | |
| 20. | There are opportunities for promotion and increased responsibility in this organization | 1 | 2 | 3 | 4 | 5 | 6 | | |
| | Sum | | | | | | | | |
| | Average | | | | | | | | |

**Figure 2.7**   Diagnosing barriers to change

| No. | Statement | Scores | Ave | Spread |
|-----|-----------|--------|-----|--------|
| 21. | This organization sets realistic goals | 1  2  3  4  5  6 | | |
| 22. | Performance is regularly reviewed by my boss | 1  2  3  4  5  6 | | |
| 23 | There are occasions when I would like to be free to make changes in my job | 1  2  3  4  5  6 | | |
| 24. | People are cost-conscious and seek to make the best use of resources | 1  2  3  4  5  6 | | |
| 25. | In my work area objectives are clearly stated and each person's role is clearly identified | 1  2  3  4  5  6 | | |
| 26. | There is a constant search for ways of improving the way we work | 1  2  3  4  5  6 | | |
| 27. | We cooperate effectively to get work done | 1  2  3  4  5  6 | | |
| 28. | Encouragement and recognition is given for all jobs and tasks in this organization | 1  2  3  4  5  6 | | |
| 29. | Departments work well together to achieve good performance | 1  2  3  4  5  6 | | |
| 30. | This organization's management team provide effective and inspiring leadership | 1  2  3  4  5  6 | | |
| 31. | This organization has the capacity to change | 1  2  3  4  5  6 | | |
| 32. | Our work is always necessary and effective | 1  2  3  4  5  6 | | |
| 33. | All individual work performance is reviewed against agreed standards | 1  2  3  4  5  6 | | |
| 34. | The work structure in this organization is arranged to produce general satisfaction | 1  2  3  4  5  6 | | |
| 35. | Conflicts of views are resolved by solutions which are understood and accepted | 1  2  3  4  5  6 | | |
| 36. | I feel motivated by the work I do | 1  2  3  4  5  6 | | |
| 37. | Other departments are helpful to my own department whenever necessary | 1  2  3  4  5  6 | | |
| 38. | My boss's management style helps me in the performance of my own work | 1  2  3  4  5  6 | | |
| 39. | Creativity and initiative are encouraged | 1  2  3  4  5  6 | | |
| 40. | People are always concerned to do a good job | 1  2  3  4  5  6 | | |
| | *Sum* | | | |
| | *Average* | | | |

**Figure 2.7**  Diagnosing barriers to change (cont.)

## 2.4 Diagnosing your and the organization's readiness for change

Before embarking on the change process, you may want to ensure that:

- the organization is ready and willing to change, and people are mentally prepared to accept the change
- you are ready and willing to manage the change process.

### Willingness of the people to accept the change

Figure 2.8 (pp. 32–3) contains a series of questions designed to help you consider whether people in the organization are willing to accept the change. This checklist deals with a range of implementation problems. Set out below is a series of techniques and principles which can help to alleviate them.

QUESTIONS 1 TO 3

These deal with implementing change:

- Has there been unsuccessful past experience of change?
- Do we have a risk-averse culture?
- Are there communication problems?

1. Keep everyone informed by making information available; explaining plans clearly; allowing access to management for questions and clarification.
2. Ensure change is sold realistically by making a practical case for change; explain change in terms which the employee will see as relevant and acceptable; show how change fits business needs and plans; spend time and effort on presentations.
3. Prepare carefully by making a full organizational diagnosis; spend time with people and groups, building trust, understanding and support.
4. Involve people by getting feedback on proposals; get people to fill out the checklists; discuss the data from these checklists.
5. Start small and successful by piloting a receptive group of employees and in departments with a successful track record; implement changes in clear phases.
6. Plan for success by starting with changes that can give a quick and positive pay-off; publicize early success; provide positive feedback to those involved in success.

QUESTIONS 4 TO 6

These deal with effects of change:

- What are people's expectations of change?
- What are the objectives of change?

1. Clarify benefits of changes by emphasizing benefits to those involved and to the company.
2. Emphasize where the new systems utilize existing knowledge and skills.
3. Minimize surprises by specifying assumptions; focus on outcomes; identify potential problems.
4. Communicate plans by being specific in terms familiar to the different groups of employees; communicate periodically and through various media; ask for feedback; do not suppress negative views but listen to them carefully and deal with them openly.

QUESTIONS 7 TO 9

These deal with ownership of change:

- Are procedures, systems, departments, products and services seen as a problem?
- Who planned the changes – top management or a staff department?

1. Plan visible outcomes from change.
2. Clarify views by exploring concerns about the change and examining impact on the day-to-day routines.
3. Specify who wants change and why; explain longer-term advantages; identify common benefits; present the potential of change.

QUESTIONS 10 TO 12

These deal with top management:

- Will top management support changes openly?
- Will top management promote necessary resources?
- Is the management performance appraisal process an obstacle to change?

1. Build a power base by becoming the expert in the problems involved; understand top management concerns; develop information and formal support; develop a strong and polished presentation in top management language.

| *Question* | *Answer* |
|---|---|

1. In the past, new policies or systems introduced by management have been:
   - seen as meeting employees needs
   - not well understood
   - greeted with some resistance
   - vigorously resisted
2. Employees may be best described as:
   - innovative
   - independent
   - apathetic
   - conservative or resistant to change
3. The most recent and widely known change in the organization is viewed as:
   - a success
   - moderately successful
   - having had no obvious impact
   - making the situation worse
4. Expectations of what change will lead to are:
   - consistent throughout the organization
   - consistent among senior management but not otherwise
   - not at all consistent
   - unclear
5. What can people affected by the changes give you about the organization's business or strategic plan?
   - a full description
   - a description of where it affects their own department or activity
   - a general idea
   - nothing
6. Outcomes of the change have been:
   - specified in detail
   - outlined in general terms
   - poorly defined
   - not defined
7. Present work produces to be affected by the change are seen as needing:
   - major change
   - significant alteration
   - minor improvement
   - no change
8. The problems to be dealt with by the changes were first raised by:
   - the people directly involved
   - first-line management and in supervision
   - senior management
   - outside management
9. The proposed change is viewed by end users as:
   - crucial to the organization's future
   - generally beneficial to the organization
   - beneficial only to part of the organization
   - largely a matter of procedure

**Figure 2.8** Readiness for change

| Question | Answer |
| --- | --- |

10. Top management support for the proposed change is:
    - enthusiastic
    - limited
    - minimal
    - unclear
11. Top management has:
    - committed significant resources to the change
    - expects the change to be implemented from existing sources
    - has withheld resources
    - has not planned the resources needed
12. The management performance appraisal and review process is:
    - an important part of management development
    - a helpful problem-solving process
    - routine
    - an obstacle to improvement
13. The proposed change deals with issues of relevance to the business:
    - directly
    - partly
    - only indirectly
    - not at all
14. The proposed change:
    - makes jobs more rewarding financially and otherwise
    - makes jobs easier and more satisfying
    - replaces old tasks and skills with new ones
15. The proposed change is technically:
    - similar to others undertaken in the recent past
    - novel
    - unclear
16. Are employees adaptable?
    - very adaptable
    - adaptable
    - reluctant to change
    - inflexible
17. Are employees working in teams?
    - yes, in clearly defined teams
    - only occasionally, when certain projects arise
    - very occasionally
    - never
18. In the past, employees have:
    - been strongly committed to change
    - only been committed if they benefited personally
    - not been particularly committed to change
    - not been prepared to accept change

**Figure 2.8**   Readiness for change (cont.)

2. Specify who wants change and why; explain longer-term advantages; identify common benefits; present the potential of change.

QUESTIONS 13 TO 15

These deal with acceptance of change:

– Do the planned changes fit other business plans?
– Is there a clear sense of direction?
– Do the proposed changes place greater demands on people?
– Does the change involve new technology or expertise?

1. Identify relevance of change to plans by reviewing plans and specifying how change fits; incorporate changes into on-going developments; if possible, frame changes in terms of the organization's style.
2. Implement changes using flexible or adaptable people, who are familiar with some or all of the change; in a part of the business where there are strong supporters for change; recognize why people support change (career, rewards, company politics).
3. Do not oversell change. Be clear about conflicts with present practices; encourage discussion of them.

QUESTIONS 16 TO 18

These deal with building an effective team to implement change:

– Will team members be inflexible in dealing with change?
– Will managers need to work hard to ensure commitment to changes?

1. Ensure that teams have clear and agreed goals.
2. Involve all members of the team in ways they each see as relevant and using their own skills/expertise.
3. Be prepared to face and deal with conflict.
4. Encourage constructive feedback.

**Your readiness to manage the change**

Finally, you can assess your own preparedness to act as a change agent within your organization by using the key to scoring given in Table 2.1 to work through the questions in Fig. 2.9. You should work through this series of questions twice. The first time through, you consider the competences needed of a change agent within the organization, scoring as in the first column of Table 2.1. The second time through, you attempt to assess your

**Table 2.1**  Key for scoring questionnaire in Fig. 2.8

| Score | Scoring the organization's needs | Scoring your competence |
|---|---|---|
| 1 | Not important | Inadequate |
| 2 | Of some importance | Poor |
| 3 | Important but not essential | Average |
| 4 | Definitely of importance | Very good |
| 5 | Of vital importance | Excellent |

own competence, scoring as in the second column of Table 2.1. Your own profile must be better than or equal to the requirement for a change agent in the organization. From this you can identify your own strengths and weaknesses, and hence identify your own development needs.

## 2.5 Project health checks

In Chapter 14, we give further diagnostics, to help you undertake an internal audit both of how well your organization supports change projects and of the projects you establish to manage the change process. These health checks can be undertaken before projects start, and once they are underway to ensure they have been properly established. You can also use them during the start-up process to help focus on the right issues. They can be applied at all levels of management – project director, project manager, team leader and team member – to ensure uniformity of understanding of the need for change, and the projects established to implement it.

## 2.6 Summary

1. Diagnostic techniques can help the change agent identify:
   - The need for change
   - Drivers and barriers to change
   - The readiness and willingness of people to change
   - Their readiness to act as change agent.
2. Gap analysis can help identify the need for change. Performance gap can be caused by failings in:
   - Efficiency and effectiveness
   - Business portfolio
   - Technology employed, products and markets
   - Culture and strategy.
3. Barriers to change arise from people's resistance, or the inability of the organization to diagnose it.
4. The organization will be ready and willing to change when:
   - People are ready to accept the change

| Preparing for change | Organization | Individual |
|---|---|---|
| 1. Identifies problems and causes systematically | 1  2  3  4  5 | 1  2  3  4  5 |
| 2. Remains calm under pressure | 1  2  3  4  5 | 1  2  3  4  5 |
| 3. Involves others when appropriate | 1  2  3  4  5 | 1  2  3  4  5 |
| 4. Builds an open climate for decision making | 1  2  3  4  5 | 1  2  3  4  5 |
| 5. Sets and agrees objectives | 1  2  3  4  5 | 1  2  3  4  5 |
| 6. Draws out the input and contribution of others | 1  2  3  4  5 | 1  2  3  4  5 |
| 7. Checks for agreement to proposals | 1  2  3  4  5 | 1  2  3  4  5 |
| 8. Reviews objectives carefully | 1  2  3  4  5 | 1  2  3  4  5 |
| 9. Seeks all information relevant to a decision | 1  2  3  4  5 | 1  2  3  4  5 |
| 10. Is effective in presenting ideas and proposals | 1  2  3  4  5 | 1  2  3  4  5 |

| Planning changes | Organization | Individual |
|---|---|---|
| 1. Identifies opportunities and solutions | 1  2  3  4  5 | 1  2  3  4  5 |
| 2. Evaluates options critically | 1  2  3  4  5 | 1  2  3  4  5 |
| 3. Communicates information and views clearly | 1  2  3  4  5 | 1  2  3  4  5 |
| 4. Generates imaginative solutions to problems | 1  2  3  4  5 | 1  2  3  4  5 |
| 5. Identifies problems of implementation, resources required and appropriate priorities | 1  2  3  4  5 | 1  2  3  4  5 |

| Implementing changes | Organization | Individual |
|---|---|---|
| 1. Identifies what needs to be done to achieve change | 1  2  3  4  5 | 1  2  3  4  5 |
| 2. Achieves deadlines and has appropriate priorities | 1  2  3  4  5 | 1  2  3  4  5 |
| 3. Identifies impact of changes on people | 1  2  3  4  5 | 1  2  3  4  5 |
| 4. Identifies and deals with pressure/stress on self | 1  2  3  4  5 | 1  2  3  4  5 |
| 5. Identifies and deals with pressure/stress on others | 1  2  3  4  5 | 1  2  3  4  5 |
| 6. Allocates tasks sensibly | 1  2  3  4  5 | 1  2  3  4  5 |
| 7. Coordinates plans and actions effectively | 1  2  3  4  5 | 1  2  3  4  5 |

| Sustaining changes | Organization | Individual |
|---|---|---|
| 1. Makes the time to review progress and problems | 1  2  3  4  5 | 1  2  3  4  5 |
| 2. Discusses problems and issues openly | 1  2  3  4  5 | 1  2  3  4  5 |
| 3. Provides relevant positive feedback to people | 1  2  3  4  5 | 1  2  3  4  5 |
| 4. Identifies areas for improvement | 1  2  3  4  5 | 1  2  3  4  5 |
| 5. Builds well on success, keeping motivation high | 1  2  3  4  5 | 1  2  3  4  5 |
| 6. Builds team spirit | 1  2  3  4  5 | 1  2  3  4  5 |
| 7. Sets out to increase the use of resources | 1  2  3  4  5 | 1  2  3  4  5 |
| 8. Allows enough time for change | 1  2  3  4  5 | 1  2  3  4  5 |

**Figure 2.9**  Change agent questionnaire

 - The management structures are in place to deliver it successfully
 - The change agent is ready and willing to manage the change process.


## References

1. Carnall, C.A., *Managing Change in Organizations*, Prentice Hall, 1990.
2. Harvey-Jones, J., 'Morgan Cars', in *Troubleshooter*, BBC TV, 1990.
3. Foreman, S.K., 'Project Selection: Markets and Technologies', in *The Commercial Project Manager*, Turner, J.R. (ed.), McGraw-Hill, 1995.
4. Porter, M.E., *Competitive Strategy*, Free Press, 1980.
5. Porter, M.E., *Competitive Advantage*, Free Press, 1985.
6. Ohmae, K., *The Mind of the Strategist*, Penguin, Harmondsworth, 1983.
7. Rowe, A.J., Dickel, K.E., Mason, R.O. and Snyder, N.H., *Strategic Management: A methodological approach*, 3rd edition, Addison-Wesley, 1989.
8. Turner, J.R., *The Handbook of Project-based Management: Improving the processes for achieving strategic objectives*, McGraw-Hill, 1993.
9. Adams, J.L., *Conceptual Blockbusting*, Penguin, 1987.

# 3

# Projects for implementing change

Tony Grundy, Rodney Turner and Kristoffer Grude

## 3.1 Introduction

Several years ago, Tony Grundy was asked to design a project management training programme for a major building society. When he tried to find appropriate case studies, he drew a blank. There were no appropriate cases focusing on using project management to implement change in service industries, let alone in the financial services sector. This was remarkable. Not only was the financial services sector going through rapid change, it was also beginning to use project management as a way of coping with that change. The same was true of other service industries, especially retail, IT and telecommunications (which have a high services ingredient) and health care. The reason why service and other industries undergoing rapid change were not thought by the high priests of traditional project management to be worthy of their attention is captured in the frustration of a consultant working on a culture change team in a major oil company: '*People seem to treat project management as if it were rocket science. But what we are doing is trying to apply its simple and more basic principles to managing our way through soft as well as hard issues.*'

There has been a tendency by both traditional authors in project management and the software industry to overcomplicate the subject, turning it perhaps not into rocket science, but complex applied mathematics. However, it is possible to apply simple qualitative techniques to help manage change effectively. With the complex mathematics stripped away, project management can be extremely valuable for implementing change.

In this chapter, we explain project management as a process for implementing change, and illustrate its use for designing and managing change through a simple case study derived from a real example. In Chapter 15, we describe more extensive case studies of the use of project management processes to manage change in the Life Administration Division of the Prudential and in the Norwich Union.

## 3.2 Project management as a process for implementing change

Figure 3.1 illustrates a simple, structured process which shows how project management can be applied to manage change. This process consists of several steps and within each step there are several activities. Some managers may view this model as being relatively complex. We have experienced cases where managers have reacted against *simpler models* of managing change through projects than this, saying that they are too complex and bureaucratic for their needs; and yet other managers who look at more complex models and say they are too simplistic for their complex and difficult projects. For instance, a simpler five-stage process might be:

- Diagnosis
- Planning
- Implementation
- Control
- Learning.

Even this triggers responses such as:

- 'We seem to spend 95 per cent of our time on implementation.'
- 'We do some planning; but what on earth is diagnosis?'
- 'We wouldn't have time for learning as such; we would be on to the next project.'
- 'I don't recognize these stages at all; they just all blur into one.'

We offer Fig. 3.1 as a relatively simple, structured approach. If your projects are more simple than this, then you can pick and choose those elements of the model which meet your needs; if they are more complex, then you can embellish the elements of the model through further reading of the references given. In this section we describe the steps in Fig. 3.1, and in the next we illustrate some of them through a change project at a telecommunications company, called here TriMagi.

### Step 1: Business strategy

The first step is to develop a business strategy. Without a clear definition of where the business is going, and how it is expected to develop, it is not possible to identify changes which will contribute to that development and those which are irrelevant. Indeed, without a clear idea of business strategy, changes may be implemented which are actually detrimental to

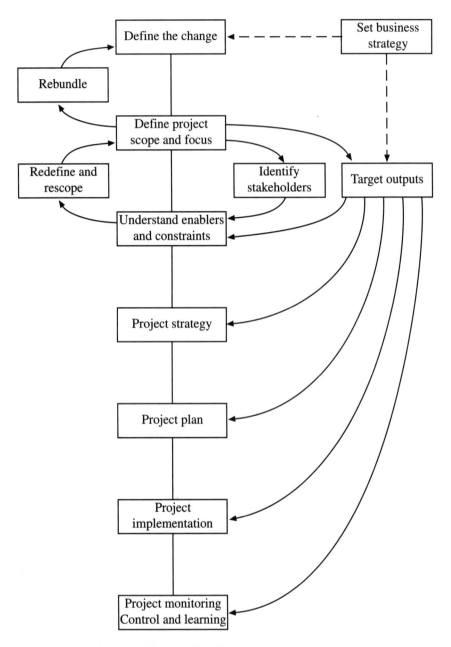

**Figure 3.1**  Projects for implementing change

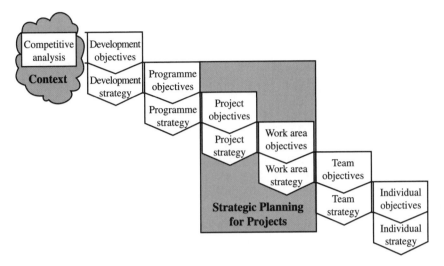

**Figure 3.2** Cascade of objectives in a change programme

the development of the business. Techniques for identifying business strategy were covered in section 2.2. The business strategy will identify a need to change the organization's:

- Products
- Markets
- Technologies
- Computer support
- Skill base
- Organizational and management structure
- Strategic alliances
- Suppliers.

**Step 2: Target outputs**

These requirements for change will lead first to development objectives. However, as the change programme, and its constituent projects, develop, this will lead to objectives at lower and lower levels of management, Fig. 3.2.[1] This cascade of objectives illustrates quite clearly the contribution of people at different levels of the organization to the overall development of the organization, through the programme and projects of change. At the development level, the objectives will be relatively long term and heuristic. However, as you move to lower levels, they become more short term, definitive and even quantitative.

In the jargon of project management, the rocket science, this cascade of objectives is called a *product breakdown structure*.[2] In the jargon of the strategist, you will hear these objectives called, at different levels, aims, goals, targets, objectives and so on. You can look on it quite simply as objectives at different levels of the organization. Managers at one level have objectives, and they derive a strategy for achieving those objectives. That strategy will define lower level objectives, which will be delegated to other, lower level, managers. However, you see that the process is initiated by the business strategy. This cascade illustrates quite clearly that each project will be part of a larger programme of change. What you often find in development programmes is that the individual projects cannot be justified in their own right. They only have value to the organization as part of the overall programme. Youker[1] illustrated this through a World Bank project on which he was involved to invest in a palm nut plantation in Malaysia. The programme of which it was part was to develop a palm nut oil industry, and the development required was economic development of Malaysia, including the creation of new jobs. Other projects in the programme included:

- Distribution mechanisms to take nuts to factories
- Factories to process nuts into oil
- Distribution mechanisms to take oil to customers

as well as the develoment of other plantations. The point is that without these other projects, all you will have is mountains of worthless nuts. You can put a value on the nuts from world market prices, but you can only realize that value when you put in place distribution mechanisms, and you get a higher value when you process the nuts into oil.

**Step 3: Defining the change**

The business strategy and cascade objectives define the need for change and the programmes and projects of change which will deliver it. (Throughout this book, we refer to the projects alternatively as *change projects* or *improvement projects*. There is nothing significant in these words other than that they are fairly widely used.) The diagnostic techniques described in Section 2.2 will help you in this process. Development workshops are also very effective in both identifying the need for change, defining the change and launching individual projects. The use of workshops is illustrated in both the TriMagi case study in the next section and the Prudential case study in Chapter 15.

**Step 4: Defining project scope and focus**

Now the individual projects must be defined. A technique for doing this is to define the purpose, scope and objectives of each project.

PURPOSE

This is the reason for doing the project; the business, programme and/or change objectives it is expected to fulfil. The purpose may also describe the expected benefit from doing the project, in quantitative or qualitative terms.

SCOPE

This is a high level description of what will be done to achieve the purpose. It may put forward several alternatives, indicate the preferred one, and say, briefly, what that solution entails in terms of work to be done. The scope also serves to ring fence the project, so it will also indicate what will not be done. There are several reasons for indicating what will not be done. There may be several reasons for excluding work:

- Some work may be unnecessary for achieving the change objectives, so it must be excluded to avoid people trying to slip their own, covert, objectives into the project – try to avoid 'nice to haves'.
- Some work may be shared between several simultaneous change projects, for example redeployment, training or marketing, and so a single project is set up to undertake it. It is not excluded from the original project to thus put it out of sight and out of mind, but to reinforce that the interface must be managed.

OBJECTIVES

These are measurable end points of the project. When the objectives are achieved, the project will be over and some 'facility' delivered to the operations managers, to be operated to achieve the long-term benefit or purpose. (The facility may not necessarily be an engineering product; it can be one or more of the possible project deliverables listed in Step 1 above.) Even primarily engineering or IT projects will require cultural or organizational changes, including changes to people, their numbers, skills, and values, the organizational structure and the management systems.[2,3]

Case Study 3.1 gives the possible background to a project at TriMagi, and its purpose, scope and objectives. In addition, the project definition may encompass some other issues:

- Impact on other parts of the organization
- Resource needs
- Its degree of difficulty, urgency and priority.

Some of these may be dependent on the analysis of stakeholders, constraining and enabling forces and project strategy as discussed next. As projects are defined, it may be continually necessary to return to previous steps, to define new projects, to eliminate some overtaken by new projects, and to regroup them into new programmes of work to achieve more focused programme or change objectives.

---

## Case Study 3.1 Project definition of the CRMO rationalization project at TriMagi

### TRIMAGI COMMUNICATIONS BV
### PROJECT DEFINITION REPORT

### PROJECT: RATIONALIZATION OF CUSTOMER REPAIR AND MAINTENANCE OFFICES

**Background**

With its expansion in Europe, TriMagi Communications intends to rationalize its Customer Repair and Maintenance Offices (CRMOs) in the Benelux countries, starting in its home base in Holland.

There are currently 18 CRMOs in the region. Each office is dedicated to an area within the region. An area office receives all calls from customers within the area reporting faults. The fault is diagnosed either electronically from within the office, or by sending an engineer to the customer's premises. Once diagnosed, the fault is logged with the field staff within the office, and repaired in turn. Each area office must cope with its own peaks and troughs in demand. This means that the incoming telephone lines may be engaged when a customer first calls, and it can take up to two days to diagnose the fault.

To improve customer services, the company plans to rationalize the CRMO organization in the region, with three objectives:

- Never have engaged call receipt lines within office hours
- Achieve an average time of two hours from call receipt to arrival of the engineer at the customer's premises
- Create a more flexible structure able to cope with future growth both in the region and throughout Europe, and create 'enquiry desks', to deal with all customer contacts.

This improvement can be achieved by changing the CRMO structure using new technology recently developed by the company's R&D department. In the new structure there will be three call receipt offices, two diagnostic offices and four field offices servicing the entire region. It would be possible to have just one office each for call receipt and diagnosis, but that would make the service exposed to technical failure.

Incoming calls will be switched to a free line in one of the call receipt offices. They will be logged automatically and passed on to a diagnostic office. The diagnostic office will try to diagnose the faults electronically, which should be possible in 90 per cent of cases. The diagnostic offices are also able to discover faults before the customer notices them. The diagnostic offices will pass the faults to the field offices to repair the faults, and diagnose the remaining 10 per cent.

The field offices will be nominally assigned to an area within the region, but will share cases to balance workloads.

**Purpose:** The purpose of the project is to rationalize the CRMO organization:

1. To improve customer service so that:
   - All customers calling the receipt offices obtain a free line
   - All calls are answered within 10 seconds
   - The average time from call receipt to arrival of an engineer on site is two hours.
2. To improve productivity and flexibility so that:
   - The costs are justified through productivity improvements
   - The call receipt offices can be made part of a unified 'enquiry desk'
   - There are no redundancies so that all productivity improvements are achieved through natural wastage, redeployment or growth.

**Scope:** The work of the project includes:

- Changing from the existing structure of 18 area offices to three call receipt offices, two diagnostic offices and four field offices
- Investigating which of two new CRMO networking technologies is appropriate for the new structure, and to implement that chosen
- Refurbishing the nine new offices to current standards
- Training and redeploying staff to meet the needs of the operation of the new CRMOs
- Installing hardware to connect the CRMOs to the new Customer Information System, and implementing a statistical package to analyse fault data.

The work of the project excludes:

- Any staff who are surplus to requirements within the CRMO structure and who will be passed to central personnel for redeployment on other expansion projects
- With the implementation of the new Customer Information System, the call receipt offices may within the next two years be incorporated into unified 'enquiry desks' dealing with all customer contacts. However, it will not be the project team's responsibility to achieve that integration.

**Objectives:** The CRMO Rationalization Project will be completed when the CRMO facilities have been installed and are operational in nine offices – three call receipt offices, two diagnostic offices and four field offices – with:

- Appropriate networking technology and supporting statistical Management Information System (MIS) required to achieve the stated customer service levels

- Appropriate operating systems and procedures required to achieve the customer service levels and productivity improvements
- Appropriate numbers of trained staff, and no surplus staff
- The first offices operational within five months and the work complete within nine months.

**Work areas**: In order to achieve the project's objectives, the following areas of work are required:

A  *Accommodation*  Refurbish new offices, install hardware and furniture. (There is only one floor area available in the region large enough to take the first call receipt and fault diagnosis offices. The remaining eight offices must be housed in existing CRMO space.)

T  *Technology*  Decide on networking technology to be used, implement statistical MIS, implement networking technology in new offices.

O  *Organization*  Communicate all changes to the staff involved, define the operation of the new CRMOs, train and redeploy staff to fill new positions.

T  *Project*  Plan the project, organize the resources, obtain financial approval.

The last is required to allow for the actual management of the project, and will deliver the last of the objectives listed above.

---

### Step 5: Identifying stakeholders

Next, you must identify all the people who have an involvement in, have an interest in or are influenced by the change, called the *stakeholders*. Turner[2] suggests that there are three main groups of possible stakeholders:

1. *The primary team* are those people assigned to the project full-time, for its duration, principally the project manager and his or her immediate assistants.
2. *The secondary team* are those people who contribute to the project on a part-time or temporary basis.
3. *The tertiary team* are those people influenced by the project or interested in its work or outcomes, but who have no direct involvement in the work. Within the tertiary team there are 3 sub-groups:
   - *Reference groups* are those people who have an interest in the work of the project, including managers, professional colleagues and families of the primary and secondary team
   - *The affected* are those people influenced by the project's work and objectives, including people made redundant, redeployed, recruited, reskilled or retrained through changed working practices
   - *Consumers* are those people who consume the project's product, including users of the service produced.

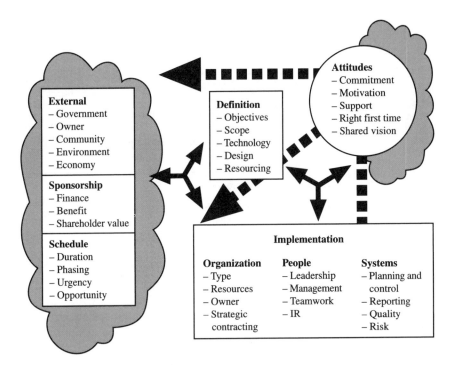

**Figure 3.3**   Strategic management of projects

The stakeholder analysis grid, Fig. 1.3, is a way of analysing the impact of the various groups. By definition (almost) the primary and secondary groups lie on the right-hand side of this grid, and the tertiary groups on the left-hand side. Any others can lie top and bottom. Chapter 8 describes in detail how to manage the stakeholders.

### Step 6: Understanding enablers and constraints

You will now be able to identify and analyse the driving and constraining forces for change. The diagnostic techniques described in section 2.3 will help. As a result of this analysis it may be necessary to return to Step 4 to change decisions made there, or even to Steps 3 or 1. (Step 2 is updated throughout the process.)

### Step 7: Project strategy

Before beginning to plan the project in detail, it is worth while setting a basic strategy for its implementation. Figure 3.3 suggests a six-element model for deriving a project strategy.[2] The elements of this model include:

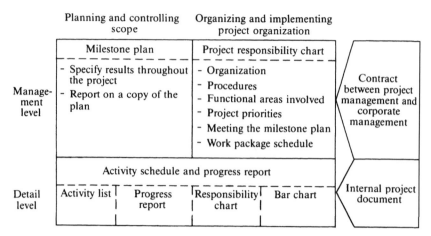

**Figure 3.4**  Three essential plans for a project

1. *Attitudes* You must ensure attitudes to change are positive in the organization and at all levels of management. If they are wrong at any level – senior, middle or junior – you will have an uphill struggle.
2. *Definition* We discussed above the need to ensure good definition, of the business objectives, the change required and the programmes and individual projects for change.
3. *Implementation* You must ensure that you have a clear, well-defined approach to managing the change projects. This does not have to be project management, the rocket science, but a clear strategy for the application of tools and techniques. Your implementation strategy may cover the planning and control systems, organizational and people issues.
4. *Context* The situation in which the change project exists must be supportive. There are three elements to the context:
   - *Environment* The support the project receives from people in its immediate surroundings, including government, stakeholders, sponsors, etc.
   - *Sponsorship* Support the project receives from the sponsor and the benefit they expect in return.
   - *Duration* The sponsor expects that return within a certain time for their sponsorship to be repaid. This can impose urgency on the project which must be addressed and managed.

**Step 8: Project plans**

Figure 3.4 illustrates the essential plans you need to manage a change project. The elements of this model are as follows.

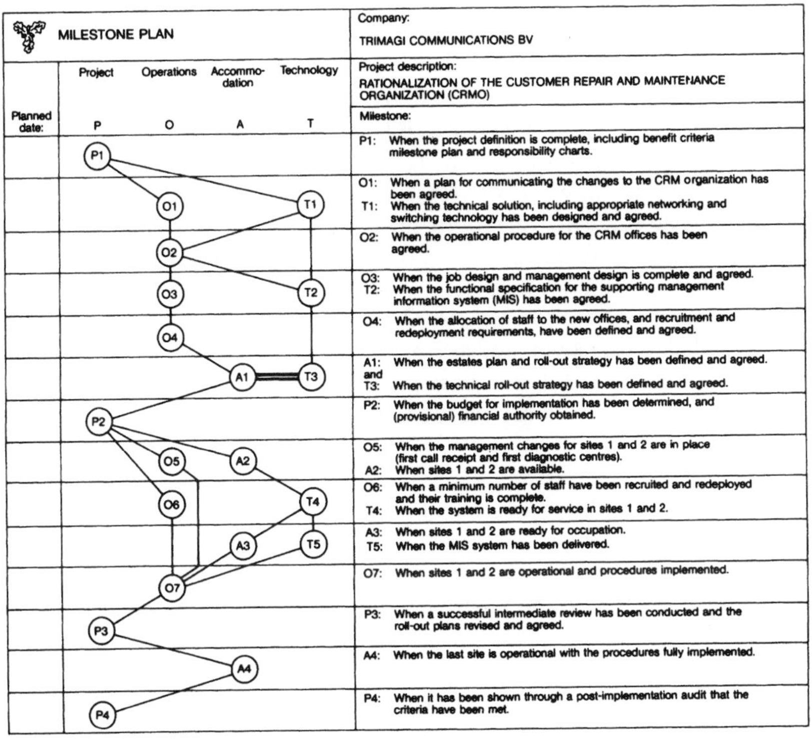
MILESTONE PLAN
Company:
TRIMAGI COMMUNICATIONS BV
Project description:
RATIONALIZATION OF THE CUSTOMER REPAIR AND MAINTENANCE ORGANIZATION (CRMO)
Project
Operations
Accommo- dation
Technology
Planned date:
P
O
A
T
Milestone:
P1: When the project definition is complete, including benefit criteria milestone plan and responsibility charts.
O1: When a plan for communicating the changes to the CRM organization has been agreed.
T1: When the technical solution, including appropriate networking and switching technology has been designed and agreed.
O2: When the operational procedure for the CRM offices has been agreed.
O3: When the job design and management design is complete and agreed.
T2: When the functional specification for the supporting management information system (MIS) has been agreed.
O4: When the allocation of staff to the new offices, and recruitment and redeployment requirements, have been defined and agreed.
A1: When the estates plan and roll-out strategy has been defined and agreed.
and
T3: When the technical roll-out strategy has been defined and agreed.
P2: When the budget for implementation has been determined, and (provisional) financial authority obtained.
O5: When the management changes for sites 1 and 2 are in place (first call receipt and first diagnostic centres).
A2: When sites 1 and 2 are available.
O6: When a minimum number of staff have been recruited and redeployed and their training is complete.
T4: When the system is ready for service in sites 1 and 2.
A3: When sites 1 and 2 are ready for occupation.
T5: When the MIS system has been delivered.
O7: When sites 1 and 2 are operational and procedures implemented.
P3: When a successful intermediate review has been conducted and the roll-out plans revised and agreed.
A4: When the last site is operational with the procedures fully implemented.
P4: When it has been shown through a post-implementation audit that the criteria have been met.

**Figure 3.5** Example milestone plan for a change project

MILESTONE PLAN

This defines at a strategic level what the project will deliver. Through 15 to 20 milestones, the project team define the intermediate goals they will deliver to achieve the project's objectives. Figure 3.5 is an example milestone plan for the change project at TriMagi defined above. Notice that the milestones are grouped into areas of work, or result paths, to help the project team achieve an overall balance to their approach to the project.[2,3] A simple plan like this can be a powerful tool for creating a vision for the project, and gaining the commitment of all the people involved in the change project to the intermediate milestones and the date by which they have to be delivered.

RESPONSIBILITY CHART

This shows the responsibility of the various groups of people involved in the project to delivering the project objectives. Against each milestone in the rows of the chart are placed a series of symbols to represent what each group of people will do to deliver that milestone, the names of the groups being at the head of the column. The chart at the milestone level defines the involvement of groups, rather than individuals. Figure 3.6 is a chart for the CRMO Project at TriMagi. This uses symbols developed by Andersen et al.[2,3] to represent the roles and responsibilities (refer to the key in the centre top of the chart). This chart also has a column at the extreme right for showing how much work each milestone entails, and space for a bar chart (Gantt Chart in the jargon of project management, the rocket science) to show when it will happen.

The milestone plan and responsibility chart are best derived at a workshop attended by the key managers on the project (champion, project manager, work area managers, resource providers, senior users).[2] For a project of up to a few months' duration, these two are the only plans you need.

ACTIVITY SCHEDULE

When each milestone itself stretches to a couple of months' work, then you will want to develop activity plans for selected milestones. Figure 3.7 is one plan for a milestone on the CRMO project at TriMagi. The activity plans should be developed on a rolling wave basis (that is when work on the milestone is about to start), at a workshop attended by the individual project team members who will do this work. They will now be the named resources in the columns of the chart.

## Project implementation

With these simple plans you can encourage people to do work milestone by milestone, having them develop their own activity schedules as they are about to start.

## Project monitoring, control and learning

As the project progresses, you must monitor progress and determine whether you are likely to achieve your objectives as assumed in the plan, in particular, will they be achieved within the original time, cost and quality assumptions? Figure 3.8 shows this monitoring carried out at two levels. The project manager gathers reports from the team against the activity schedules, Fig. 3.9, and feeds summarized reports to the project's sponsors on the milestone plan, Fig. 3.10. The top cycle may be over a longer frequency than the bottom cycle. You must also make predictions about how the project will perform, by forecasting the likely completion. There is a strong view that you cannot control the past, only the future. This is

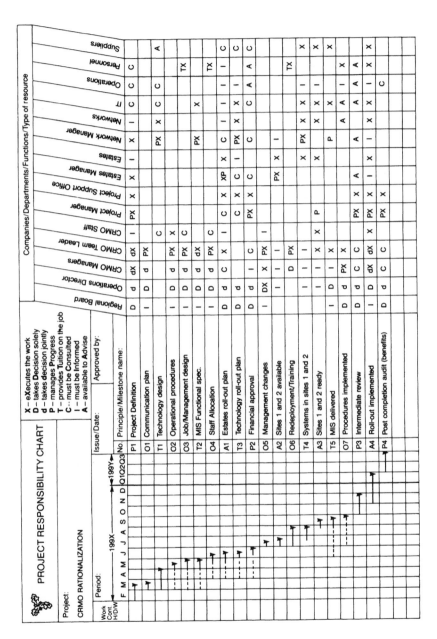

**Figure 3.6** Example responsibility chart at the milestone level for a change project

51

Figure 3.7 caption below.

**ACTIVITY SCHEDULE**

Project: CRMO RATIONALIZATION
Milestone No./Name: P1: PROJECT DEFINITION
Issue/Date: A/2 Jan
Approved by: JRT

Work Cont. H/D/W — Period: 199X Week Number

Key:
- X – eXecutes the work
- D – takes Decision solely
- d – takes decision jointly
- P – manages Progress
- T – provides Tuition on the job
- C – must be Consulted
- I – must be Informed
- A – available to Advise

Companies/Departments/Functions/Type of resource

| No. | Activity/Task name | Regional Board | Operations Director | CRMO Managers (2) | CRMO Team Leader | CRMO Staff | Project Manager | Project Support Office | Estates Manager | Estates | Network Manager | Networks | IT | Operations | Personnel |
|---|---|---|---|---|---|---|---|---|---|---|---|---|---|---|---|
| 10 | Produce project proposal | C | D | d | dX | | PX | A | A | | A | | A | A | A |
| | Hold project definition workshop | | DX | d | X | | PX | X | | | | | | | |
| | Define required benefits | C | D | d | dX | | PX | X | I | I | I | | I | I | I |
| | Draft project definition report | | D | d | dX | | PX | X | X | | X | | X | | |
| | Hold project launch workshop | C | D | X | X | | PX | X | C | | C | | C | A | C |
| | Finalize milestone plan | | D | d | d | | PX | X | C | | C | | C | A | A |
| | Finalize responsibility chart | D | D | d | d | | PX | X | C | | C | | C | | A |
| | Prepare estimates – time | | | | A | | P | X | A | | A | | A | A | A |
| | Prepare estimates – cost | | | A | A | | P | X | A | | A | | A | A | A |
| | Prepare estimates – revenue | | A | A | A | | P | | | | | | | | |
| | Assess project viability | | D | d | d | | PX | X | C | | C | | | C | C |
| | Assess risks | | D | d | d | | PX | X | C | | C | | C | C | C |
| | Finalize project definition report | D | d | d | dX | I | PX | X | X | I | X | I | IX | | I |
| | Mobilize team | | D | d | dX | I | PX | X | | | | | | | I |

Figure 3.7 Example activity schedule for a change project

52

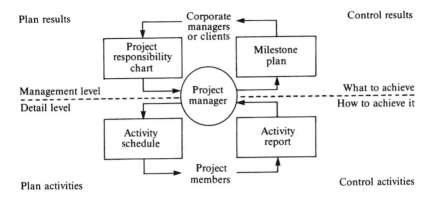

**Figure 3.8**   Monitoring and control on two levels

forward-looking control. Hence, you forecast completion by planning the remainder of the project, starting from now, in much the same way as you planned originally. If your new plan begins to diverge from the original plan, you have four choices:

- Find a new way of doing the project to recover your original plan
- Provide extra resources and funds for the project to maintain the time-scale
- Let the timescale slip
- Do less work, reducing the functionality of the product, but maintaining the quality of that which you do complete.

These are in decreasing order of desirability.[4] The second option can sometimes have the opposite effect – adding resource delays the project further as the existing project staff take time out to brief the new staff.[5]

## 3.3 Implementing change at TriMagi

We close this chapter by illustrating the application of the ideas to a change project at a company called, here, TriMagi. At the time in question, TriMagi had a turnover in excess of £100 million, with operations in a dozen countries and a complex portfolio of products, markets, technologies and distribution channels. Following Fig. 3.1 (p. 40), we describe how project management was used to:

- Conduct a strategic analysis
- Define a new business strategy
- Manage the change project to implement that strategy.

**Figure 3.9** Reporting progress at the team level against the activity schedule

| PROGRESS REPORT | Consequence for Milestone Plan: |
|---|---|

Suggested text on Milestone Report:
WORK ON TARGET FOR PLANNED
COMPLETION FOR 12TH MAR

| Work done | Work to do | Est'd compl'n | Quality accept | Resp'y chart kept | Change req'd | Waiting time | Special problem |
|---|---|---|---|---|---|---|---|
| 5 | 0 | | | | | | |
| 4 | 0 | | | | | | |
| 2 | 0 | | | | | | |
| 7 | 0 | | | | | | |
| 13 | 0 | | | | | | |
| 2 | 1 | 3/3 | | | | | |
| 1 | 1 | 3/5 | | | | | |
| 1 | 1 | 5/3 | | | | | |
| 1 | 1 | 5/3 | | | | | |
| 0 | 1 | 5/3 | | | | | |
| 0 | 1 | ✓ | | | | | |
| 0 | 3 | ✓ | | | | | |
| 0 | 5 | ✓ | | | | | |
| 0 | 3 | ✓ | | | | | |

**ACTIVITY SCHEDULE**

Project: CRMO RATIONALIZATION
Milestone No./Name: P1: PROJECT DEFINITION
Issue/Date: A/2 JAN
Approved by: JRT

Period: 199X Week Number

| Work Cont HDW | 4 | 5 | 6 | 7 | 8 | 9 | 10 | No. | Activity/Task Name |
|---|---|---|---|---|---|---|---|---|---|
| 4 | | | | | | | | | PRODUCE PROJECT PROPOSAL |
| 4 | | | | | | | | | HOLD PROJECT DEFINITION W'SHOP |
| 2 | | | | | | | | | DEFINE REQUIRED BENEFITS |
| 8 | | | | | | | | | DRAFT PROJECT DEFINITION REPORT |
| 12 | | | | | | | | | HOLD PROJECT LAUNCH W'SHOP |
| 2 | | | | | | | | | FINALIZE MILESTONE PLAN |
| 2 | | | | | | | | | FINALIZE RESPONSIBILITY CHART |
| 2 | | | | | | | | | PREPARE ESTIMATES - TIME |
| 2 | | | | | | | | | PREPARE ESTIMATES - COST |
| 1 | | | | | | | | | PREPARE ESTIMATES - REVENUE |
| 1 | | | | | | | | | ASSESS PROJECT VIABILITY |
| 3 | | | | | | | | | ASSESS RISKS |
| 5 | | | | | | | | | FINALIZE PROJECT DEFINITION REPORT |
| 3 | | | | | | | | | MOBILIZE TEAM |

X – eXecutes the work
D – takes Decision solely
d – takes decision jointly
P – manages Progress
T – provides Tuition on the job
C – must be Consulted
I – must be Informed
A – available to Advise

Named Functions/Named Persons/Named Resources

| Activity | REGIONAL BOARD | OPERATIONS DIRECTOR | CRMO MANAGERS (2) | CRMO TEAM LEADER | CRMO STAFF | PROJECT MANAGER | PROJECT SUPPORT OFFICE | ESTATES MANAGER | ESTATES | NETWORK MANAGER | IT | OPERATIONS | PERSONNEL |
|---|---|---|---|---|---|---|---|---|---|---|---|---|---|
| PRODUCE PROJECT PROPOSAL | C | D | d | dX | | PX | A | A | | A | | A | A | A |
| HOLD PROJECT DEFINITION W'SHOP | | DX | | X | | PX | X | | | | | | | |
| DEFINE REQUIRED BENEFITS | C | D | d | dX | | PX | | | | | | | | |
| DRAFT PROJECT DEFINITION REPORT | C | D | d | dX | | PX | X | I | | I | | I | I | I |
| HOLD PROJECT LAUNCH W'SHOP | | | X | X | | PX | X | X | | X | | X | | |
| FINALIZE MILESTONE PLAN | D | d | d | | | PX | X | C | | C | | C | A | C |
| FINALIZE RESPONSIBILITY CHART | D | d | d | | | PX | X | C | | C | | C | A | A |
| PREPARE ESTIMATES - TIME | | | A | | | P | X | A | | A | | A | A | A |
| PREPARE ESTIMATES - COST | | | A | | | P | X | A | | A | | A | A | A |
| PREPARE ESTIMATES - REVENUE | A | A | A | | | P | X | | | | | | | |
| ASSESS PROJECT VIABILITY | D | d | d | | | PX | | | | | | | | |
| ASSESS RISKS | D | d | dX | | | PX | X | C | | C | | C | C | C |
| FINALIZE PROJECT DEFINITION REPORT | D | d | d | d | | PX | X | C | | C | | C | | C |
| MOBILIZE TEAM | | D | d | dX | I | PX | X | X | I | X | I | IX | | I |

Additional comments

– problem description  LAUNCH WORKSHOP DELAYED 3 DAYS
MILESTONE PLAN REQUIRED ADDITIONAL MODS

– likely cause  OPERATIONS DIRECTOR UNAVAILABLE
CRMO 1 HAD ADDITIONAL COMMENTS

– possible consequence  COMPLETION DELAYED 3 DAYS

– suggested action  NONE – TIME CAN BE RECOVERED

– supporting information

Signed: LJN    Date: 26/2/9X

Manager's comments:

MONITOR

Signed: JRT    Date: 1 MAR 9X

**MILESTONE PLAN**

| | | | | Company:<br>TRIMAGI COMMUNICATIONS BV | Project Manager:<br>SVK | | |
|---|---|---|---|---|---|---|---|
| | | | | | Plan issue:<br>A | Approved by:<br>JRT | Date:<br>04 Feb |
| | Project | Operations | Accommodation | Technology | Project description:<br>RATIONALIZATION OF THE CUSTOMER REPAIR AND MAINTENANCE ORGANIZATION (CRMO) | | |
| Planned date: | P | O | A | T | Milestone: | Date: | Report: |

| Planned date | Milestone | Report |
|---|---|---|
| 01 Jan | P1: When the project definition is complete, including benefit criteria milestone plan and responsibility charts. | 07 Jan Completed |
| 01 Feb / 01 Mar | O1: When a plan for communicating the changes to the CRM organization has been agreed.<br>T1: When the technical solution, including appropriate networking and switching technology has been designed and agreed. | 04 Feb Plan agreed<br>04 Mar Completed |
| 15 Mar | O2: When the operational procedure for the CRM offices has been agreed. | 18 Mar Completion predicted 22 Mar<br>Awaiting engineering input |
| 15 Apr / 15 Apr | O3: When the job design and management design is complete and agreed.<br>T2: When the functional specification for the supporting management information system (MIS) has been agreed. | 18 Mar Work started where possible<br>18 Mar Draft functional spec prepared |
| 1 May | O4: When the allocation of staff to the new offices, and recruitment and redeployment requirements, have been defined and agreed. | |
| 1 May | A1: When the estates plan and roll-out strategy has been defined and agreed.<br>T3: When the technical roll-out strategy has been defined and agreed. | |
| 1 May | P2: When the budget for implementation has been determined, and (provisional) financial authority obtained. | |
| 01 Jun / 01 Jul | O5: When the management changes for sites 1 and 2 are in place (first call receipt and first diagnostic centres).<br>A2: When sites 1 and 2 are available. | |
| 15 Jul / 15 Jul | O6: When a minimum number of staff have been recruited and redeployed and their training is complete.<br>T4: When the system is ready for service in sites 1 and 2. | |
| 01 Aug / 15 Aug | A3: When sites 1 and 2 are ready for occupation.<br>T5: When the MIS system has been delivered. | |
| 01 Sep | O7: When sites 1 and 2 are operational and procedures implemented. | |
| 01 Oct | P3: When a successful intermediate review has been conducted and the roll-out plans revised and agreed. | |
| 01 Mar | A4: When the last site is operational with the procedures fully implemented. | |
| 01 Apr | P4: When it has been shown through a post-implementation audit that the criteria have been met. | |

**Figure 3.10**   Reporting progress at the project level against the milestone plan

### Business strategy

Over a period of four months, the senior and middle managers worked to devise a strategic plan to drive change, Fig. 3.11. This involved several cross-functional project teams. Every one of these sub-projects was completed on time, except for the *decision workshop*, involving the top team, and this overran by 120 per cent. This was because management underscoped the range and difficulty of the decisions to be made. In part this was inevitable, as it was hard to foresee the radical nature of the decisions which emerged. On the other hand, previous experience pointed to the need for some contingency, in case decisions took longer to crystallize and work through. However, senior management chose to assume the process would work without delay. The success of the *early analysis* in running to time and cost and in delivering the anticipated results was very much attributable to effective project management. For each module of the process in Fig. 3.11, there:

– Were clear outputs specified

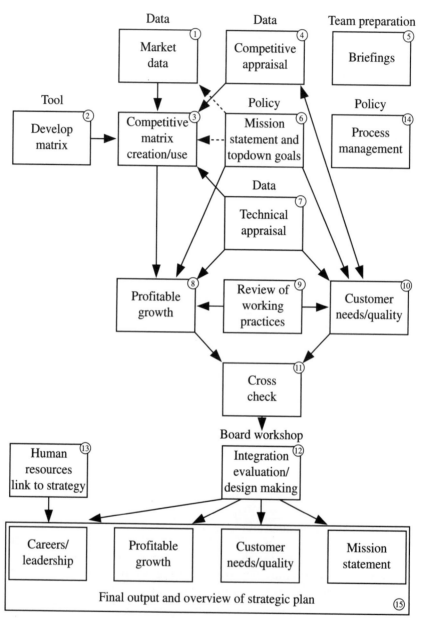

**Figure 3.11** Strategic plan for TriMagi

- Were additional processes and inputs
- Was a project team
- Was a project sponsor
- Were defined relationships with other projects.

These were distilled into a report filling no more than two sides of A4 for each module (the lesson here being to strive for simplicity when managing complex change).

## Defining the change

Out of the *decision workshop*, a number of change initiatives were identified. These in turn needed scoping and defining as change projects and included:

- Simplifying business processes
- Developing more sophisticated account management
- Implementing market and competitor monitoring systems
- Reducing the cost of many products
- Continuing market analysis of several European countries
- Implementing a framework of business measures to integrate strategic, operational and financial controls
- Withdrawing from certain activities.

This agenda looked both large and unmanageable before each of these areas of change were themselves defined as projects. Each of these projects was defined and scoped as follows:

1. Its key objectives and detailed outputs were defined.
2. Its impact on different parts of the organization was assessed.
3. Formal analysis of key stakeholders was performed using the stakeholder analysis grid in Fig. 1.3. This helped in suggesting creative influencing strategies.
4. More specific forces enabling and constraining change were identified using force field analysis.
5. Resource needs were identified.
6. From this the *degree of difficulty* of the project was assessed.
7. Furthermore, the *degree of urgency and importance* of each of the change projects was assessed, and the various projects marked on the importance/urgency grid, Fig. 3.12.

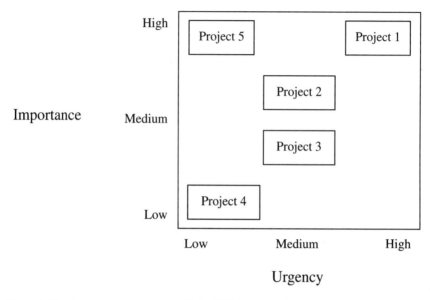

**Figure 3.12**   Importance/urgency grid for TriMagi's projects

This final step enabled the management to prioritize and phase each project, and so reduced the shock felt when the extent of the change projects actually required was first revealed.

### Understanding enablers, constraints and stakeholders

The phases of definition of project scope and focus were thus bound up with:

– Understanding stakeholders
– Understanding enabling forces and constraints
– Targeting outputs.

This allowed projects to be redefined and rescoped. Only then could a project strategy be formulated. Certain generic constraints were highlighted during this exercise. Some of these were 'hard', such as the problem of constrained resources and a fixed headcount. Some were 'soft', suggesting difficulties in implementing change given the prevailing organizational culture. Although culture had been identified as an issue in the earlier strategic plan, this had then been put to one side as being 'too difficult for the time being'. Subsequently, a project was initiated to diagnose the required changes to culture. This project explored options for achieving the culture shift. Hence, project management can be used for managing soft and hard organizational issues.

### Implementation strategy – project plan

Each change project thus had defined:

- Scope and milestones
- Focus and key issues involved
- Strategic, financial, operational and organizational objectives
- Links to other change projects
- A supporting budget
- An allocated project.

These were not detailed, but defined in a succinct way as bullet points and visual pictures, rather than as a more conventional, detailed project plan. Case Study 3.1 and Figs. 3.5, 3.6 and 3.7 illustrate possible project plans at TriMagi for an assumed change project. (Although this project is based on a real example, it is in fact from another telecommunications company. That company has a turnover of £14 billion, and global operations. The project concerned was adapted for illustrative purposes.)

### Project implementation and feedback

Despite these efforts at structured project management of this major change project, there were still many problems. As with many change projects, the programme of change became impeded by a number of internal and external factors. These included:

- A (largely unexpected) economic downturn
- Internal restructuring
- A change in senior management
- An intensified pressure to reduce costs.

With such internal and external factors there can be a temptation to allow improvement projects to drift, until such time as they are typically scrapped. After an abrupt change in managing director, the moribund improvement projects were reviewed. The projects were rapidly reprioritized and refocused into the following:

- Simplified business processes
- Cost reduction of many products

- Overhead reduction and restructuring
- Withdrawal from several business areas
- Culture change.

Other issues which needed to be addressed in the medium term were put on hold so these key projects could be mobilized. However, having a map of all the projects and how they interrelated was a constant reminder to management that the issues, and hence the relevant improvement projects, were on the critical path of strategic change. Although these adjustments to early project plans met with some cynicism, the fact that the change programme was being managed in a structured way allowed these changes to be made without disruption. Without rigorous project management, it is likely that the whole programme of change would have collapsed.

### Lessons from managing change through projects

A number of key lessons can be drawn from the experience of managing change at TriMagi:

1. Project management is not a discipline you apply to just one stage of the change process (such as the definition of the strategy); it applies throughout all stages.
2. It can also deal equally effectively with soft and hard issues (the cultural and technical change described by Andersen et al.[3] and Turner.[2]
3. During major change, projects are typically reshaped, regrouped and refocused. This fluidity is quite normal, but the processes need to be channelled and controlled.
4. In major change programmes, projects often need to survive changes in members of senior management. They must therefore be robust and have a clear rationale so that they can be endorsed by any new leader.
5. No sensible project strategy can be formulated without considering how difficult it will be to implement the associated cultural change process. This requires a thorough analysis of the enabling and constraining forces affecting the change, particularly arising from the impact of key stakeholders.
6. It is imperative to assess the total set of change projects being undertaken in the organization at any one time, in order to compare the workload with organizational capacity and capability. This may lead to some reprioritization of projects by considering their importance, urgency and degree of difficulty.
7. During times of organizational trauma, it is particularly difficult, but nevertheless essential, to hold a change project together during any period of uncertainty over leadership and direction.

8. Where there are problems in securing the necessary infrastructure for change projects to progress, these bottlenecks may themselves be eliminated via improvement projects. This might include, for example:
   - An intervention project aimed at changing culture or management style
   - A project targeted at recruiting a significant new resource.
9. There needs to be a clear link between project output and company strategy. Ambiguous or poorly defined change projects are likely to fail. The project team and key stakeholders must know explicitly how the project is linked to corporate strategy.

## 3.4 Summary

1. A structured approach is required to planning and implementing change. This structure may include the following steps:

   - Business strategy
   - Target outputs
   - Defining the change
   - Defining project scope and focus
   - Identifying stakeholders
   - Understanding enablers and constraints
   - Project strategy
   - Project plans
   - Project implementation
   - Project control.

## References

1. Youker, R., 'Defining the hierarchy of project objectives', in *Proceedings of the PMI 24th Annual Seminar/Symposium*, San Diego, Project Management Institute, October 1994.
2. Turner, J.R., *The Handbook of Project-based Management: Improving the processes for achieving strategic objectives*, McGraw-Hill, 1993.
3. Andersen, E.S., Grude, K.V., Haug, T. and Turner, J.R., *Goal Directed Project Management,* Kogan Page, 1987.
4. Mills, R.W. and Turner, J.R., 'Projects for Shareholder Value', in *The Commercial Project Manager: Managing owners, sponsors, partners, supporters, stakeholders, contractors and consultants*, Turner, J.R. (Ed.), McGraw-Hill, 1995.
5. Brooks, F.P., *The Mythical Man Month*, Addison-Wesley, 1974.

# 4

# Organizing for change: A versatile approach

Rodney Turner and Reza Peymai

## 4.1 Introduction

Having defined the work of the project, we need to consider how it should be organized to involve both the project team and the operations personnel whose working lives are being changed. The standard management model for the first three-quarters of this century was the functional, hierarchical, line management structure. So ingrained was this approach that it was the structure adopted on many early projects. More recently, matrix management approaches have been adopted and this has led to consideration of issues such as whether resources are located in a project office or at their normal place of work, and the balance between the project managers and operations managers.[1] However, the matrix management approach led to stresses, because:

- It was not always clear who was in control of the project, the project managers or the operations managers
- Where it was clear, operations personnel would still give their loyalty to the operations managers because it was they who controlled career progression and annual bonuses
- Managers had difficulty assigning priority between operations and projects.

This conflict is captured in the projectivity model described later. The problem arose to a certain extent because line and matrix management structures encourage both operations and project managers to focus on needs of the job and the organization, and not on those of the customer. Many organizations implementing *total quality management* programmes in the 1980s and 1990s, found focusing on the needs of the customer forced them to adopt novel approaches, particularly ones based on defining management processes to deliver products to customers, rather than ones based on defining management functions or tasks which specify how the organization will work internally.[2,3]

In this chapter, we describe an approach called *process management* which provides customer focus and allows routine and project-based work to be mixed in a versatile way. We describe how the traditional systems approach to both operations and project management leads to lack of customer focus, and the conflict across the operations/project interface because of different systems employed. We show, in contrast, how *management by projects* was adopted to provide customer focus,[4,5] but sacrifices the ability to learn from prior experience. We introduce process management and illustrate its use by an organization in the building industry as part of its total quality management programme. By judging organizations against their level of customer focus and the novelty of their work, we propose appropriate organization structures for the four management environments: traditional operations management, traditional project management, management by projects, and process management. We then propose a structure for the *versatile organization*, in which organizations mix these four management approaches into an ever-changing granular structure, with the functional hierarchy providing the cement. We close by illustrating the concepts through BT, a company which recognized that its old, hierarchical, line structure gave it internal focus, but has now gone some way towards the implementation of a versatile organization structure, through a major change project called Project Sovereign.

## 4.2 Operations management versus project management: Routine versus novel

### Operations management

Up to the 1950s, virtually the only organization structure used was the hierarchical, functional, line organization structure – the 'bureaucratic' organization structure.[6] Within these organizations, people fulfil well-defined roles to achieve historical objectives. The concept is that if people do today what they did yesterday, then they will achieve the same objectives today. These organizations provide security and stability, and competitive advantage comes through ever-increasing efficiency, gained through *habitual incremental improvement*.[1] Long-term stability enables the organization to routinely achieve short-term production targets (tactical objectives). However, the structure has many weaknesses:

1. The organizations are based on a command-and-control structure, supposedly derived from a military model. Instructions are sent down the hierarchy. There is no need for feedback, because there is no need for

deviation from the instructions. However, this is a distortion of the military model. Von Moltke, a general from Germany's Second Reich, is quoted as saying: 'I have never known a battle plan to survive the first contact with the enemy'. Flexibility is required, because we cannot predict the future, and so we may need to adapt our plans in the light of the actual events encountered. This requires feedback mechanisms.

2. The structure results in 'over-the-wall' working. People in different cells in the organization do not need to communicate. They all perform well-defined routine tasks, in accordance with instructions passed down the hierarchy. Any cross-communication goes up and down the organization via the lowest common boss. When one cell finishes their work on a product it is passed 'over-the-wall' to the next cell, with no contact between them. There is a scene in the film *1984*, made in 1984, where Winston Smith is sitting in his cubicle in the Ministry of Information. A hole in the wall opens and papers are pushed through. He takes them, burns some, modifies the others and pushes them through another hole in the wall. Orwell[7] in writing the novel was describing life as he saw it in 1948, and so this is his metaphor for the bureaucratic organization structure.

3. The organization is totally inflexible. It cannot respond to rapid change and it cannot respond to differing customer requirements. People are working to rigidly defined roles, communication via the lowest common boss is slow and product development has to take place as a relay race, since once passed over the wall the new product cannot be passed back.

4. The organization is internally focused, existing for its own sake. Roles and procedures become established and become more important than customer requirements, reinforcing the inflexibility of the organization. This syndrome was blamed for the fall of IBM.[8]

This becomes the way organizations implement quality procedures such as BS5750 or ISO 9000. They write standing instructions which reinforce the well-defined roles and procedures, reduce the need for communication and feedback, reinforce the walls between the cells of the organization and make internal procedures more important than customer requirements. Whether this is an inherent flaw in the quality procedures or a fault in the way they are implemented remains a moot point. The British Standards Institute will tell you the latter.

### Project management

Two things happened in the 1950s which demanded a flexible, responsive approach to management. These were rapid weapons development required by the Cold War, and the rapid economic development brought on by the

Marshal Plan. Project management provided cross-functional working and communication, which enabled multi-functional teams to work together on rapid product development.[9] Short-term flexibility enables the organization to achieve long-term strategic objectives. However, project management as it developed tends still to be based on a command and control structure and have a systems rather than a customer focus.

Project management is meant to be the flexible approach, with progress fed back to the centre, so the plans can be adapted accordingly. However, somehow changing the plan has become equated with bad project management, even though the original plan is less likely to be correct than it is in the operations environment, because it is based on less historical experience. Perhaps we have one Robert Falcon Scott to blame for that. In the race for the South Pole, he adhered rigidly to his plan, even when it was obvious that it did not reflect the conditions as encountered, whereas Amundsen changed and adapted his. Nobody had been to the South Pole before and so nobody could predict the precise conditions that would be encountered. Unfortunately, even though Amundsen was successful and Scott was not, Scott has been the role model for British project management.

Morris[10] says: 'The most pervasive intellectual tradition to project management . . . is the systems approach', and Kerzner[11] calls his book: *Project Management: A systems approach to planning, scheduling and control.* Hence, in project management as it has developed, the internal systems have become more important than customer requirements, and this is reflected in the quality procedures adopted for project management. A standard mantra of project managers is to say that a successful project is to deliver to time, cost and quality, and by quality they mean to deliver a specification written and frozen at an early stage of the project. Recent research shows that successful project management is delivering value for the owner,[12] and a key element of achieving that is delivering *useful* functionality for the customer.

**Projectivity**

A further problem arises because project management is meant to implement change in the operations environment, and yet the different systems adopted mean that there is a clash of cultures. A basic paradox exits. Projects are transient, they exist only for the short term, but are created to deliver medium- to long-term strategic development objectives. Operations are continuous, they exist for the medium to long term, but are focused on achieving short-term tactical objectives. This leads to the adoption of the *projectivity model*, Fig. 4.1, to describe the need to manage the interface between operations management and project management.[1] The need to manage this interface arises because of the starkly different

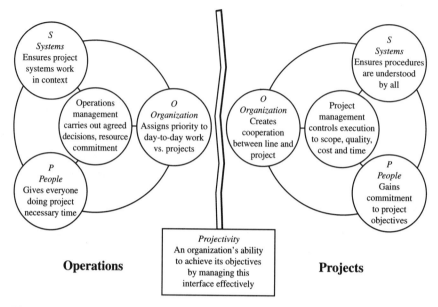

**Figure 4.1** The projectivity model

cultural approaches that exist on either side of it, because these two environments adopt very different approaches to their internal management. The word *projectivity* was introduced to reflect an organization's ability to achieve its development objectives by managing this interface. The projectivity model is about trying to make the people on either side of the interface appreciate the systems used on the other side, and in particular helping the people on the other side to fit in with your approach. The responsibility of the operations manager is to ensure the organization delivers adequate resources to enable the selected project to take place. They must support projects by ensuring:

- Staff are given time to meet their project goals
- Project systems are understood in the operations environment
- The project has priority alongside the daily operations.

The responsibility of project managers is to manage the achievement of results. In particular, to manage the interface with operations effectively, the project manager must:

- Ensure all participants understand and are committed to the project's goals
- Ensure that the projects systems and documents are understood by all

– Create cooperation between project and operations by communicating project plans in a form in which they and their consequences are understood and accepted.

Thus the projectivity model recognizes that the systems adopted by both operations management and project management are internally focused, designed for the benefit of the environment in which they are applied, not for the benefit of customers. It tries to manage the conflict this creates, not eliminate it.

## 4.3 Management by projects: Customer versus systems

*Management by projects* is an approach which tries to eliminate the operations/project interface, by making project-based working the norm for the organization.[4,5] All work is treated as unique and novel, and so a novel and transient approach is adopted for its management, meeting the particular requirements of each customer. This leads to the adoption of a flat, flexible organization structure, involving working in transient project teams, which in turn leads to a degradation of the organization's expertise, customs and culture.[1] This ultimately threatens the quality of the organization's products, as there is a greater chance of getting it wrong if a new approach is adopted every time. Hence organizations seem to be presented with a dilemma; do they:

– Rigidly apply internally defined procedures to the detriment of customer requirements?
– Develop new procedures for every job to meet the unique requirement of every customer, hence losing the ability to learn from prior experience, and increasing the chance of achieving a poor quality product?

Process management tries to overcome this by adopting a versatile approach, which recognizes differing customer requirements, but follows flexible guidelines to maximize learning from prior experience.

## 4.4 Process management: Providing customer focus to routine work

A customer-oriented approach, called *process management*,[2] has been successfully adopted for the management of routine work in the construction industry. Clemmer[3] describes the motivation for process management:

A key change in moving from a traditional organization to a team based one is bringing planning and thinking back together with implementing and doing. To

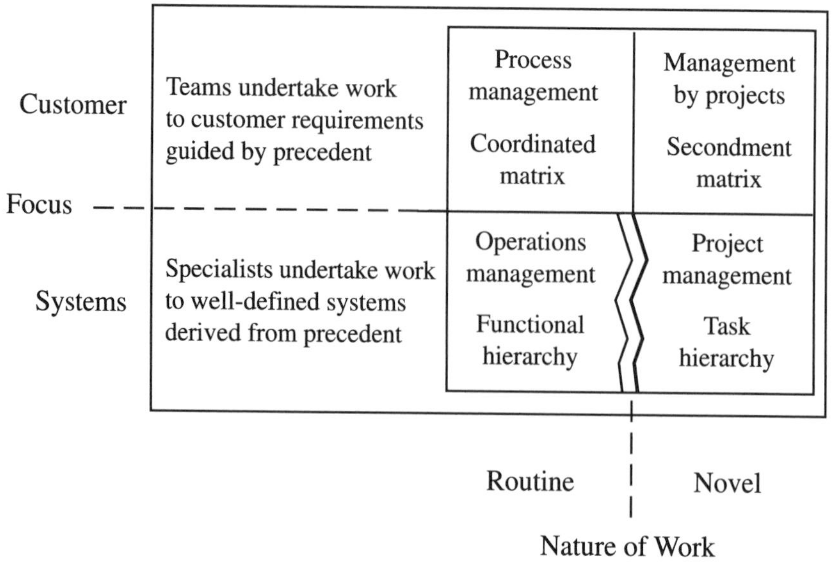

|  |  | Routine | Novel |
|---|---|---|---|
| Customer | Teams undertake work to customer requirements guided by precedent | Process management<br><br>Coordinated matrix | Management by projects<br><br>Secondment matrix |
| Focus |  |  |  |
| Systems | Specialists undertake work to well-defined systems derived from precedent | Operations management<br><br>Functional hierarchy | Project management<br><br>Task hierarchy |

Routine   Novel

Nature of Work

**Figure 4.2** Four management approaches

maximise the level of ownership for making it work, the thinking and doing are brought as close as possible to the customers and the people making, serving, or supporting the organization's basic products or services.

Thus process management provides customer focus for routine work, Fig. 4.2. What this illustrates is that adopting a customer focus eliminates the interface between operations and project management. Both environments must now be flexible in their approach, and rather than defining their work in terms of responsibilities and systems, they are responsive to the customers' requirements and the processes which must be undertaken to deliver products which meet them. Project management may create flexibility. However, customers are becoming less loyal, and more ruthless, and hence flexibility is not enough. Organizations must now demonstrate versatility. Process management does exactly that, allowing a 'flexible' manager (project manager) also to become a 'versatile' manager (process owner). The most important aspect of this change is the manager is now responsible not only for executing the project, but also for improving the process for delivering products or services to customers. For this manager, the beginning is not 'when the job has been won', but 'win a job'. Similarly, the end of the process is not 'when the project is complete', but 'when the process has been further improved'. The project manager needs to build a record of improvement ideas generated by the project team during the project, and to refer to them at the end of the project to improve the process. You no longer have 'project management' but a process of project management on a journey of continuous improvement.

Peymai[2] describes the implementation of process management in a service industry, building. He describes how process management can be applied to the management of design, procurement and site security functions. Although the building industry might appear to be project-based, these three functions in particular are fundamentally routine, and are therefore managed as operations. When his organization first obtained quality registration, under BS5750 (the first building contractor in the UK to be so registered), they defined their procedures in terms of the systems operated by each department. This produced a very functional approach, describing what departments are responsible for, rather than what they do to deliver products to customers. The organization divided itself into projects and routine operations and found it had to manage the projects/operations interface as described in the projectivity model above. Their experience was that the implementation of BS5750 made the organization more inward looking, indeed made each department more inward looking, reinforcing the walls between the departments. The quality of the product delivered to the customer actually fell, even though (or perhaps because) they were now working to improved internal procedures.

On implementing process management, the work of all departments became a service to the project manager, who is the primary internal representative of the customer. Process-based teams were established to provide the service to project managers. However, these process-based teams must not lose sight of the fact that they are undertaking routine tasks and they can therefore maximize the opportunity for learning from prior experience, and increasing product quality through habitual incremental improvement. Peymai[2] reports that by adopting process management the organization improved the quality of the product, but also reduced costs by eliminating waste and rework.

## 4.5 The versatile organization

Figure 4.2 proposes appropriate organizational structures for the four management approaches taken from the traditional five used in project-based management in Fig. 4.3.[1] The four management approaches in Fig. 4.2 are:

– Operations management
– Project management
– Processes management
– Management by projects.

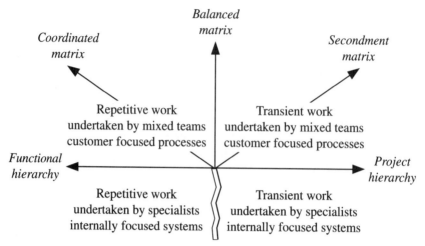

**Figure 4.3** Five organization structures

## Operations management

This is appropriate when the customers' requirements are unchanging, and the products can be delivered using well-defined and highly refined systems. Then it is possible to adopt a functional hierarchy, with people fulfilling defined roles. With time it is likely the roles will become skill based, rather than product based. However, in the modern business environment, customers' needs and expectations change more than ever before. Operations management would find it difficult to maintain a pure and strict functional hierarchy without incorporating some degree of process management in order to keep abreast of the changes.

## Project management

This is appropriate when there are clearly defined project objectives and methods of achieving them, that is on what Turner and Cochrane[13] describe as Type 1 Projects in their goals and methods matrix (Fig. 4.4). Then it is possible to adopt a project hierarchy, with people undertaking well-defined activities. Inevitably, the activities become systems-based rather than product-oriented (see Fig. 4.2).

There is a major divide between project management and operations management which many organizations find impossible to cross.

## Management by projects and process management

These are required when the customers requirements are varying, or the methods of achieving them are varying. Management by projects should

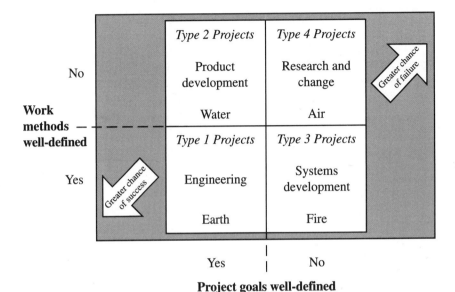

**Figure 4.4** The goals and methods matrix

be used for Type 2, 3 or 4 Projects, and a secondment matrix is appropriate, with the project manager remaining the primary interface with the customer, but with the process managers providing support. Process management should be used where the products are fundamentally routine but with minor variations required by different customers. A coordinated matrix is the appropriate structure, with the primary interface with the customer via the process managers, but with project managers coordinating the bespoke variations. (In the secondment matrix, the project manager sets the work of the project personnel day by day, while the process manager oversees how it is done. In the coordinated matrix, the process manager sets the daily schedules, while the project manager sets the overall targets. The terms are explained further in Turner.[1])

The flat, flexible and versatile organization is able to move easily between process management and management by projects dependent on the changing requirements of its customers (Fig. 4.5). This organization structure shows process and project teams delivering customer requirements of varying uniqueness. These teams vary in size and composition to meet the changing customer requirements, with people moving between the teams and the functional organization which forms the cement holding the cells together. The functional 'cement' also holds the knowledge that the organization develops through the learning and review which follow each job, so that it becomes the store for the systems, customs and culture of the organization.

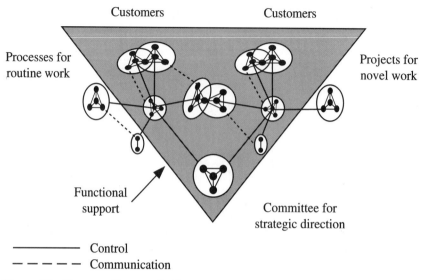

Customers          Customers

Processes for                                    Projects for
routine work                                     novel work

Functional
support

Committee for
strategic direction

———————— Control
— — — — — Communication

**Figure 4.5** The versatile organization

Figure 4.5 also shows some of the teams being formed by people from outside the parent organization. The cells in this structure will be cross-functional teams working on small projects or processes. However, larger jobs will require the teams to collaborate, communicating with each other and forming informal contracts on how they will support each other to deliver products to the organization's customers. Such an organization is sometimes called a *fractal organization*.[14] In this flat, versatile organization, a small central committee provides strategic direction and vision, but does not command and control. Hastings[15] provides pathfinder case studies of organizations adopting structures similar to this. Benneton is one with a similar structure, although in this case most of the cells are outside the parent organization; only the committee providing strategic direction and the design department are inside. We refer to the versatile organization as the 'network organization', to differentiate from more traditional matrix organizations.

## 4.6 Total quality management (TQM) and customer focus in BT

The aim of *quality management* is to achieve *zero defects*. When you ask who judges zero defects in your products or services, the answer is your customers; only they know whether your products meet their requirements absolutely. Organizations adopting quality management have found that this realization has led them to question their systems and structures. Often they are designed for the benefit of the organization and its efficient operation, not for the benefit of customers. The roles fulfilled by people in the organization are for the sake of efficient operation, not for the delivery of products or services which meet the customers' requirements. The UK's largest company, BT, reached this conclusion in 1989, leading them to undertake a major reorganization, called Project Sovereign.[16,17] The aim of Project Sovereign was: 'To turn British Telecom into a truly customer oriented, quality global company', with the specific objective of: 'Reshaping BT from five existing divisions to seven new ones, corresponding more directly to customer sectors and the international market'.

The old divisions were geographically and technology based, representing the way BT operated. Indeed, the geographical organization may have reflected the customer interface with the old mechanical and electro-mechanical switching technology. However, that changed with modern electronic switching. The old organization structure now existed only for its own sake. Under the new structure, three major divisions are Business Communications, Personal Communications and World-wide Networks.

In making the change, BT recognized that approximately half their operations are project based, involving novel, unique and transient activities. Therefore in adopting the new organization structure, they widely adopted management by projects as their operational philosophy. However, in some areas they went too far, adopting management by projects even though the nature of the work was fundamentally routine. This misses the point. Projects, being novel, unique and transient, involve risk. It is not possible to eliminate this risk, as there is no prior experience. Hence, rather than spending time in planning, the management approach must focus on managing the risk. On the other hand, if an organization applies a project-based approach to the management of routine work, it will lose the opportunity of learning from its previous experience (which in itself will eliminate the risk). This does not mean that an organization undertaking routine work cannot adopt a customer-focused approach. Many organizations have tried. The UK public sector, through its Citizens' Charter, is becoming more customer focused. A food canning company, described by Turner,[1] was adopting TQM in the late 1980s, and was in the process of changing the management of its factories from being functionally based to product based (which is as close as they could come to customer orientation in fast moving consumer goods).

## 4.7 Summary

1. There have been two traditional approaches to management:

   – *Operations management* Which exists long term to meet short-term objectives, where the product is passed 'over-the-wall' between functions of the organization. Procedures define how functions work.

- *Project management* Which exists short term to meet long-term objectives. This is meant to provide flexible, cross-functional working, but has traditionally been system oriented and often inflexible.
2. Projectivity measures an organization's ability to achieve its development objectives by managing the interface between these two incompatible environments.
3. Management by projects tries to eliminate the interface by making project-based management the norm for the organization. However, it fails to recognize that some work is fundamentally routine. Process management addresses the routine work, providing a flexible approach which defines how products are processed by the organization.
4. This provides four potential management approaches:
   - Operations management
   - Project management
   - Process management
   - Management by projects

   depending on whether the work follows predefined systems or is flexible in its response to customer requirements (first two versus last two), and whether it is fundamentally routine or fundamentally novel (first and third versus second and fourth).
5. The versatile organization is a flat, flexible structure, providing customer focus, and in which process management and management by projects exist side by side, held together by a weak functional organization. BT has adopted a structure along these lines for about 70 per cent of its business.

## References

1. Turner, J.R., *The Handbook of Project-based Management: Improving the processes for achieving strategic objectives*, McGraw-Hill, 1993.
2. Peymai, R., 'An investigation into the use and application of process management in the construction industry', MBA Dissertation, Brunel University, 1993.
3. Clemmer, J., *Firing on All Cylinders*, Macmillan, 1992.
4. Gareis, R. (ed.), *The Handbook of Management by Projects*, Manz, 1990.
5. Gareis, R. (ed.), *Proceedings of the International Conference on Management by Projects Implemented*, Vienna, Project Management Austria Institute, June 1993.
6. Weber, M., *Wirtschaft und Gesellschaft*, Mohr, 1956.
7. Orwell, G., *Nineteen Eighty-four*, Secker & Warburg, 1949.
8. Cassidy, J., 'The rise and fall of IBM', *The Sunday Times*, **3**, pp. 2–3, 28 March 1993.
9. Morris, P.G.W., *The Management of Projects*, Thomas Telford, 1994.
10. Morris, P.G.W., 'Managing Project Interfaces: Key points for project success', in *The Project Management Handbook*, 2nd edition, ed. Cleland, D.I. and King, W.R., Van Nostrand Reinhold, 1988.

11. Kerzner, H., *Project Management: A systems approach to planning, scheduling and controlling*, 3rd edition, Van Nostrand Reinhold, 1989.
12. Mills, R.W. and Turner, J.R., 'Projects for Shareholder Value', in *The Commercial Project Manager: Managing owners, sponsors, partners, supporters, stakeholders, contractors and consultants*, McGraw-Hill, 1994.
13. Turner, J.R., and Cochrane, R.A., 'Goals and Methods Matrix: Coping with projects for which the goals and/or methods of achieving them are ill defined', in *International Journal of Project Management*, **11**(2), 1993.
14. Warnecke, H.J., *The Fractal Company: A revolution in corporate culture*, Springer-Verlag, 1993.
15. Hastings, C., *The New Organization: Growing the culture of organizational networking*, McGraw-Hill, 1993.
16. MPA, *Project Sovereign, Proceedings of Seminar 48*, Oxford, Major Projects Association, June 1992.
17. MPA, *Beyond 2000: A source book for major projects*, 3rd edition, Snow, P. (ed.), Major Projects Association, 1994.

# PART TWO
# LEADING THE
# ORGANIZATION

---

Part Two looks at the change agent's role in managing downwards, outwards and upwards within the organization, as shown in Fig. 0.1. The first two chapters deal with the management of the team of individuals who will achieve the specific task. They deal with management as described in traditional books oriented to the functional, hierarchical organization. In those organizations, the manager's role is to pass instructions down from on high to the people within his or her command and motivate them to deliver their objectives. The project manager as change agent has a similar role. However, it is made more difficult within the project-based environment for several reasons, including:

- There is no prior history to show that one way of delivering the objectives will be better than another
- The people within the project team may not be within the project manager's direct line authority, but may have divided loyalty to functional managers and professional managers.

The subsequent two chapters explain how the project manager sells the project to the rest of the organization, and how he or she obtains political support from more senior managers.

In Chapter 5, Phil Austin, Rodney Turner and Lynn Thurloway describe the management of project teams and individuals within the team. The bottom of Fig. 0.1 illustrates John Adair's model which shows that in managing their subordinates' work, managers must manage the task, the team undertaking the task and the individuals within the team. We dealt with the management of the task in Chapter 3. In Chapter 4, we described how to create an organization to undertake the task. In Chapter 5, we explain how to turn that organization into a team and how to manage that team and the individuals in it. We consider team types and levels, team formation and maintenance, team roles and the creation of balanced teams. We then describe how to develop and empower individuals and motivate and reward them. We also consider the counselling and disciplining of team members.

In Chapter 6, David Rees, Rodney Turner and Mahen Tampoe compare managers and leaders. They describe the role of the manager and styles and traits of effective project managers. They then consider whether leadership is something more than management and describe models of inspirational leadership.

In Chapter 7, Susan Foreman explains internal marketing. She describes types of internal marketing, key components and how to implement an internal marketing programme.

In Chapter 8, Bob Graham and Eric Gabriel describe how to influence the wider organization. Bob Graham describes how to develop an influence strategy, based on risk/reward factors. He then explains how to influence the team and the rest of the organization, and discusses the power of information. A note is also included on how to develop a stakeholder management strategy. Eric Gabriel concludes the chapter by describing the role of the project champion.

# 5
# Project teams and individuals

Phil Austin, Rodney Turner and Lynn Thurloway

## 5.1 Introduction

Effective teams offer sustainable competitive advantage. This is especially so in the management of projects, where the level of uniqueness and uncertainty creates dependency on the team. Project management software is now available to all, and hence it is in being able to create effective teams where lasting differentiation is possible. The way teams are structured can have significant influence over their motivation and effectiveness. High profile teams set up in a network structure tend to perform and deliver specific results within tight time constraints. Phil Austin worked in a mechanical engineering-based company where this approach was effective in developing a new product range consisting of hundreds of electronic components, which was introduced into the company within eighteen months. It is when the challenges facing the team are particularly difficult that high-performing teams can be realized. There are parallels with team sports, in that we all want to be on the winning team. So provided the right climate is created for the team to perform and the individual team members to perform and to gain benefit from the work of the team, the goals are adequately defined and there is a competent and respected leader, then the potential for high-achieving teams is great.

How do we create high-performing teams? Indeed, can we create them or are they just a freak of organizational life? We will deal with this issue in this chapter. We examine team types, roles and effectiveness, and consider how individual behaviour and personality can affect the roles people adopt in teams and describe how this can affect overall team performance.[1-3] Psychometric tests can be used to identify an individual's preferred role when working in a team. We then consider the development, motivation, empowerment and counselling of individual members of the team.

## 5.2 Managing the team

A team is a group of individuals with a common identity and a psychological attachment, with shared values, norms and standards of behaviour, who work together to achieve a common objective.[4] Handy says the concept of shared identity is essential, because without it the team just remains a collection of individuals. What sets project teams apart is that they and their work is unique, novel and transient.[5] The team exists for a short period of time to undertake an assignment which nobody has done before. Because the team is novel, it has no shared identity and norms at the outset. It takes time to develop these, which delays achievement of the team's objective. Furthermore, because the objective is novel, it carries uncertainty and risk, and takes time to define. Because of perceived urgency imposed by the transience, development of the team's values and project's objectives can often be rushed, but, for the project to be successful, they must be done properly before the team begins work.

Each team is unique, because it consists of individuals, each with their own personality, knowledge and experience. The knowledge and experience of the team members are usually considered during the building of the team, as to complete any task, especially a project, particular skills are required. However, recently there has been considerable interest in examining the way individuals interact together in a team, and the roles that our personality and behaviour encourage us to take within the team.[1-3] Differences between teams can also arise through differences of industry, company culture and management level. Different industry sectors have different historic approaches to structuring teams. For instance, the construction industry has tended to adopt a more autocratic, directive style, whereas the IT industry has tended to adopt a more participative, facilitating style. Some company cultures have a particular influence over the ways in which teams operate. The Mars Corporation, for instance, has a very strong style governing the way teams are formed and managed. We consider types and levels of team, building and maintaining effective teams and balancing team roles.

### Types and levels of team

In Chapter 3, we identified three levels of team working on a project:

#### THE PRIMARY GROUP

This is the set of people who work face-to-face and know everyone else in the group. On a project, they are the immediate project team, or task force, whether full-time or seconded part-time, see Chapter 3.

THE SECONDARY GROUP

These are the people who work part-time on the project and contribute to the work of the primary team, but are not part of the task force. On a project, these are the functions which contribute through the network organization. However, they must be treated as part of the larger project team, if the team is to be effective.

THE TERTIARY GROUP

These are people who influence the work of the primary and secondary teams, or who are affected by their work, but have no direct contribution. The tertiary group has three parts: those influencing the work of the project, and those affected by the facility delivered or the product of the facility. The first may consist of family and friends, peer groups or professional bodies. The second group are people who live in the neighbourhood in which the facility is to be built (NIMBYs – Not In My Back Yard) or who will use or operate the facility after it is commissioned, or they may be people whose lives will be irreversibly changed (even by being made redundant) by the operation of the facility. The final group are the consumers; the people who will buy the product produced by the facility. (Sometimes they are the users, but often not.) The expectations of all of these groups of people must be managed if the project is to be successful, as they have a powerful ability to disrupt.

There are different organizational approaches to structuring these teams. Figure 4.3 identifies five basic approaches based on line and matrix structures. The versatile, network approach has attractions for organizations because it is easy to create teams without having to take on additional staff and easy to break them up. This is being reinforced by teams working apart, perhaps internationally, and even in different time zones. With modern electronic communications, these 'teams apart' can be as cohesive as teams located in the same building.[6] People now talk of 'virtual teams', sometimes synonomously with 'teams apart'. At Henley Management College, we had a discussion about what differentiates a 'virtual team' from a 'team'. The only thing we could decide upon was lack of psychological attachment because you do not know the faces of other people in the team. However, people from Reuters told Rodney Turner that with video conferencing even the psychological attachment exists, so we concluded that there is no such thing as a 'virtual team'.

## Team formation and maintenance

The members of a team must identify themselves with the team, and develop a common set of values or norms, before they can work together effectively. The process of forming a team identity and a set of values takes time. Project teams typically go through five stages of formation,[7] as follows.

FORMING

The team forms with a sense of anticipation and commitment. Their motivation is high at being selected for the project, their effectiveness moderate because they are unsure of each other.

STORMING

As the team begins to work together, they find that they have differences about the best way of achieving the project's objectives, perhaps even differences about its overall aims. They also find that they have different approaches to working on projects. These differences may cause argument, or even conflict, in the team, which causes both the motivation and the effectiveness of the team to fall.

NORMING

Hopefully some accommodation is achieved. The team members begin to reach agreement over these various issues. This will be by a process of negotiation, compromise and finding areas of commonality. As a result of this accommodation, the team begins to develop a sense of identity and a set of norms or values. These form a basis on which the team members can work together, and effectiveness and motivation begin to increase again towards the plateau.

PERFORMING

Once performance reaches the plateau, the team can work together effectively for the duration. The manager's role is to maintain this plateau of performance. For instance, after the team has been together for too long, the members can become complacent, and their effectiveness fall. If this happens, the manager may need to change the structure or composition of the team.

MOURNING

As the team reaches the end of its task, one of two things can happen. Either the effectiveness can rise, as the members make one concerted effort

**Table 5.1**  Characteristics for measuring effective team performance

| *Task-oriented characteristics* | *People-oriented characteristics* |
|---|---|
| Technical success | High involvement, energy |
| On time, within budget | Capacity to solve conflict |
| Achieves performance of product | Good communications |
| Committed, results oriented | Good team spirit |
| Innovative, creative | Mutual trust |
| Concern for quality | Membership self-development |
| Willingness to change | Effective organizational interface |
| Ability to predict trends | High need for achievement |

to complete the task, or it can fail, as the team members regret the end of the task and the breaking up of the relationships they have formed. The latter will be the case if the future is uncertain. Again, it is the manager's role to ensure that the former rather than the latter happens.

During these five stages, the team's motivation and effectiveness first decreases, before increasing to reach a plateau, and then either increasing or decreasing towards the end. The manager's role is to structure the team formation processes in such a way that this plateau is reached as quickly as possible, the effectiveness at the plateau is as high as possible, and the effectiveness is maintained right to the very end of the task. This structured process is called *project start-up* and is discussed below.

How do we measure the effectiveness of the team? We could say a team is effective if it successfully delivers its project objectives within time, cost and quality constraints. However, that assessment is very subjective, since our opinion of successful project objectives can depend on our own covert objectives. Furthermore, the team may have been performing effectively, but the project's objectives were impossible. Thamain[8] suggests that the team performance is measured against several factors which show how well the team members are working together. These factors he splits into task- and people-oriented characteristics, Table 5.1. Thamain also identifies six drivers for effective team performance and six barriers, Table 5.2.

## Project start-up

*Project start-up*[4,9] is a structured process used to minimize the duration of the hiatus in the performance of the team during team formation and to get the team working together effectively. This process may be repeated throughout a project, whenever there is a significant change in the team. The process of project start-up can also be used to gain the commitment of the team and to brief the team members.

**Table 5.2** Drivers for and barriers to effective team performance

| Drivers for effective performance | Barriers to effective performance |
|---|---|
| Professionally interesting and stimulating work | Unclear project objectives |
| Recognition of accomplishment | Insufficient resources |
| Experienced management | Power struggle and conflict |
| Qualified direction and leadership | Uninvolved, disintegrated senior management |
| Qualified project team personnel | Poor job security |
| Professional growth potential | Shifting goals and priorities |

OBJECTIVES OF START-UP

The objectives of project start-up are:

- To create a shared vision or mission, by identifying the project's context, its purpose and objectives
- To gain acceptance of the plans, by defining the work, project organization and quality cost and time
- To get the project team functioning, by agreeing its mode of operation and the channels of communication
- To build the team spirit, creating the common identity, norms, values and psychological attachment.

The emphasis of start-up can change at any time during the project life-cycle. During feasibility, the emphasis will be on agreeing the background, purpose and objectives of the project; during design, it will be on agreeing the project model; and during execution it will be on briefing the team and gaining the team members' commitment to earlier decisions. Building team spirit will remain an objective throughout the life-cycle.

METHODS OF START-UP

There are three standard techniques of project start-up:

- *Project or stage launch workshops* Where key people develop plans in a joint team-building process
- *Start-up or stage review report* Which collates the results of the analysis undertaken during start-up or from a previous stage in accessible form for use during the subsequent stage
- *Ad hoc assistance* From in-house project management professionals (such as a project support office), external consultants or members of other project teams.

These three techniques may be used individually or in any combination. The choice depends on several factors. Firstly, the different methods require varying amounts of time, so you must ensure key team members are willing to devote the necessary time. Without it most methods will fail. Secondly, the methods have different efficacy in achieving the objectives and so should be chosen depending on the requirements of the current stage. Thirdly, through project start-up, you should try to build as much historical experience into the project definition as possible, to minimize the uncertainty. You should choose a method which does that for the case in hand. Launch workshops may be held extensively throughout a change project, to initiate stages of the change project, or other significant parts of it, especially problem and solution definition when it is vital to take account of the views of all the parties involved. Launch workshops are discussed further below.

The start-up or *stage review report* is prepared at the end of one stage to launch the next. A report for launching Proposal and Initiation may be a one- or two-page *project scope statement*. During the feasibility study, this is expanded into a *project definition report* or *client requirements definition*, used to launch Design and Appraisal. At the end of that stage, a full *project manual* or *project requirements definition* may be produced in support of the design package and used to launch *project execution.*[5]

Ad hoc assistance may be from:

– Internal professionals, such as the project support office
– External consultants.

The advantage of this method is that it provides additional resources with special skills, who may motivate key people. Having someone to share ideas with can be stimulating. A disadvantage is that there can be some confusion over responsibilities, which can lead to wasted effort.

LAUNCH WORKSHOPS

These are a way of initiating the current stage of the project. Indeed, mini workshops may be held at the start of work packages, in accordance with the rolling wave principle. A workshop held at the start of Proposal and Initiation is called a *project definition workshop*, and at the start of Design and Appraisal, a *design initiation* or *kick-off meeting*. (A similar meeting, a *project initiation meeting*, may be held at the start of Execution and Control.) In addition to sharing all the other objectives of start-up, launch workshops are a powerful way of gaining commitment and building team spirit. Many of the other objectives can be achieved by people working in smaller groups. By coming together, especially off-site in a neutral environment, they may develop a common understanding and resolve items of confusion, disagreement or conflict through discussion. If people are briefed after a meeting (presented with a *fait accompli*), they may nod their heads in agreement, but you often find they do not truly accept what they are told. If people agree to a course of action in a meeting, you find they have internalized that agreement, but if they have not, it is difficult for them to avoid their commitments later because several people have heard them make them. A typical agenda for a workshop is:

1. Review the current project definition
2. Define the objectives of the current stage
3. Develop solutions and criteria for evaluation
4. Prepare a milestone plan for the current stage
5. Prepare a responsibility chart for the current stage
6. Estimate work content and durations for the work packages
7. Schedule the work packages
8. Assess risk and assumptions
9. Prepare initial activity schedules
10. Prepare a management and control plan.

We find most effort goes into the milestone plan and the responsibility chart, as these are the most effective uses of group working. They can be developed using white-boards, flip charts and Post-it notes. Involving everyone present around a white-board, gains their commitment to the plans produced; whereas working around a table with pen and paper can isolate members of the team from the working process. A workshop typically lasts one to three days. We usually allow two hours per item, except items 5 and 6 for which we allow four hours. However, it is important not to stick rigidly to a timetable, but to allow discussion to come to a natural conclusion, as people reach agreement and a common understanding. We sometimes include project management training as part of the timetable, which extends the duration by about a day.

**Team roles and balancing the team**

People tend to adopt different roles within a group, dependent on their personality and inclination. These roles must be balanced if the team members are to work effectively together. Belbin[1,2] offered one classification of team roles, Table 5.3. (The last role is not one of Belbin's but is, in our view, essential.) To be effective, a team needs a balance of these various types of person. In reality, you do not have the luxury of selecting one of each type of person from a limitless pool to make up your ideal team. You are left trying to create your team, probably from people who are assigned

**Table 5.3**   Classification of team roles

| Team role | Characteristics | Contribution |
|---|---|---|
| Plant | Creative, imaginative, unorthodox | Solves difficult problems |
| Resource investigator | Extrovert, enthusiastic, communicative | Explores opportunities. Develops contacts |
| Coordinator | Mature, confident, a good chairperson | Clarifies goals, promotes decision making, delegates |
| Shaper | Challenging, dynamic, enjoys pressure | Overcomes obstacles through drive |
| Monitor–evaluator | Sober, strategic, discerning | Sees all options. Judges accurately |
| Teamworker | Cooperative, mild, perceptive, tactful | Listens and builds. Reduces conflict |
| Implementer | Disciplined, reliable, conservative | Turns ideas into practical actions |
| Completer | Painstaking, conscientious, anxious | Searches out omissions. Delivers on time |
| Specialist | Single-minded, self-starting, dedicated | Provides scarce knowledge and skills |
| Comic | Unflappable, robust, resilient | Relieves tension |

to it. However, you will find that people can fulfil several of the roles; that they have several strengths. What is more, people's strengths may vary according to the circumstance. Part of the skill of the effective team leader is to achieve a balance of the various types from the range of people available.

Another classification system was developed by Margerison and McCann.[3] They offer a framework for building teams based on research with managers and teams from all over the world. They suggest that there are two key approaches to work behaviour; and within each approach they identified two opposite orientations:

- People adopt roles or behaviours that are necessary to ensure the work is executed successfully: advising roles or organizing roles
- People undertake the roles or behaviours they prefer to do: exploring roles or controlling roles.

Margerison and McCann proposed that, in a balanced team, the four quadrants of the resulting matrix of required behaviours and preferred behaviours will be adequately covered. They developed the matrix by identifying nine key roles, to form their team management wheel, shown in Fig. 5.1. Margerison and McCann clearly related their roles to work and, like Belbin, suggest that these roles have implications for team building and team management. Although there are similarities between the work of Belbin and that of Margerison and McCann, one key difference is the

| | *Exploring behaviour*<br>preferred external orientation, divergent activities | | | |
|---|---|---|---|---|
| *Advising roles*<br>support roles<br>required to get<br>things done | Creator–<br>innovator | Explorer–<br>promoter | Assessor–<br>developer | *Organizing roles*<br>required to<br>build and deliver<br>product or service |
| | Reporter–<br>adviser | Linker | Thruster–<br>organizer | |
| | Upholder–<br>maintainer | Controller–<br>inspector | Concluder–<br>producer | |
| | *Controlling behaviour*<br>preferred internal order, following plans,<br>convergent work | | | |

**Figure 5.1**  Team roles as defined by Margerison and McCann

role of the linker. In the team management wheel, the role of the linker is seen as important to the coordination and integration of the team and their work. The linker focuses on networking, utilizing their interpersonal skills and building bridges between the team and others in the wider organization. This role appears to be more widely accepted than Belbin's chairperson role. Furthermore, Margerison and McCann suggest that the role of linker may not necessarily be undertaken by the person who is the dedicated or designated leader, that is by the project manager, but that other members of the team may undertake this role at different stages of the team life or project according to the requirements of the tasks and team.

### From individuality to team performance

A problem encountered by project managers, especially at start-up, is getting a group of individuals to act collectively, to think as a team, and to commit to the notion of individual and team responsibility. We saw that without a clear commitment on an individual and team basis, people who work on project teams are little more than a group of individuals, and the key benefits gained from team working, especially synergy, are lost. Indeed, it is this group identity and responsibility that Handy[4] say differentiates a team from a collection of individuals. Katzenbach and Smith[10] suggest that, for high team performance, team managers should concentrate on team performance and team basics issues, Fig. 5.2, rather than team-building issues. Results can then be more successfully delivered, with team behaviour a clear outcome. The outer boxes indicate what teams can deliver; the inner circles describe the elements of the disciplines that can make it happen.

In reality, it is probably a combination of team building and focusing on performance issues that helps a team to work together. This is because it is

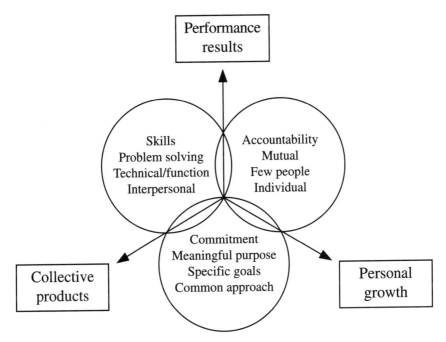

**Figure 5.2** Focusing on team basics

not just a question of mobilizing and motivating individuals to unite and look forward, but also of addressing key concerns which individuals might have. For example, individuals are influenced in their current situation by their past experiences of working on projects, their perceptions or experiences of working with the project manager and their personal values and goals. In order to get individuals to commit to team working, therefore, the 'personal' aspects that are brought into the project situation have to be recognized and in an ideal situation would be addressed throughout the project. Hence, a key to moving people from an individualistic approach to a team approach is good communication and a supportive, honest approach from the project manager. Many people have suggested key characteristics of high-performing teams and methods that facilitate moving from a situation where individuality dominates to one where true team work is evident. Many suggestions are similar and identify that teams which perform together well have:

- Common, clear, challenging and relevant goals and objectives
- Understanding of the interdependency of members in terms of skill and contribution
- Specific, individual performance goals that can be seen to clearly contribute to the success of the team

- An understanding of individual aspirations, so effort can be made to integrate these with project objectives
- Clear procedures and processes that are agreed upon and accepted by all team members
- Good communication and non-threatening interpersonal relationships
- Good relations between the team and the wider organization
- Good communication and links outside the team and up the hierarchy
- Committed and focused leadership, with a flexible and responsive style
- Time allowed for the team to grow together
- Festivals celebrating minor team and individual successes, as well as the successes at the major milestones.

## 5.3 Managing the individuals

We now consider how to manage individuals within the team. Managers tend to have a preference for focusing on the task, the team or the individual.[11] In particular, it is possible to operate at one of two extremes:

- The team is functioning well, with everyone working to a common vision, yet individuals feel abused
- The individuals within the team feel prized and well regarded, but the team itself is falling apart and failing to meet its objectives, because the members do not share a common identity.

The effective manager needs to achieve a balance between the needs of the task, the team and the individuals within the team (see Case Study 5.1). In this section we discuss how to manage the individual, and consider:

- Developing and empowering individuals
- Motivation and reward
- Counselling and disciplining.

## Case Study 5.1 Balancing task, team and individual

A film, *Twelve O'clock High,* based on a true story about an American bombing squadron based in England during the Second World War, illustrates this balancing. The film opens with planes landing following an unsuccessful raid. Ten planes went out, and only eight return, one of which is badly damaged. The pilot of the damaged plane is lowered from the cockpit on a stretcher, with the squadron leader watching. The squadron leader accompanies the pilot to the ambulance, gets in and goes off, leaving the other crews stood around saying, 'What about us? We completed the mission!' The squadron is falling apart because the leader is totally people focused. He is sacked and replaced by a new squadron leader (played by Gregory Peck). He is task and team focused. Under him the team comes together and begins to achieve its task. Ten planes go out; ten planes come back. However, he ignores the needs of the individuals in the team, and they ultimately turn on him. The film closes with the new squadron leader having a nervous breakdown. (That last scene is apparently not in the book on which the film is based, but was presumably added for dramatic affect.)

## Developing and empowering individuals

The need to develop and empower individuals is linked to the need to motivate. Commitment to the project is essential for its success, and a way of encouraging this, especially in a networked organization, is to pay attention to developing team members and assisting their career development. This is not just important for the individual's own career, but also for ensuring competitive advantage for the organization. Staff competence and attitude is increasingly providing unique and enduring competitive advantage to organizations. Technological advantage and systematized advantage, such as ISO 9000 quality systems, are only temporary, as competitors quickly catch up. However, raising the general competence of individuals within the organization, and ensuring that such competence is unique and continually developing, is a way of achieving sustained advantage. There are three principles for managing and positively developing people:

1. Be sure that goals are:
   - Quantified where possible
   - Understood
   - Reasonable but challenging
   - Documented.
2. Keep in touch with progress; be involved and solve problems as much as is necessary, but ensure responsibility remains with the member of staff.
3. Be prepared to revise the goal if it becomes out of date.

It is part of the project manager's role to create a situation in which staff can perform their tasks so as to deliver the project effectively. As a first option, project managers should try to delegate responsibility for work to team members (through a responsibility chart, Chapter 3) and, only if there is no one else available, actually carry out the work themselves. Graham[12] says:

Project managers often say they could accomplish any task if only they had the 'right people'. One common characteristic of these right people is that they can operate with the minimum of instruction and supervision. They seem to know what to do without being told.

The Hawthorne experiment, Case Study 5.2, shows how subtle the impact of empowerment can be.

## Case Study 5.2 The Hawthorne Affect

The Hawthorne experiment is an oft quoted example about the management of people, and how subtle empowerment can be. This was a study into productivity carried out some decades ago within a US company, Western Electric, at their Hawthorne plant. They were trying to determine what impact certain improvements to the working environment had on productivity levels of staff. Improvements were made, and with each improvement there was an increase in productivity. The interesting observation came when, as a control, the experimenters made conditions worse and productivity went up even further. It was concluded that when workers receive special attention from management, productivity improves regardless of any actual change in working conditions. It is only the long-term impact of the changes which can be used as a guide to their efficacy. There are two further messages from the Hawthorne experiment:

1. As a change agent, you cannot be sure of the impact of your changes until some time after making them. The initial impact will almost always be to show improvement.
2. Making the observation affects the system. Heracleitus (Chapter 1) said you cannot step into the same river twice at the same point. The idea is that you can step off the bank at the same place, but the water has flowed on. If you put your toe in to test the water before you go swimming, the water you swim in will not be the water you put your toe into. But worse, because putting your toe in changes the flow of the river, the water you go swimming in is not the water you would have swum in had you not put your toe in. The same is true for organizations, as the Hawthorne experiment shows.

### Motivation and reward

How do you make the people on your project work harder to achieve the project's goals? Money is not always the prime motivator some believe it to be. People clearly need a certain level of financial reward which matches their circumstances, and gives a measure of the status of their job, but, equally, they want their work to be meaningful and their contribution recognized. We all need a degree of feedback from managers and peers. We welcome praise, provided it is genuinely given and clearly deserved. Faint praise is not a motivator and can lead to a lack of respect and trust, and to a lowering of standards. If no feedback is given, team members may try to elicit at least negative feedback by not doing the job well. Harrison[13] proposed three categories of motivator on a project. Many of the theories of motivation combine these three elements:

1. *Participation: the project as motivator*   Staff should be encouraged to participate in decision making. This idea has been commonplace for some time and applies to all management, not just project management. It emerged as a reaction to the 'scientific management' principles developed in the early part of this century.
2. *Expectancy: the reward system as motivator*   Managers have personal ambitions and career goals, and so will be motivated to work on projects if doing so will help realize their career ambitions.
3. *Achievement: goal and target setting as motivator*   The need to achieve is in itself a strong motivator. This is particularly relevant to projects, because outcomes or deliverables tend to be recognizable and distinguishable, due to the assignment of clearly defined responsibilities and work packages.

One theory that has stood the test of time is Maslow's hierarchy of needs.[14] He proposed that people have certain needs, Table 5.4, which must be fulfilled in order, starting with the most basic. As one becomes fulfilled, the next takes over, but the first begins to lose its ability to motivate. In developed countries, the lower order needs are largely fulfilled by the structure of society, so people are motivated by higher order. You need to be careful in interpreting the needs too literally. For example, people may accept a degree of physical risk in interesting and challenging jobs, which may seem to conflict with 'safety' needs. You also need to recognize that the needs only motivate over a longer timescale (measured in months or years). They will not make someone miss their daughter's fifth birthday party to work overtime to ensure an urgent order is shipped. Turner[5] proposed an adaptation of this, based on work by Kanter.[15] He proposed five motivational factors, which expand on recognition and achievement, Table 5.5, based on the assumptions that:

– A project-based environment has three essential features, Table 5.6, which requires a different approach to the motivation of personnel than more traditional environments
– Most people working on projects have satisfied the bottom three needs in Maslow's hierarchy, and are therefore motivated by the top two. Indeed, one feature of projects is that they are less able to satisfy the need for belonging, at least in the medium to long term.

**Table 5.4**  Maslow's hierarchy of needs

| Need | Description |
| --- | --- |
| Sustenance | The need for food, water and air to survive |
| Security | The need for shelter, security, stability, and freedom from threat to physical safety |
| Belonging | The need for friends and companionship |
| Recognition | The need for self-respect and esteem of others |
| Achievement | The need for self-fulfilment, to grow and learn |

Mention must be also made of Herzberg's work.[16] He postulated two types of motivational factor:

- *Hygiene factors* Which in themselves cannot motivate, but their absence demotivates
- *Motivators* Which increase the level of satisfaction, and hence motivate.

In Table 5.5, we proposed Progression as a motivator, and said that money and company cars are a measure of this. They are therefore hygiene factors; on their own they cannot motivate, but without them progression cannot motivate either, and so their absence demotivates. Hygiene factors tend to be related to lower levels of Maslow's hierarchy and motivators to higher levels. Since most people in the developed world are motivated by the higher levels, absence of the hygiene factors undermines the lower levels, but only higher levels motivate.

**Table 5.5**  New motivational factors

| Motivational factor | Elements |
| --- | --- |
| Purpose | People believe in their work and its importance to the organization<br>– Creates a vision for the project<br>– Helps align project and functional objectives |
| Proactivity | People want freedom to manage their own career development<br>– Emphasizes achieving results, rather than fulfilling roles<br>– Delegates professional integrity |
| Profit sharing | People share in the entrepreneurial culture<br>– Encourages them to value it<br>– Encourages employees to solve problems and satisfy customer needs |
| Progression | People value the opportunity to learn new things and tackle new problems<br>– Increases self-esteem and achievement<br>– Unfortunately, money and company cars measure achievement |
| Professional recognition | People want to be acknowledged for their contribution<br>– Allows people to achieve recognition<br>– Not the anonymity of the bureaucrat |

**Table 5.6**  Features of a project-based environment impacting motivation

| Feature | Elements |
| --- | --- |
| Matrix or network structures | – No clear indicator of title, status or rank<br>– Multiple reporting lines, tasks, functions, professional discipline<br>– Split loyalty between task and career development |
| Flat, flexible structures | – Fewer career milestones, see Case Study 5.3<br>– Remote from career decision makers<br>– Remote from people setting the strategy of the organization |
| Transient existence | – Projects cannot in themselves provide a career structure<br>– Annual objectives are aligned with the functional hierarchy<br>– Not able to satisfy a long-term need to belong |

## Case Study 5.3 Fewer career milestones

In the late 1980s, BT had 13 levels of management, from the most junior to the chairperson; not many for a bureaucratic organization. A management trainee of 25, wanting to be chairperson at 55, had to progress through one grade every two-and-a-half years; a reasonable rate of progression. In the early 1990s, as a result of a change project called Project Sovereign, the number of layers was reduced to seven. Now the future chairperson takes five years to progress through each grade, giving fewer career milestones, and greater opportunity to go astray.

### Counselling and discipline

Many managers find counselling and discipline difficult. Is there a better way of dealing with staff who are under-performing or need disciplining, other than simply terminating their employment, which can be less than satisfactory? A prerequisite for both counselling and discipline is a clear understanding by the team members of precisely what is expected of them. Their standards of performance need to be clearly stated and accepted. The objectives must also be updated as and when events make them obsolete. Once these are in place, then both the manager and the team member know clearly what the goals are, and effective discussions can take place should the individual consistently fail to meet his or her goals. Counselling involves the manager in discussing the individual's unacceptable performance with them, and agreeing what can be done to improve performance. For it to be effective, there must be mutual respect, and the issue must be dealt with by careful and thorough examination of the situation, using supportive evidence. It must be a fair and reasonable assessment. The manager can do this by writing down what the objectives were, what the shortfall has been, and giving their honest opinion of why performance is unacceptable. This must then be discussed with the individual openly and honestly, seeking their view on the issue. It is also important to allow the individual an opportunity to debate the manager's views, but it is also important to concentrate on the facts as they appear and not unsupported feelings. Once the individual has accepted the facts as true and accurate, action can be discussed as to what must be done to improve performance. There should be action on both the manager and the individual, and progress reviews should be scheduled and agreed. If the facts are not accepted by the team member, it may be necessary to follow the company's, hopefully, established discipline route. If you go this route, meetings must be carefully logged, and the facts must be irrefutable, as the end point may be dismissal.

## 5.4 Summary

1. Effective teams are the key to the effective delivery of projects. To obtain effective teams requires careful management of the team and its dynamics, and of the individuals within the team. These requirements of the team and its constituent members must be balanced.

2. A team is a group with a common identity and shared norms. There are three levels of project team:
   - *The primary team* The people working full-time on the project
   - *The secondary team* People working occasionally on the project in a matrix environment
   - *The tertiary team* People with a view on the project, or affected by it, but not involved in the work.

3. The stages of team formation and maintenance are: forming; storming; norming; performing; mourning. Thamain suggests measures for team performance. These are task based, measuring the team's effectiveness at delivering its task, and people based, measuring how well the individuals work together.

4. Structured project start-up processes can:
   - Create a shared vision for the project
   - Gain acceptance of the plans
   - Get the project team functioning
   - Be used to brief the project team.

5. Methods of start-up include launch workshops, reports and *ad hoc* assistance.

6. Both Belbin and Margerison and McCann suggest you need to balance team roles for high performance.

7. Managers need to meld a group of disparate individuals into high-performing teams. Such teams have:
   - Common, clear, challenging and relevant goals and objectives
   - Understanding of the interdependency of members in terms of skill and contribution

- Specific, individual performance goals which contribute to the success of the team
- An understanding of individual aspirations, integrated with project objectives
- Clear procedures and processes that are agreed upon and accepted by all team members
- Good communication and non-threatening interpersonal relationships
- Good relations between the team and the wider organization
- Good communication and links outside the team and up the hierarchy
- Committed and focused, flexible and responsive leadership
- Time allowed for the team to grow together
- Festivals celebrating minor and major successes.

8. People are empowered by setting goals to achieve rather than defining their tasks. Goals should be:
   - Quantified where possible
   - Understood
   - Reasonable but challenging
   - Documented.

9. Individuals will be motivated to achieve the project's goals if they are aligned with their own goals. Many theories of motivation combine the three elements:
   - *Participation* The project as motivator
   - *Expectancy* The reward system as motivator
   - *Achievement* The goal and target setting as motivator.

10. Turner suggests five motivating factors for people working in a project-based environment:
    - *Purpose* People believe in the importance of their work
    - *Proactivity* People manage their own career development
    - *Profit sharing* People share in the entrepreneurial culture
    - *Progression* People value the opportunity to learn new things
    - *Professional recognition* People want to be acknowledged for their contribution.

## References

1. Belbin, R.M., *Management Teams: Why they succeed or fail,* Heinemann, 1981.
2. Belbin, R.M., *Team Roles at Work,* Butterworth-Heinemann, 1993.
3. Margerison, M., and McCann, D., *Team Management,* Mercury Press, 1990.
4. Handy, C.B., *Understanding Organizations,* Penguin, 1982.
5. Turner, J.R., *The Handbook of Project-based Management: Improving the processes for achieving strategic objectives,* McGraw-Hill, 1993.
6. Hastings, C., *The New Organization: Growing the culture of organizational networking,* McGraw-Hill, 1993.

7. Tuckman, B.W., 'Development Sequence in Small Groups', *Psychology Bulletin,* 1965.
8. Thamain, H.J., 'Teambuilding in project management', in *The Project Management Handbook*, 2nd edition, Cleland, D.I., and King, W.R. (eds), Van Nostrand Reinhold, 1988.
9. Fangel, M., 'To start or to start-up? – That is the key question of project initiation', *International Journal of Project Management*, **9**(1), 1991.
10. Katzenberg, J.R., and Smith, D.K., *The Wisdom of Teams*, Harvard Business School Press, 1993.
11. Adair, J., *Effective Leadership*, Pan, 1983.
12. Graham, R.J., *Project Management as if People Mattered*, Primavera Press, 1990.
13. Harrison, F.L., *Advanced Project Management*, 3rd edition, Gower, 1990.
14. Maslow, A.H., *Motivation and Personality*, Harper & Row, 1954.
15. Kanter, R.M., 'The new managerial work', *Harvard Business Review*, November 1989.
16. Herzberg, F., 'One more time: How do you motivate employees?', *Harvard Business Review*, **46**(1), January 1968.

# 6

# On being a manager and leader

David Rees, Rodney Turner and Mahen Tampoe

## 6.1 Introduction

In the last chapter we considered the need to manage the project team and the individuals within the team as an essential part of managing the project. We now turn to the manager. We consider the role of the manager and what he or she does to manage the process of change. We suggest qualities of effective managers and management styles they may adopt in different circumstances. We then consider the question of whether leaders are more than, or even different from, managers. We conclude that there is a difference, and describe qualities of good leaders. We might think that Ronald Reagan was a good leader, but weak manager; John Major an effective manager, but poor leader. Good managers manage the process effectively, not just of delivering the task but also building the team and satisfying the needs of the individuals. (Some people go as far as saying managers are people who administer the status quo. However, that clearly does not apply to project managers who deliver results from work which is unique, novel and transient.) Good leaders inspire their teams to achieve levels of performance well beyond their normal abilities, for extended periods of time; they inspire them to take unpleasant, even unpopular, decisions, and to choose and adhere to difficult options. They win and maintain respect through the good and bad times (see Case Study 6.1). We propose models of inspirational leaders.

## 6.2 The role of the manager

So what do managers do? Their main responsibility is to manage the team and its work *to deliver the promised results*; it is the leader's responsibility to create the climate for success. Five functions of management[1] are illustrated in Fig. 6.1 and are as follows:

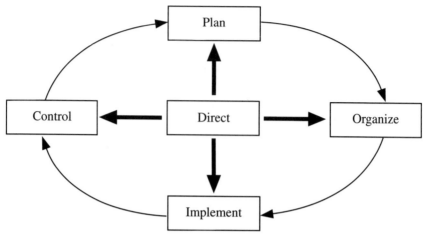

**Figure 6.1** Five functions of management

- Planning the work to be done to achieve the defined objectives
- Organizing the team of people to do the work
- Implementing by assigning work to people
- Controlling progress
- Directing the people involved in the project.

## Case Study 6.1 Two prime ministers compared

Comparing Margaret Thatcher and John Major illustrates this point. Mr Major was a good party manager, who was an effective chief whip, but as Prime Minister has been unable to inspire his party to form a common policy over Europe, and lost the respect of his 'team' to the point where the Chief Secretary to the Treasury publicly disagreed with his boss, the Chancellor of the Exchequer, who in turn publicly disagreed with his, the Prime Minister, over the likelihood of a common European currency. Mrs Thatcher, on the other hand, inspired her party to unity through five years in opposition and ten years as prime minister:

- Through the Callaghan government
- Through the recession of the early 1980s
- Through the Falklands' war
- Through the miners' strike
- Through the Westland crisis when two cabinet ministers lost their jobs.

It was when she lost respect over the poll tax that her premiership crumbled. Having lost respect over one issue, it became impossible to maintain it over others. (It also illustrates a view of Rodney Turner's, that a person should not occupy one position of leadership for more than ten years. ICI and the USA are right to limit the terms of their chairperson and president to eight and ten years, respectively. The French are wrong to allow their president to serve for 14 years, as the growing disillusionment with President Mitterand in the closing years of his presidency illustrated.)

## Directing

The project manager as change agent must manage the commitment of people in three directions, Fig. 0.1, through all five functions. It is possible for a good manager to take a procedural approach to all, and perform effectively. However, managing the procedures and process well is a necessary requirement for effective performance, but not a sufficient condition, as we describe in Section 6.4. Previously,[2] we have used the word 'leading' for the fifth function, but we have used the word 'directing' here to differentiate from the leadership as we describe it later. Directing can be purely procedural. Fayol[1] uses the word 'commanding' but that word carries all the connotations of a bureaucratic, command and control structure. Directing can be more, it can involve conducting the people involved in the project and, in managing the team, that may involve the following.

### MOTIVATING AND REWARDING

Motivating and rewarding ensures all team members know their work is appreciated and recognized. This we will keep returning to as an essential part of the role of effective managers and leaders.

### KEEPING PERSPECTIVE

It is important to keep a sense of perspective to maintain team equilibrium and balance. Teams which have worked together for a long time fall into the trap of becoming insular. This manifests itself in the team seeing other groups as inferior, being resistant to change or outside influences, attributing shortcomings to others and in other ways setting themselves apart from the rest of the organization. Although a strong team spirit and pride is good, it can be counter-productive if turned into vanity and aloofness because it can result in alienation. It is the project manager's role to make sure that the team keeps its perspective.

### GROUP DECISION MAKING

This means knowing when to draw on the decision-making skills of the group and when to make individual decisions. Research has shown that group decision making does not necessarily mirror that of the individual opinions in the group. For example, a strong leader may influence the group to make a high-risk decision to which individual members would not have agreed. Similarly, dissenting voices can either remain unheard or find themselves overruled or ignored.

SUPERVISING AND MAINTAINING GROUP BEHAVIOUR

This harnesses group potential. Groups can behave in ways uncharacteristic of the individuals in the group. Well-structured, positive teams can achieve more than any individual. Group behaviour can also be destructive to the group and to those who depend on its work. Irrational group behaviour can take over from more moderate and modest individual acts.

EVERYONE MUST GAIN

This is the essential factor in negotiating the contract through the planning process, as described throughout this book, and in motivating the team, as described in the last section.

## 6.3 Effective project managers

What makes an effective project manager? Handy[3] suggests three criteria for effective managers:

- *Management traits* Effective managers have certain common traits
- *Management styles* Effective managers adopt certain styles
- *A contingent approach* Effective managers adapt their styles to suit the circumstances.

### Traits of effective project managers

It is now more common to talk in terms of 'competencies' for doing the job. Many major organizations have invested considerable effort in defining competency models for people performing all jobs within the organization, whether a management job or other functions, professions or disciplines. Indeed, people now differentiate between 'competence' and 'competency':[4]

- *Competence* Is an ability or 'behaviour' which makes a person adequate at their job
- *Competency* Is a 'behaviour' which delivers superior performance.

We have identified six traits for effective project managers, as follows.

PROBLEM-SOLVING ABILITY AND RESULTS ORIENTATION

Effective managers are usually of above average intelligence, able to solve complex problems by analysing the current situation and recognizing patterns. Problem solving pervades project management. The achievement of the project's purpose is a problem, as is the completion of each stage of the life-cycle. Furthermore, the control process is also one of problem solving, planning recovery to overcome variances from plan. Without a problem-solving ability, a project manager would be lost. This ability at problem solving should be coupled with results orientation. The purpose is not to complete work for work's sake, but to achieve the desired ends. The solution to the problems should deliver the planned objectives and defined purpose, not necessarily complete the originally agreed work. The end justifies the means, or *All's well that ends well.*

ENERGY AND INITIATIVE

The project manager must be able to continue managing under considerable pressure and against considerable odds. This requires the manager to be energetic and fit. This energy will be coupled with initiative to see the need for action, and the resolve to take such action. This initiative should extend to the management of one's own career as well as the task at hand (see Table 5.5).

SELF-ASSURED PERSONALITY

The manager must have the self-assurance to know what they are doing is right. This does not mean they must be extrovert or brash; the manager can be self-effacing while still self-assured. They must be resolute, confident in their opinions and judgement. Often, it is better to take action based on incomplete information, being ready to modify the action as new information comes to light, than to dither endlessly looking for the perfect solution. The self-assured manager also delegates readily to their team, confident in the ability of team members and their own ability to motivate the team. Sometimes, especially in the IT industry, you see good technologists promoted into managerial positions who are very reluctant to delegate because they believe, quite rightly, that they can do the work better than anyone else. They work themselves into an early grave, while their team members are idle and consequently demotivated.

SENSE OF PERSPECTIVE

Managers need to be able to look beyond the project team, and to see how they fit into the organization as a whole. This need for perspective extends to the work of the project. The manager must be able to move freely through all three levels of the project hierarchy, and above as well, to understand the detailed work of the project and how it will deliver the project's objectives, and to understand how the project's objectives will meet the needs of the parent organization. This ability is known as a *helicopter mind*.

GOOD COMMUNICATION SKILLS

Similarly, project managers must be able to communicate at all levels, from the managing director down to the janitor. They must be ambassadors for their project, able to sell it to senior managers and win their support; they must be able to talk to their peers, functional managers and resource providers to win cooperation; they must be able to brief and motivate the project team; and they must be able to talk to the janitor, because often the latter knows better than anyone how the project is progressing, Case Study 6.2.

---

## Case Study 6.2 Communicating at all levels

As a post-doctoral research fellow, Rodney Turner had an office in one of a pair of semi-detached houses. The research fellows had offices in one house while the other was being renovated. When the other was complete, they would all move across while the first was renovated. Rodney was due to go to the USA for a month. A week before he left, the janitor, a retired Welsh miner called Frank, asked when he was going to be away. From 20 August to 20 September, Rodney said. Frank said that they were due to move into the other house on 14 September, so it might be worth while for him to put his books in a tea chest before he left. Rodney thought that was a good idea, but when he asked the secretary to the administrator of the Engineering Department for a tea chest she denied any knowledge of the move. So he asked the builders, but they said they would not be finished until late October. He locked his office door, and went off to the USA. When he came back, he found his door forced and that the move had taken place on 14 September, the very day Frank had predicted. Of course, he had spoken to the University Estates people as they came to survey the work.

---

NEGOTIATING ABILITY

The project plan is a contract on two levels (Fig. 3.4):

-  Between the project manager and sponsor, agreeing what the project team will deliver to the organization, and the support the organization will give in return to enable the team to deliver the contracted results

– Between the project team members on another level, agreeing how they will work together to deliver the results to the project manager.

Like all contracts this must be negotiated through bipartite discussions. Project managers rely on their ability to negotiate, because they do not have direct line authority over their resources as functional managers do. They must win and maintain the cooperation of other people through their ability to negotiate and persuade.

## Styles of effective project managers

There are many models on the styles adopted by effective managers.[5,6,7,8] Most of these judge managers against one or two parameters and characterize managers along a one-dimensional continuum or in a two-dimensional matrix. Often the two-dimensional matrix can be reduced to a one-dimensional continuum, because two styles presented side-by-side (usually bottom left and right) are starkly different (as in Fig. 4.2). The parameters against which managers are judged include:

– Focus on people or relationships
– Focus on tasks
– Use of authority
– Involvement of team in decision making
– Involvement of team in decision taking
– Flexibility versus application of rules and procedures.

Decision making is where options for action are formulated; decision taking is where one of those options is chosen for implementation. Figure 6.2

| Parameter | Blake and Mouton Grid [5] | Tannenbaum and Schmidt[6] | Hershey and Blanchard[7] | Bonoma and Slevin Grid[8] |
|---|---|---|---|---|
| 1. People focus | Two-dimensional grid based on parameters one and two but encompassing three | | Two-dimensional grid based on parameters one and two but including three as a line through grid | |
| 2. Task focus | | | | |
| 3. Use of authority | | One-dimensional model based on parameter three but encompassing four and five along the line | | Two-dimensional grid based on parameters four and five but encompassing three |
| 4. Joint decision making | | | | |
| 5. Joint decision making | | | | |

**Figure 6.2**   Theories of management styles

**Table 6.1** Four styles adopted by project managers

| Parameter | Bureaucratic | Autocratic | Democratic | Laissez-faire |
|---|---|---|---|---|
| Team decision making | Low | Low | High | High |
| Team decision taking | Low | Low | Low | High |
| Flexibility | Rule-based | Flexible | Flexible | Flexible |

summarizes the models. Only one, the Bonoma–Slevin grid, was specifically related to the styles of project managers. The rest relate to managers in functional, hierarchical organizations, and hence the focus is on task and not goal in the second parameter. Sometimes the two-dimensional matrices imply four styles, but use of one of the styles is virtually impossible. It is difficult, for instance, to involve the team in the decision taking without first having involved them in the decision making, although the Bonoma–Slevin grid seems to imply that this is a possible style.

We find that project managers will usually adopt one of four styles, which can be described by the last three parameters, Table 6.1. Although three parameters might imply eight styles, four of the styles are incompatible. You cannot, for instance, adopt a rule-based style but pretend to involve either yourself or your team in the decision making or taking. That would lead to dissonance and failure. The four styles are as follows.

DEMOCRATIC

The democratic manager consults the team, but decides the best course of action. Note that this is different from the *laissez-faire* style below, which is almost anarchic, not democratic. This style may be appropriate during the feasibility and planning stages of a project, when you want to encourage people to contribute their ideas.

AUTOCRATIC

The autocratic manager dictates to the team what should be done and how. This style may be appropriate during execution and close-out, when the specification and design of the facility has been decided, real money is being spent and early completion of the project is required to achieve the revenue returns.

BUREAUCRATIC

The bureaucratic manager manages through rules and procedures. This style is usually only appropriate on projects with low risk, with little expected change, because the bureaucratic manager is unable to respond to change. This probably means it will only be appropriate during the close-out stages of a project.

*LAISSEZ-FAIRE*

The *laissez-faire* manager allows the team to manage themselves. They behave like all the other members of the team, and are there to advise if required. This style is appropriate during the early developmental or feasibility stages of a project, or on research projects.

TYPES TO BE AVOIDED

There are styles which should be avoided. The first is the technocrat, to whom the science is more important than the results, the means more important than the ends. This person searches for the ideal solution, rather than achieving an adequate solution which satisfies the customer's requirements. They are usually unable to delegate, because they have no faith in their project team's ability to achieve the perfect result. Taken to extreme, the bureaucrat can be ineffective. They pedantically follow procedures, assured in the knowledge that they have done the job correctly, even if not effectively. A third is the salesperson, who is very good at selling the project, but not at delivering results. All three of these characteristics, technical ability, application of best practice and the ambassadorial role, are strengths if applied in moderation, but they become weaknesses when applied to excess, and become more important than delivering results of the project.

## Situational management

Many managers have a preferred style. Effective managers adopt styles appropriate to the team and task at hand. The four styles described above can be related to four team types proposed by Frame,[9] Table 6.2. Adopting an inappropriate style and team structure can cause dissonance, sending

**Table 6.2**  Management styles and team structures

| Style | Team type | Description |
|---|---|---|
| Democratic | Matrix | Teams of mixed discipline working on several tasks |
| Autocratic | Task or functional | Teams each of a single discipline working on separate tasks |
| Bureaucratic | Surgical | A single professional supported by others with specific duties |
| *Laissez-faire* | Ego-less | Teams of professionals with shared responsibility for decisions |

different messages to the team. Silburn[10] showed that it is quite common for managers to adopt a preferred style different to that which the team members would prefer their manager to adopt. Using the Bonoma–Slevin Grid, he found almost no constancy between the styles adopted by managers and the styles preferred by their teams, or, surprisingly, the direction of the gap between the preferred styles. Only once, across five companies, nine project managers and eighteen teams (each manager had two teams working on different projects), did the style of the manager correspond with the style desired by one of his teams, but in that particular case the manager's second team showed almost the greatest gap in preferred style. Surprisingly, sometimes the team wanted greater involvement in the decision making or decision taking, and sometimes less. In the case where there was a correspondence between preferred style of the manager and the team, the manager was adopting a fairly *laissez-faire* style and that was what one team wanted. The other team wanted a completely autocratic manager, with no involvement in the decision making or taking. That may indicate that the team was reacting against the manager's *laissez-faire* style, or that the members of the team were risk averse. Silburn found that the impacts of this style gap were:

- Reduced team and individual performance
- Teams thinking that some of the work they were asked to do was unnecessary
- Reduced team and individual morale
- Difficulty in coping with the project manager's style
- High staff turnover
- Teams isolating themselves from the project manager by minimizing communication.

## 6.4 Leadership

We have described the role of managers, their traits (competences) and styles, and said it is possible to take a procedural approach to these roles and achieve effective performance. However, we now try to consider what superior characteristics (or competencies) make one person an inspiring leader and another 'just' an effective manager. We have called this book *The Project Manager as Change Agent*. An agent is someone who promotes something or somebody. They initiate new ideas, and influence others to buy. So an agent is someone who initiates, promotes and influences others. These are essential leadership activities. Cleland[11] suggested that leadership exists at all levels of the organization, from chairperson to factory worker and even janitor. Everyone, not just managers, can have a role of inspiring others to go that extra mile for the organization:

- Hotel managers are leaders; they lead people to a fair settlement of a customer complaint
- Car salespeople are leaders; they lead people to important buying decisions
- Supermarket shelf-fillers are leaders; again, influencing people's buying decisions.

Over the centuries much has been written on leadership, but it remains one of the most ephemeral aspects of human behaviour. Its description has usually been more effective through case study than models, although models have been attempted and some are described here. To be world class at anything – tennis player, opera singer, manager or leader – requires four things:

- Innate ability
- Initial training
- Career-long development
- Continuous practice.

When Rodney Turner was at school in the 1960s, the suffragen bishop of Auckland, who was Visitor at his school, talked about a three-legged stool. Remove one leg and the stool collapses. Here we have a four-legged stool. Remove one leg and with careful balance the stool can stay up, but easily topples; remove two and it collapses. It is in the area of leadership (as opposed to management) that innate ability seems to play a far more important part than elsewhere. It is almost as if the legs are placed unevenly around the stool, so that if a leg is removed it cannot remain upright, even with careful balancing. However, by identifying what inspiring leaders do, we can try to develop our own competency. We describe models which try to describe what more it is that leaders do than managers; we introduce a leadership competency model developed by BP; and finish by explaining a concept of SMART objectives.

**Leaders versus managers**

A simple model of the difference between managers and leaders was provided by Kotter.[12] He described leadership as being about providing 'constructive and adaptive change', the role of the project manager as change agent, whereas management is about 'providing consistency and order'. Table 6.3 contrasts management and leadership as defined by Kotter[12] at the stages of the management lifecycle Fig. 6.1. In terms of

**Table 6.3**   Management versus leadership, as defined by Kotter[12]

| Life-cycle stage | Management | Leadership |
|---|---|---|
| Planning | Planning and budgeting | Establishing direction |
| | Setting the path to achieve results | Developing the goal |
| | Allocating resources | Developing the strategy to achieve it |
| Organizing | Organizing and staffing | Aligning people |
| | Identifying individuals | Communicating direction |
| | Defining roles and responsibilities | Influencing the team |
| | Creating control systems | Obtaining understanding and cooperation |
| Executing and controlling | Controlling and problem solving | Motivating and inspiring |
| | Monitoring progress against plan | Enthusing the team to overcome problems |
| | Resolving issues | Satisfying basic human needs |

Margerison and McCann's team development grid, shown in Fig. 5.1, this shows a strong preference for exploring rather than controlling, and a slight preference for advising rather than organizing. Tampoe and Thurloway[13] developed the focus on both role and goal orientation, and the balance between team and personal motivation, to achieve leadership by aligning personal goals with project goals, Fig. 6.3.

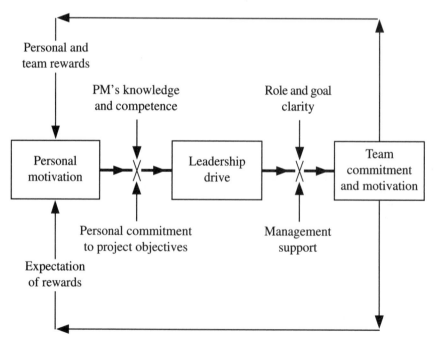

**Figure 6.3**   Project leadership model

**Table 6.4** The performance triangle, as defined by Clemmer and McNeil

| Performance factor | Gestion | Administration | Leadership |
|---|---|---|---|
| Focus | Equipment, expertise, products | Administrative systems | People |
| Predictability | High, based on science | Medium, based on probabilities | Low, an art form |
| Controls | Physical laws | Legal and accounting principle | Emotional commitments |
| Tracking results | High, measurable output | Medium, measurable process | Low, perceptions, attitudes |
| Financial thrust | Scientific breakthroughs | Cost containment | Revenue enhancement, value added |
| Key elements | Manufacturing, delivery, services | Budgets, rules, plans, controls | Vision, values, environment, behaviour |
| Key words | Research, facts, precision | Efficiency, objectives, structure | Feelings, motivation, pride |

Table 6.4, adapted from Clemmer and McNeil,[14] compares the differences between the Roman *gestion*, administration and leadership over six performance indicators. What we have called gestion, they called technology, and what we have called administration, they called management. We do not agree with their vocabulary, thinking that management combines gestion, administration and the directing of teams and individuals. What all these models of leadership focus on, compared to effective management, is the achievement of goals and results rather than the doing of tasks. This is what differentiates them from the models of management styles shown in Table 6.1. Although some of those are billed by other people as leadership theories, we believe they describe management styles because they are about completing tasks and wielding authority, not about inspiring people to achieve difficult results. An adherence to just 'achieving the task' caused UK industry in the 1960s and 1970s to fall behind many of its competitors, particularly the Japanese. We have now learnt that review and reflection upon 'how we are achieving the task' can lead to a concept of continuous improvement that the Japanese term *Kaizen*.

**Leadership competency**

BP have developed a competency model for leadership,[4] Figure 6.4. This identifies attributes of the leader which he or she must bring to the role. These cannot be further developed through training. There is then a list of competencies, which can be developed through training (as that is the point of a competency model). Many of these are subjective. However, by being

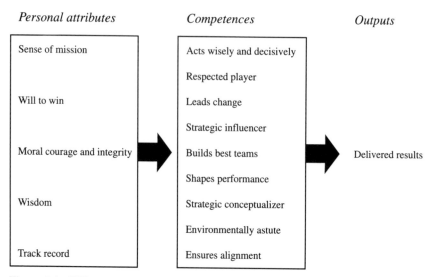

**Figure 6.4**   BP's competency model for leadership

aware of the need to develop these attributes in themselves and the need to influence others, perceptions of how effective they are at using them, prospective leaders can use simple tools and techniques, many described in this book, to help develop their competency in these areas. The output from this competency model is desired results, again showing goal, rather than task orientation in inspiring leaders, and highlighting a weakness in many of the management style models summarized above.

What is surprising about this model is the lack of mention of communication skills. Perhaps it is assumed to be an essential element of the others. However, all the great leaders of history – Churchill, Hitler, Peron, Napoleon – were great orators. The presidential elections in the United States in 1960 and 1992, and in France in 1981 and 1988, are said to have been lost by the television debates. The general election in the UK is also said to have been won for John Major by his soap-box speeches, and lost for Neil Kinnock by his head-butting speech at Labour's premature victory parade. The ability to inspire through communication is so central to inspirational leadership that it would seem to require individual mention. Although oratory skills are to a certain extent innate, they can be developed. Max Atkinson, visiting professor in Communication Skills at Henley Management College, trained a woman with little previous experience in public speaking in oratory skills, and she went on to achieve a standing ovation at an annual conference of the Social Democratic Party in the early 1980s, even though her speech is said to have had little substance.

## SMART objectives

We have seen that many views of leadership involve a focus on the achievement of goals rather than the fulfilling of tasks, and that an essential part of leadership is the ability to communicate the goals, and gain the commitment of others to them. A concept which is now a little clichéd, but none the less effective, is that the goals or objectives should be SMART (see Case Study 6.4). SMART objectives are:

*S*pecific
*M*easurable
*A*chievable
*R*ealistic
*T*imeframed.

### SPECIFIC

To be specific, an objective must be a goal, not a process; achieve something, not do something; reach a destination, not undertake a journey. So often one reads so-called objectives which are the latter, and not the former, and the managers (non-leaders) wonder why they fail to inspire people.

### MEASURABLE

To be measurable, you must be able to say when the goal has been achieved. Undertaking the journey is not measurable, because you cannot say you are heading in the right direction; being halfway there is not measurable, because you cannot say what unexpected diversions there will be.

### ACHIEVABLE

The objective must be achievable with the technology and skills available to the team. There is a fine balance between setting goals which are too easy to achieve and hence will not inspire superior performance and goals which are unachievable and hence will demotivate.

### REALISTIC

Goals can be achievable, but not realistic at the time, or within the timeframe set. Again, unrealistic goals can demotivate.

### TIMEFRAMED

The team must be given a clear end date by which to achieve the goal, or again it will not motivate. This is another problem with defining objectives in terms of processes rather than outputs. You find the musical chairs approach to management, saying 'We will run around until the music stops, and see what we can achieve!' – hardly an inspiring approach to leadership.

---

### Case Study 6.4 John F. Kennedy addressing the American people

I believe this nation should commit itself to landing a man on the moon and returning him safely to earth before the decade is out... No single space project will be more impressive to mankind or to the long-range exploration of space... We chose to go to the moon and back in this decade not because it is easy, but because it is hard, because that goal will serve to organize and measure the best of our energies and skills, because that challenge is one we are willing to accept, one we are unwilling to postpone, and one we intend to win... But, in a very real sense, it will not be one man going to the moon, it will be an entire nation.

---

## 6.5 Summary

1. Managers plan, organize, implement, control, direct. Directing is:
   - Motivating and rewarding
   - Keeping perspective
   - Encouraging group decision making
   - Supervising and maintaining group behaviour
   - Ensuring everyone gains.
2. Traits exhibited by effective project managers are:
   - Problem-solving ability and results orientation
   - Energy and initiative
   - Self-assured personality
   - Sense of perspective
   - Good communication skills
   - Negotiating ability.
3. Four main styles used by managers are:
   - Democratic
   - Autocratic
   - Bureaucratic
   - *Laissez-faire.*
4. Truly effective project managers adapt their style to the task, the team and the individuals.
5. Great leaders inspire their teams to go that extra mile. They sometimes use SMART objectives:
   - *S*pecific
   - *M*easurable

- *A*chievable
- *R*ealistic
- *T*imeframed.

## References

1. Fayol, H., *General and Industrial Management*, Pitman, 1949.
2. Turner, J.R., *The Handbook of Project-Based Management: Improving the processes for achieving strategic objectives*, McGraw-Hill, 1993.
3. Handy, C.B., *Understanding Organizations*, Penguin, 1982.
4. Euroform, 'Capitalising on Competencies', in *Proceedings of the Euroform Conference*, Euroform, January 1995.
5. Blake, R.R. and Mouton, S.J., *The New Managerial Grid*, Gulf Publishing Company, 1978.
6. Tannenbaum, R. and Schmidt, W.H., 'How to Choose a Leadership Style', *Harvard Business Review*, March–April, 1988.
7. Hershey, P. and Blanchard, K.H., *Management of Organizational Behaviour*, 5th edition, Prentice Hall, 1988.
8. Slevin, D.P. and Pinto, J.K., 'Project leadership: Understanding and consciously changing your style', *Project Management Journal*, **24**(2), 1993.
9. Frame, J.D., *Managing Projects in Organizations*, Jossey Bass, 1986.
10. Silburn, N.L.J., 'The leader and the led: perspectives on leadership styles by those managing and those being managed in a project team', MSc Dissertation, Henley Management College, 1995.
11. Cleland, D.I., 'Changing dimensions in leadership', in *Proceedings of PMI's 25th Seminar Symposium*, Vancouver, Project Management Institute, October 1994.
12. Kotter, J.P., *A force for change: How leadership differs from management*, The Free Press, 1990.
13. Tampoe, F.M.C. and Thurloway, L., 'Project management: the use and abuse of techniques and teams', *International Journal of Project Management*, **11**(4), November, 1993.
14. Clemmer, J. and McNeil, A., *Leadership Skills for Every Manager*, Piatkus Books, 1986.

# 7
# Internal marketing

Susan Foreman

## 7.1 Introduction

Marketing is traditionally considered as an organization's interface with the external environment. However, very few organizations can, or desire to, draw clear and distinct barriers with their environment and in particular their customers. Indeed, in the service sector and in project environments, managers are encouraged to develop close working relationships with customers and to bring them closer and into the organization. In many projects the development and the delivery of the project cannot be separated from the client. Thus the quality of project outcomes are directly related to the management and *marketing* activities of project managers. The more entwined organizations and customers become, the more important it is to consider the need for marketing *inside* the organization, in addition to the external marketing with which we are more familiar.

This chapter considers the nature and role of marketing inside the organization. We begin by discussing the evolution of internal marketing, and we then consider internal customers and the need to recruit and develop employees who are able to deliver quality service to clients. Different types and components of internal marketing are examined, and we close by describing internal marketing programmes.

## 7.2 What is internal marketing?

Internal marketing has become an accepted and frequently used part of marketing. However, there are several different definitions of internal marketing, reflecting the several different forms that exist. One of the most comprehensive reviews of the status of marketing in the service sector[1] shows the development and current status of internal marketing and identifies it as a specific topic of importance. The work in this area distils

116

internal marketing down into two key areas which form the basis of internal marketing:

1. '... that internal customers must be sold on the service and be happy in their jobs before they can effectively serve the final customer,' Berry.[2]
2. 'Everyone in the organization has a customer,' Gronroos.[3]

The common theme is that there are customers inside the organization; indeed, Sasser and Arbeit[4] suggested 'personnel is the first market of a service company'. It is important to capture the full value of the employees (or internal customers) as they have an important role in the development of general business activities, project management and the marketing strategy. Indeed, managers are neglecting a key customer group if internal customers are ignored and managers focus only on external customers. Essentially, therefore, marketing tools and concepts might be used as effectively with employees as the internal customers. A key ingredient, therefore, in internal marketing is the understanding of employee needs and wants prior to the development of marketing programmes as in the external market.[5] In treating the employees as customers there is a relationship between levels of work effort and job performance (although a missing link in research) and in the practice of internal marketing are the linkages between employee satisfaction and external customer satisfaction.

## 7.3 Types of internal marketing

The origin of internal marketing was in service firms. However, it also has origins in project management and consumer and industrial sectors as well[6,7] – wherever all employees can be considered as part of the internal market who must deliver excellent service to customers in support of the organization's overall strategy. The internal market of an organization can be treated as one mass market, or marketing can be applied to specific groups of customers in the organization. Internal marketing is something which the firm (in totality) can apply to its entire market of employees (in totality). However, this mass approach which does not take into account the different needs of internal customers (employees) in the organization is often rejected in favour of dividing the whole firm into groups, for example the source of marketing activities tends to be departments, project teams, groups or functions within the organization. Similarly, all internal customers (employees) are frequently not the target of internal marketing efforts – rather, only one department, project team, group or function might be.

There are different types of internal marketing activity. Figure 7.1 classifies internal marketing by its source and the audience whom internal

| | | Who is the focus for internal marketing? | |
|---|---|---|---|
| | | Group | Organization |
| Who applies | Organization | Type II | Type IV |
| internal marketing? | Group | Type I | Type III |

**Figure 7.1** Perspectives on internal marketing

marketing activities are aimed. The vertical axis considers who is the internal marketer: the entire organization or a department group or team within it? The horizontal axis considers whom the internal marketing effort is aimed at: all employees; or a specific group, team, function or department within the organization. From this, four different types of internal marketing can be identified, labelled Type I, Type II, Type III and Type IV.

### Type I: Internal marketing between departments

... intra-organizational marketing of goods and services – where one organizational unit or staff group markets its capabilities to other units in the same company – Harrell and Fors[7]

This type sees one department, group or function as marketer and another as customer(s). So, for example, many departments, particularly the information systems department, have become business units in their own right within organizations, encouraged to compete with external suppliers and market themselves to the organization. Furthermore, their customers inside the organization (departments, project teams) have been encouraged to choose between the comparable services provided by internal and external suppliers, therefore internal suppliers must become self-sufficient and meet internal customers' needs 'profitably'.[8] A Management Information Systems (MIS) department might focus its efforts on marketing to a sales department or specific project teams.

### Type II: Internal marketing to the internal customer

Everyone in the organization has a customer – Gronroos[3]

Here, the organization as a whole markets to specific groups, functions or departments within itself. One objective could be to encourage this group or team to engage in behaviour that supports or enhances some organizational initiative. For example, the organization as part of initiatives on efficient customer service may focus on those employees in departments that have most contact with the customer. Bream *et al.*[9] describe the internal marketing of hospitals, who focus on developing a strong positive image of nursing to their nurses which are coupled with incentives, in order to lessen the organization's reliance on temporary agency nurses.

In the professional service sector, Hartley and Lee[10] highlight that the development and maintenance of business is through effective customer relations where all employees have a role to play in the effective management of customer relationships, which can be achieved only when employees, too, are considered as customers. Even those employees who are removed from the customer also have a role to play in the ultimate delivery of customer satisfying service.

## Type III: Internal marketing from a group to the whole organization

Commitment – Putting policy into action[11]

Groups, departments or functions marketing to the whole organization are representative of the internal marketing in the Type III quadrant. Here, internal marketing may, for example, be practised by service functions in an organization, such as human resources. Human resources (HR) management has begun to adopt many of the tools of marketing to build and develop relationships with the rest of the organization. There have been a number of descriptions of internal marketing by HR departments to communicate their role and to enhance the visibility of HR. Collins and Payne[12] suggest that the 'manager who seeks mutual benefit through working closely with the HRM department is involved in a similar exchange process to that which takes place between consumers and companies everywhere.'

There is a two-way exchange as managers in the human resource management function could benefit from a more market-oriented approach inside the organization and managers who use that in managing the employee exchange. Alternatively, marketing to the organization also occurs in more specific ways. Leonard-Barton and Kraus[12] describe the diffusion of innovation to internal markets who may be made up of top management on one hand and users on the other. The aim is to encourage the adoption of technology through the use of an internal marketing approach. The approach in this example has three strands; firstly, the identification of needs and wants to ensure satisfaction with the technology; secondly, the 'preparation of the user organization to receive the innovation'; and finally, the implementation and 'ownership' of the technology.

## Type IV: Internal marketing of the organizational focus

Human resource management interface[11]

In the fourth quadrant, the organization is the marketer, and is also the market. This type has received considerable attention recently. Indeed, it is sometimes viewed as the origin of internal marketing. It is the type of internal marketing referred to originally by Berry[14] (where employees are considered to be customers and jobs are considered to be like products), and by Kotler[15] (the marketing concept requires internal marketing if external marketing is to be successful). The competent practice of internal marketing seems to complement the effectiveness of external marketing programmes in its capacity for influencing customer satisfaction. Gronroos[16] deems the focus of internal marketing to be on how to obtain and retain customer-conscious employees. Thus, 'internal marketing' becomes a useful and effective metaphor for seeing the customer in every individual, and the individual in every customer. It has been suggested that Type IV internal marketing is necessary to ensure that the organization attracts, selects and retains the best employees, and that these see, appreciate and value their role in the delivering of excellent quality of service to external customers.[17] While this is the most common application of Type IV internal marketing, it is not the only one, and there have been a number of variations on this theme. An important role for internal marketing is the implementation of marketing strategy.[18] The internal marketing programme parallels the conventional external marketing programme directly, and the 'external' marketing strategy is marketed to all the organizational constituents in order to get the support so necessary to the success of its implementation.

## 7.4 Key components of internal marketing

The ultimate goal of internal marketing is to encourage effective marketing behaviour: the ultimate goal is to build an organization of marketers willing and able to create true customers of the firm – Berry and Parasuraman[17]

While there are different types of internal marketing, there are also three important components of internal marketing. These components are focused on employees as internal customers in the organization, and are:

– Offering a vision that employees can believe in
– Developing the full potential of employees
– Rewarding employees.

Here, there are close links with human resource activities in the organization; the organization needs to select and recruit the right employees in marketing terms – those who not only perform their jobs well but will be part-time marketers and 'create true customers for the firm'.[17] This involves more than recruitment; it means organizations should compete for the right employees by using traditional marketing methods of market research, segmentation, targeting and positioning. The recruitment and retention of employees is also dependent on whether the organization can offer employees a vision that they can believe in. The vision offered by the organization plays an important role in determining the level of commitment employees have to serving each other and then the ultimate customer – developing employees who are sold on the organization in body and in spirit. The demands on employees in organizations in competitive environments are such that providing a vision employees can believe in offers a dimension which can enhance working life.

Reward is another important component of internal marketing. For a long time organizations have, for example, rewarded sales forces financially for achieving sales volume and value targets. Reward can be more than providing pay increases or the provision of profit-share options for increases in sales; organizations such as British Airways and Rank Xerox can, and do, reward people for customer service, indeed, reward can also be given for service to the organization. It is also important to remember that reward does not need to be financial; recognition, support, encouragement and so forth can be used to develop and maintain commitment in employees. While these activities are entwined with the work of the human resource department, the marketing focus is on managing the relationship with employees as the first customers of the organization who will then serve the external customer. In essence the goal is to give employees the encouragement to respond to customers' needs effectively and efficiently. Indeed, customers and clients partially assess the quality of the project outcomes, services and products by the quality of their contact with employees.

## 7.5 Developing internal marketing programmes

In many respects the mechanics of marketing inside the organization are similar to marketing activities conducted in the external environment. There are many different models to guide marketing inside organizations; the focus in the first instance must be on developing a customer orientation internally and externally. Indeed, internal marketing activities need to be coordinated and planned together to ensure a uniform and consistent approach to the marketplace.

**Customer focus**

The first step is understanding the customer and here we are considering the employee as a customer. This is first and foremost. This chapter has already emphasized the recruitment and retention of employees; the next step is to understand their characteristics, needs and behaviour patterns. This in itself is a considerable task as it is sometimes difficult to get an accurate picture of our external customers. Herb Kelleher, CEO of Southwest Airlines (the only major US airline to have turned a profit every year of its existence), said in an interview about the success of Southwest Airlines:

> We find out from people, who communicate to us. We find out from their performance at their station. We serve 41 cities, and I can tell you personally about the performance of the managers of Southwest Airlines – what kind of personality they have, what kind of relationship they have with their people, whether they're strong on customer service.[18]

**Market research inside organizations**

This is more than an employee survey. Market research studies can be conducted inside the organization, whether the information required is specific or required continuously. This involves structuring the research programme and developing rigorous procedures, starting with:

- Research objectives
- Methods/procedures
- Collection
- Analysis
- Reporting.

**Market segmentation**

In the same way that organizations segment external markets, they segment the internal market. This is particularly relevant to medium and large organizations. Segmentation is a procedure concerned with dividing the marketplace into meaningful groups of customers with similar characteristics. This then enables the marketer to develop 'products' and services that are relevant to specific groups of customers and can form the basis of the marketing strategies. Piercy and Morgan[19,20] suggest that the internal marketplace can be divided on the basis of job function and role performed. Level in the organization, contact with customers, project team location and benefit are just a few examples which may also provide the appropriate base to segment the market into meaningful groups.

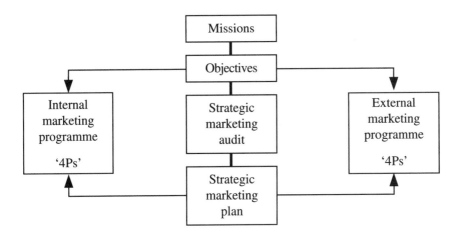

**Figure 7.2**    Internal marketing planning

**Marketing planning inside the organization**

Internal marketing planning should be consistent with the marketing approach taken in the external marketplace; where, for example, the internal marketing objective is to gain the support and commitment of the employees to the external marketing strategy. Piercy and Morgan[19,20] suggest that internal marketing should 'match and parallel' the external marketing activities, Fig. 7.2. In essence this should not be a static process, but an iterative one, where internal marketing planning is not only an output of the overall marketing planning process but should also contribute to its development. They show internal marketing programmes based on a marketing mix approach focused on customer segments inside and outside of the organization.

## 7.6 Summary

1. Internal marketing is a useful tool for gaining internal commitment to a project.
2. There are four types of internal marketing:
   - *Type I* Internal marketing between departments
   - *Type II* Internal marketing to the internal customer
   - *Type III* Internal marketing from a group to the whole organization
   - *Type IV* Internal marketing of the organizational focus.
3. There are three key components of internal marketing:
   - Offering a vision that employees can believe in

- Developing the full potential of employees
- Rewarding employees.
4. There are four elements to developing an internal marketing programme:
   - Customer focus
   - Market research inside the organization
   - Market segmentation
   - Marketing planning inside the organization.

## References

1. Fisk, R.P., Brown, S.W. and Bitner, M.J., 'Tracking the evolution of the services marketing literature', *Journal of Retailing*, **69**(1), Spring, 1993.
2. Berry, L.L., 'Perspectives on the retailing of services', in *Theory in Retailing: Traditional and Non-traditional Sources*, Stampfl, R.W., and Hirschman, E.C. (eds), American Marketing Association, 1981.
3. Gronroos, C., 'Internal marketing: An integral part of marketing theory', in *Proceedings of the American Conference on Marketing of Services*, Donnelly, J.H., and George, W.R. (eds), 1981.
4. Sasser, W.E. and Arbeit, S.P., 'Selling jobs in the service sector', *Business Horizons,* February, 1980.
5. Tansuhaj, P., Randall, D. and McCullough, J., 'Applying the internal marketing concept within large organizations: as applied to a credit union', *Journal of Professional Services Marketing*, **6**(2), 1991.
6. Gummesson, E., 'Using internal marketing to develop a new culture – the case of Ericsson quality', *Journal of Business and Industrial Marketing*, **2**, Summer, 1987.
7. Harrell, G.D. and Fors, M.F., 'Internal marketing of a service', *Industrial Marketing Management*, **21**, November, 1992.
8. Obenshain, V., 'Peer training yields speedy results', *Personnel Journal*, **71**, April, 1992.
9. Bream, T.L., Bram, K., Bantle, A.L. and Krenz, K.D., 'Beyond the ordinary image of nursing', *Nursing Management*, **23**, December, 1992.
10. Hartley, S.W. and Lee, P.L., 'Implementation of services marketing programs: Key areas for improvement', *Journal of Professional Services Marketing*, **2**, Fall/Winter, 1986.
11. Foreman, S.K. and Woodruffe, H.R., 'Internal marketing: A case for building cathedrals', in *Proceedings of the Marketing Education Group Conference*, Cardiff Business School, July, 1991.
12. Collins, B. and Payne, A., 'Internal marketing: A new perspective for HRM', *European Management Journal*, **9**, September, 1991.
13. Leonard-Barton, D. and Kraus, W.A., 'Implementing new technology', *Harvard Business Review*, Nov/Dec, 1985.
14. Berry, L.L., 'Services marketing is different', *Business*, May/June, 1980.
15. Kotler, P., *Marketing Management: Analysis, Planning, Implementation and Control*, 7th edition., Prentice Hall, 1991.
16. Gronroos, C., 'Relationship approach to marketing in service contexts: The marketing and organizational behaviour interface', *Journal of Business Research*, **20**, January, 1990.

17. Berry, L.L. and Parasuraman, A., *Marketing Services: Competing Through Quality*, Free Press, 1991.
18. Lee, W.G., 'A conversation with Herb Kelleher', *Organizational Dynamics*, **23**(2), 1994.
19. Piercy, N., *Market-led Strategic Change: Making marketing happen in your organization*, Thorsons, 1991.
20. Piercy, N. and Morgan, N., 'Internal marketing – the missing half of the marketing programme', *Long Range Planning*, **24**, April, 1991.

# 8
# Influencing the organization

Bob Graham and Eric Gabriel

## 8.1 Introduction

One of the most important abilities of the successful project leader is to influence others in the organization to act for the project. The concept of influence is used because the project leader typically does not have the command relationship of authority present in most organizations. I do not know how many times I have heard statements like 'the problem in this organization is project leaders have all of the responsibility, but none of the authority', to which I respond 'welcome to project work'. In project leadership, lack of direct authority over project team members and other stakeholders is the normal state of affairs. Successful project leaders must develop their influence in order to get the project completed. There are a variety of people in the organization who need to be influenced in favour of the project. One important group are the members of the project team. As these people typically do not report to the project leader, they must be influenced and motivated to devote their best work to the project effort. Another group is departmental directors, those people who supply the manpower resources to complete the project. Your project is only one of many they must consider, so they too must be influenced to supply good people. Another group includes the people in the financial area who supply the monetary resources. The group of senior managers must also be influenced to support the project, as projects are seldom successful without top management support. Often one or more government agencies must also be included on the stakeholder list. Finally, there are the end users, the people who will benefit most from project completion, but who often give only lukewarm support as the project progresses.

A key concept in developing influence is to treat people as if they are volunteers. That is, assume you have to develop a team only from volunteers, people have to volunteer to put their time into this project.

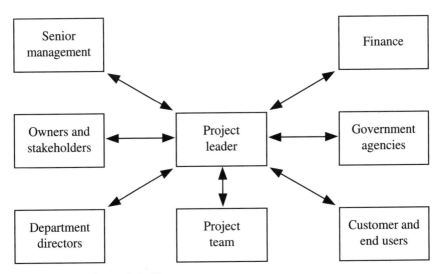

**Figure 8.1**   Project stakeholders

The following sections will outline some techniques to do that. Then, even if your project team members are not volunteers, you can influence them by treating them as if they are. The same is true for other project stakeholders such as your peers and superiors, as well as functional managers (department directors) who will be supplying the volunteers on your team. The successful project manager will develop an influence strategy for these stakeholder groups as well as for team members, and we give a seven-step process for implementing a project stakeholder influence strategy. We conclude the chapter by describing the role of the project champion.

## 8.2 Developing an influence strategy

The first step in developing an influence strategy is to identify potential stakeholders, Fig. 8.1. (Also see Figs. 0.1 and 3.3.) The second is to develop a list of key people in the various groups. Within the project team, the core team members are probably the most important. Within the senior management group, the champion who proposed this project, and those who are ultimately supplying the manpower, are probably most important. One customer may also be more important than the others. The next step is to ask yourself why these individuals should support your project; what benefit will they derive from a successful project? If you are unsure what benefit key individuals might derive, you might want to discuss it with them. From this you develop a list of potential allies, along with the knowledge of the benefits you need to deliver in order to maintain their support. These benefits are key to developing influence. An important complement to the list of 'allies' is a list of 'enemies' – key individuals who do not support the project. Although these people are not really 'enemies', they may not see the benefit of the project, or may see it as detrimental to the success of the organization. It is important to understand why these people do not support the project and work to overcome their objections as the project progresses. Remember that all enemies are potential allies, if it is in their interest (look back to Fig. 1.3).

## 8.3 The reward/risk factor in developing influence

The key factor in influencing anyone to do anything is to ensure that the rewards for doing it are greater than the risks. If people understand and value the rewards of being on your project, and you have taken the steps to minimize the risks involved in gaining that reward, you can influence them to work on, or otherwise support, the project.

### Reward: Perception of value

Projects have value for the organization and for the individuals involved. The project manager must think clearly through the questions of '*Why are we doing this project?*' and '*What are the potential benefits for the people who work on or support this project?*'. The project manager must ensure potential team members and other stakeholders fully understand the nature of these benefits.

### Risk: Perception of loss

Projects also have potential risks for the organization and for the participants. The nature of these risks is very subjective, and their evaluation is often a function of the individual's risk preference profile. To understand these risks, the project manager must ask the question '*What will the organization or the individuals potentially lose if they participate in this project?*'. Once a list of risks is developed, the project manager must work to ensure that the potential losses are minimized. This information must then be told to potential project participants and stakeholders.

The key to developing influence is to maximize the value while minimizing the risks. If the perception of value exceeds the perception of risk, individuals will be motivated to work on or support the project. If the perception of risk exceeds the perception of value, individuals will not be so motivated and may work against project completion. Further application of these principles of influence are given in the sections that follow.

## 8.4 Influencing team members

When some managers think of value for team members, they think of money. Many project leaders lament that they have little control over the salaries of their team members. However, money is only one part of motivation (see Chapter 6). There are many aspects of projects which people find inherently rewarding. The project leader must use these non-monetary rewards to maximum benefit. These inherent values may include:

- *Doing something new* By definition, a project is something new in the organization. People generally enjoy variety in their work and thus find value in doing something new and different.
- *Learning a new skill* This aspect enhances people's self-worth, and also their future marketability. Learning and applying the latest methods of technology is rewarding for many people. In addition, learning a new skill often helps people to add value to the organization, enhancing the organizational skill set.
- *Networking and travel* Projects cut across departmental lines, giving people exposure to other departments. These contacts can increase an individual's network and also knowledge about other parts of the organization.
- *Developing a unique product* Much of organizational work involves repetition. Being on a team that is doing something new and unique can be rewarding. People also find much satisfaction in being able to point to a finished product and say 'I was on the team that made that product'.
- *Positive visibility with senior management* This is an important reward for many people. People often feel it is to their advantage to be viewed positively by upper management.

On the other hand, the risks associated with something as uncertain as a project may include:

- *Negative visibility with senior management* There are two sides to the visibility coin. In some organizations, being associated with a failed project is a step toward the exit door. A good track record helps to recruit project team members. If the project leader is new at the job, they must display a lot of enthusiasm at the beginning of the project. If the project leader is enthusiastic about the potential success of the project, then potential team members feel there is a higher chance of success (which, of course, helps to actually lead to success, becoming a self-fulfilling prophesy). If the project leader is not enthusiastic, then potential team members will feel there is little chance for success and will not be motivated to join that project team.

- *No reward for project work* This is a typical problem in organizations new to project management. Reward systems and performance appraisals are departmentally based, which means employees see their promotion and salary tied to performance in the departments. The project leader, however, is attempting to get these people to join project teams and there will be little motivation to do so unless work on the project also counts as a part of the performance appraisal process. The project leader must ensure that project work is used in performance appraisal, and complete appraisals for all members of the core team. An associated risk is 'out of sight, out of mind'. Potential team members may feel that if they are not working at all times on departmental work, then the department managers will 'forget' them and overlook them if a promotion is available. Thus the project leader must have a plan for informing departmental managers about the work of their department members.
- *A more exciting project may come along* There is not much the project leader can do about this fear, except be certain that the potential team members are fully aware of just how exciting this project is going to be.

The project leader must take steps to maximize perceived benefit and minimize perceived risk (Case Study 8.1). Team members must also be made aware of the potential risks and rewards. This is an important part of the leadership role.

## Case Study 8.1 Crisis management in a consultancy

These concepts are illustrated by an example from Bob Graham's consultancy. Most of the firm's work came through projects for clients. However, the firm had difficulty getting people to volunteer for projects, particularly support staff. They typically worked at the end of the project, getting things ready for client presentations, and felt that management worked in 'crisis' mode, leaving everything to the last minute, working them overtime at the end, and that they got no reward for it. They wanted an end to the crises in order to be motivated to join project teams. Consultancy firms are responsive organizations, responding to client wants and whims. There is little chance of eliminating the crisis environment. So we worked on what they might find of value to working on projects and what they perceived as associated risk. It turned out that they valued the work as it was seen to be more exciting than departmental work. However, the risk was 'that we walk in one day, the manager yells "CRISIS", and we are stuck working through the night'. So the problems seemed to be the uncertainty of the crises and lack of reward for extra work. An examination of past crises showed a pattern, that the crises happened during the week before client presentations. With this knowledge we were able to schedule the crises and take away some of the uncertainty. We worked on the rewards by giving 'comp' time so that they could have the next Monday off after every scheduled crisis. The comp time was seen as a super bonus and project work became the most sought after work in the company.

## 8.5 Influencing others

Numerous studies of successful projects point to the need for top management support, and so this is a key part of a successful project. Influencing upper management and other stakeholders is very similar to influencing team members. The project leader must realize that influencing project stakeholders is a process, not an event. Some project leaders will hold stakeholder influencing events, such as a project start-up workshop, and feel that the influence has been set for the project. They often feel that their project will maintain a constant, high priority. However, priorities change, and stakeholder's feelings about a project and attention given to it also change with time. So while a project start-up workshop is an excellent event for gaining support for a project, it is to be seen as only one event in a long and continuous process of developing and maintaining project support.

The process of developing support begins by identifying the major stakeholders. These stakeholders may include those people asking for the results of the project, those people paying for it and those people supplying resources (people). We call these groups the upper management, the customers and the department managers. Most projects have additional stakeholders, but all projects have at least these three groups. In addition, there are often groups who feel they will not benefit from the project, and the project leader should work to develop their support. The project leader must then determine what value these various groups will obtain from a successful project; and for those that are not initially supportive of the project, what loss they feel the project will cost them. Common values received for the stakeholder groups from projects are shown as follows.

### Senior management

The common value for upper management is that the project will help to support a corporate strategy, such as entering a new market. If the strategy is successful, then the project will ultimately help to lead to higher profitability and other corporate goals. It is important that the project leader realizes just what strategy it is that the project is supporting. As projects unfold they are often financially scrutinized and are sometimes felt to be expendable at budget review time. It is important that the project leader reminds upper management of what strategy will suffer if the project does not receive continued support.

### Customers/end users

These are the people who will gain benefit from the ultimate use of the end product of the project. To satisfy the customer, the project leader must be continually in touch with what the customer wants from the product, as well as what they really expect from the product. Experienced project leaders understand that what a customer says they want, and what they really expect, are often two very different things. It is thus a task of the project leader to continually probe to discover what it is that the customers and end users really expect from the end product. There are two parts to discovering customer expectations:

1. One part is to develop a mindset of continuous exploration. This means that the project team expects and welcomes a sequence of constant changes and suggestions from the customers and end users. In the past, these changes were often seen as irritants that delayed project progress. Now they should be seen as additional information that will help to ensure project success.
2. The second part is using prototypes to evoke responses. Most people cannot really tell you what they expect from a product until they have experience of it. (It is the same in a marriage.) Developing prototypes allows them to have this experience and to say the classic line *'Well, how come it doesn't do this or that'*. Of course, the customer never asked for it to do this or that, but the experience of the prototype will uncover that they expected it.

One possible solution is to put customers on the core team. This was done at Boeing Corporation for the team developing the Boeing 777. Three customers were given office space on the shop floor and access to design decisions. In this way design engineers could easily discover what the customer both wanted and expected.

### Department directors

This group supplies people to undertake project work. It is assumed that all people working on a project will be 'on loan' from various departments in the organization. The project leader should therefore consider the needs and desires of the managers of those departments. Department managers may have a role implementing corporate strategy, so a knowledge of how the project supports corporate strategy is important in gaining their support.

However, department managers are also occupied with the more immediate task of scheduling people to perform the tasks of the department, and to support other projects. Thus the more immediate questions run along the lines of '*What people do you want, for how much of their time, and when will they be finished?*'. It is important that the project leader reviews project plans, schedules and progress with department managers on a regular basis. The more complete and accurate information they have, the better they will be able to schedule people to meet the other demands placed on their department. This will help to develop and maintain their support for your project.

**Other stakeholders**

There may be some groups or individuals, even among those mentioned above, who will not initially support the project. With these people it is important that the project leader determine what they have at risk, or what they feel they have to lose, from successful completion of the project (Case Study 8.2). Many times this feeling of risk and/or loss is due to mis-information or false assumptions. Thus, to gain their support the project leader must discover what their assumptions are, and work to inform. In fact, they must do more than inform, as talk is cheap. They must demon-strate that the results of the project will not result in the loss they expect. This is a long process and often takes place over the life of the project. But it has many rewards.

## Case Study 8.2 Installing a computer system in a college

Bob Graham was project leader of a project to install a computer system in a col-lege that had no existing system. He was hired expressly for that job, so he thought people would welcome help. However, he quickly noticed that people were resisting him in the different departments, not giving him the support that he expected. He discovered that many saw him as a 'hired gun', brought in to eliminate their jobs. Worse, many kept their jobs so that their children could attend the college at reduced tuition. So if their jobs were eliminated, their children's future would be ruined. It is easy to see why they were not in a mood to help him. Of course, there was no plan to eliminate jobs. At best, it was hoped that the computer could help to reduce the need for additional people as the college grew. But as he discussed this with people his words were met with scepticism. It was not until he automated one department, and no one lost their job, that they began to believe him and offer more support. However, through this process of discovering their fears, addressing their fears and showing that they were unfounded, he was able to turn many 'enemies' into allies. This is the process recommended for all project leaders.

## 8.6 The power/value of information

By now, you will have realized the key to motivating and influencing others lies in the power of information. The project leader needs to see himself or herself as the ultimate information disseminator. Because of the uncertainty that surrounds most projects, they tend to generate anxiety among stakeholders, usually concerning outcome, cost, final schedule and resource requirements. Information is the only tool the project leader has to relieve this anxiety. The project leader will find that he or she can have a large influence over members of the organization by providing timely and complete information about salient aspects of the project.

The first step in developing a project management information system (PMIS) is to determine what information the stakeholders need to relieve their anxiety. Some suggest you begin with a list of stakeholders and ask them what information they need. However, experience has shown the response to such a question does not reveal all that is needed. Many people find it difficult to answer questions about what data they need. They give an answer, but when the data is presented they say it is not what they wanted. This often leaves the project leader puzzled and frustrated. Most people do not think in terms of data, but rather in terms of questions. Therefore, instead of asking *'What data do you need?'*, it is better to ask *'What questions do you have about this project?'*. Then the project leader and the stakeholders can work together to develop a set of information to answer those questions. Good information is that which answers stakeholders' questions, is easy for them to understand and is there when they need it. This requires the project leader to understand the questions and associated information from the stakeholders' viewpoints. The PMIS should be developed to satisfy their needs, in much the same way as the entire project is developed to satisfy the needs of the customers/end users.

### Questions on outcome

The questions about outcome are normally of three types:

1. The first is about what the final product will do when it is completed. This is a question for the project leader as well as the stakeholders as the specifications will change as the project proceeds. The project leader must guard against suggesting a certain function will be available before it is certain it will indeed be in the final product. So answers to questions about outcome should be in two parts: one that contains features that have definitely been decided on, and the other that contains a list of features that are being considered. This list should be updated regularly and distributed automatically to all stakeholders.

2. The second question about outcome is the 'Will it be successful?' type. Stakeholders want to know how this product compares to the competition, and its probability of market acceptance. The best way to answer these questions is to summarize information gleaned from customer and end user representatives, show how the product is being designed to address their expectations, and then pass this on to the stakeholders. If this cannot be done due to competitive reasons (secrecy), then the stakeholders should be assured that it is indeed taking place.

3. A third outcome question is the 'market segment' type. Stakeholders often want to know what market the product is aiming to satisfy. The project leader needs to be continually aware of and searching for potential applications and markets for the product, and passing this information on to the stakeholders.

QUESTIONS ABOUT THE SCHEDULE

Of course, the classic schedule question is 'When will it be ready?'. Associated questions concern availability of prototypes and milestone reviews. This means that an updated schedule should be always available to stakeholders to answer these questions.

QUESTIONS ABOUT RESOURCE REQUIREMENTS

Projects have a way of using up hours of resources, much said to be unexpected. This often frustrates department directors supplying resources. Their questions normally revolve around how much resource you are going to need and when such resource will be available to the department again. Project leaders are understandably hesitant to answer such questions, as forecasts of project requirements are difficult to make when you are doing something new. In addition, initial estimates have a quality of being 'cast in stone', so future changes in requirements cause friction with department directors. Thus requirements should be presented with a 'here is what we know so far' quality. The project leader should not just produce estimates and send them to the department directors. Rather, they should go on to explain assumptions that went into making the estimate and indicate all of the factors that could cause the estimate to change. It is well known that department directors, as with other humans, are much more amenable to change if they understand the reason for the change. The project leader must ensure that they know the reasons for all changes.

In addition to providing information that answers stakeholders' questions, good information should also be there when it is most needed. Having the information available to stakeholders is often not enough. The project leader should attempt to determine when it is that the information will most likely be needed. Simple questions to stakeholders like '*When do you usually discuss this project?*' or '*What meetings do you go to where questions about this project come up?*' can often reveal the best time to provide the information. For example, if there is a regular meeting where the project is discussed, it would be good to provide the information the day before that meeting. In that way the stakeholder could arrive at the meeting with the latest information. Timely information is current information that arrives just before the person needs it.

As a final note, it is important to remember that timely, accurate information is useless unless the person who is using the information understands what they are being presented with. Many people are not comfortable with information presented on Gantt charts and network diagrams. Thus, during the first few times when information is supplied the project leader may need to personally review the format with the stakeholders in order to ensure that they fully understand what they are being presented with. If they cannot work with network diagrams and the like, then a different format should be developed with which they are comfortable. Always remember that the information is being produced in order to relieve anxiety and uncertainty. If people cannot understand the information, then it will act to actually increase the very anxiety it was designed to reduce. So the information should be made to conform to the person, rather then expecting the person to conform to the information. In summary, good information answers stakeholders' questions, is there when they need it and is easy to understand.

## 8.7 Developing a project stakeholder management strategy

We have shown that a successful project requires leading by influence rather than authority. Developing this influence requires an understanding of individuals' risk/reward relationships and the power of information. Project leaders can influence individuals to do their best if they perceive that the benefits outweigh the risks. Project leaders must use information to show people the potential rewards and the way in which risks are being addressed. Calvert[1] suggests how this may be formalized within a project stakeholder management strategy, Table 8.1. Formalizing the process ensures that stakeholder information is retained within the project while manpower and other cultural changes take place. This is particularly important on large, complex projects.

Developing influence is a process, not an event. This means the project leader can never order team members to complete a task, but must persuade them, over and over again. Such influence is more effective than authority, but takes more time. The project leader often feels the urge to just say 'Do it' in order to get things done. This may often be seen as a short-run necessity, but it leads to a long-run disaster. Use it sparingly.

**Table 8.1** Developing a project stakeholder management strategy

| Step | Process | Main questions/issues | Tools |
|---|---|---|---|
| 1. | Identify stakeholders | Who are the stakeholders?<br>What are their stakes? | |
| 2. | Investigate stakeholders | Gather information on all stakeholders | PEST analysis (Fig. 8.2) |
| 3. | Identify mission | Are stakeholders likely to be supportive?<br>Are stakeholders likely to be opponents? | |
| 4. | SWOT stakeholders | What are stakeholders strengths?<br>What are stakeholders weaknesses? | Stakeholder information sheet (Fig. 8.3) |
| 5. | Predict behaviour | What will stakeholders do? | |
| 6. | Make action plans | Formulate plans and procedures | Communication plan (Fig. 8.4) |
| | | Maintain contact with key stakeholders | PSM action plan (Fig. 8.5) |
| 7. | Implement PSM strategy | Make PSM a project policy<br>Make PSM part of project review<br>Make PSM part of change control | |

## 8.8 The project champion

One senior manager may help the project leader by championing the project's cause. We consider the *project* champion – their role, attributes required to undertake the role and specific responsibilities.

### The role of the project champion

The word champion has been applied in the past without specifically relating to a position in the organization. A champion is someone who fights for a cause, which can imply an adversarial situation and is best avoided on projects but is necessary to maintain support for one project over others. A project champion is a person in the sponsoring organization who is totally committed to the success of the project. The role may be combined with that of the project manager, but that is only likely on a minor project, without a complex client organization or with a single patron. The project manager is usually a separate individual, perhaps because he or she is managing more than one project or is concerned with hands-on operation of the project and with leading the project team. The project champion is therefore someone within the sponsoring organization with delegated responsibility

| Political | Socio-cultural |
|---|---|
| Environmental protection laws<br>Taxation policy<br>Foreign trade regulations<br>Employment law<br>Local government | Population demographics<br>Social mobility<br>Attitudes to work and leisure<br>Education |
| Interest rates<br>Inflation<br>Disposable income<br>Labour costs<br>Material costs | Rate of obsolescence<br>Speed of technology transfer<br>New discoveries<br>Research |
| **Economic** | **Technological** |

**Figure 8.2** PEST analysis

| STAKEHOLDER INFORMATION SHEET | |
|---|---|
| **Project:** | **Project manager:** |
| Stakeholder: | Supportive/adverse: |
| Useful information: | |
| Strengths: | Weaknesses: |
| Opportunities: | Threats: |
| Likely strategy: | |

**Figure 8.3** Stakeholder information sheet

| Project: Redwings Supermarket | | | Project manager: Peter Smith | | |
|---|---|---|---|---|---|
| Audience | Information | Timing | Method | Media | Responsibility |
| Local residents | Brief on project | Start of site work | Press release | Newspaper | PM |
| Close neighbours | Noise of foundation work | Ditto | Letter | Mailshot | Site engineer |
| Local residents | Completion of work | 4 weeks be-fore opening | Interview | Radio | Store manager |
| etc | | | | | |

**Figure 8.4**   Example of a communication plan

| PSM CONTINGENCY ACTION PLAN | |
|---|---|
| **Project:** | **Project manager:** |
| Contingency in case of following action: | |
| By: | |
| Action to be taken: | |
| Responsibility: | |
| Persons to be advised: | |
| | |
| | |

**Figure 8.5**   PSM Contingency action plan

from the client body for the project, with the authority to champion the pro-ject and the project manager. It may be necessary to obtain resources or take action with the stakeholders or with the participants at the highest level. The champion fulfils three distinct roles: protecting the project manager from influence by stakeholders in the parent organization; liaising with the client organization; and maintaining focus on objectives.

### Relationship with the organization

The champion's most important function is to protect the project from stakeholders with no direct contractual responsibility, but who may have divergent objectives from the project. Figure 8.6 shows that stakeholders relate to the champion only and not any other level of the project unless an appropriate mechanism has been established. Figure 8.7 shows an organization in which the client, user and other interested parties become closely involved in the project process. In this case, it may be impossible for the sponsor to act unilaterally. If the leader is perceived to be challenged or inhibited by these peer forces, the role of champion is extremely difficult to establish and maintain. It is therefore necessary that authority within the organization is clearly set out and understood by all, so that the role is a positive one, built on the expectation of success and is not, as often happens, put in a no-win situation. The difference between a champion and a hero should be noted. It is no advantage to the project to have a champion who is overcome by superior forces and does their glorious best against overwhelming odds. If the champion is not certain

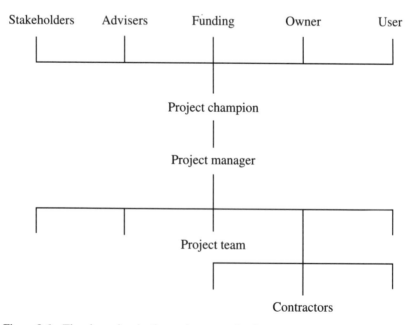

**Figure 8.6**   The champion in the project organization

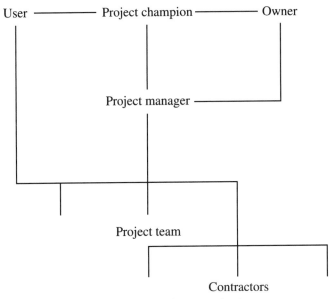

**Figure 8.7**    Closely integrated project organization

and confident of success and seen to be successful this will be transmitted through the organization, inflicting considerable damage on morale and commitment.

CLIENT COORDINATION

A major cause of poor performance on projects is for the client to be unclear about objectives, to instruct or agree to inessential changes, and to interfere in the process. An important duty of the champion is to coordinate between the various client or user interests and to shield and support the project manager when they encounter problems of this sort. The single axis between the champion and the project manager, the one acting outwards and upwards and the other leading the project team directly, is very positive and is the driving force of the project. It has the effect of giving confidence to those involved in the project by demonstrating success in defending the interests of the project in all circumstances.

THE IMPORTANCE OF OBJECTIVES

The champion should have a positive attitude in all situations, and keep attention always on the desired objectives. It is necessary to expect success at every stage and encourage in others the habit of meeting all the carefully planned targets. Where conflict occurs, as it always will when there is a conflicting requirement for resources or where there is a genuine conflict of interests and objectives, on no account should a defensive approach be adopted. This only leads to chronic conflict and adversarial attitudes. The causes of the problem are what is important and are not usually difficult to find. A mechanism should be set up to enable the counter-productive activities to be controlled and channelled for the benefit of the project.

### Attributes of the project champion

The champion requires two competencies above all:

1. They must know how to operate in and with all the organizations involved, by understanding how they work and the people who comprise them. This is usually very different from operating via the organization charts, which may not be so effective. The champion is therefore a 'high-risk' person, able to get decisions and answers from their own or other related organizations by effective operations know-how.
2. They must have an uncanny knack of knowing the right lever to pull and button to press for any eventuality.

It is a matter for debate as to whether a detailed knowledge of the relevant technology is required. Some knowledge of the technology is required, but only to a limited extent. It is required so that the champion can communicate with and have the respect of various specialists involved, and is sufficiently familiar with the terminology and approach to have credibility with those over whom he or she is to exercise authority. It can be something of a disadvantage to reveal expertise in the technology concerned. The champion may be seen to be technically authoritative and thereby be in conflict with specialists. It is also an enormous temptation to reveal that knowledge and so become involved in the process. The more this happens, the more team work can be damaged. Also, if the champion is seen to become involved in the technical detail, those with the responsibility are likely to back off. The team requires leadership and support not interference, whether expert or not. The nineteenth-century, German general, von Moltke, prided himself on his ability to keep silent in seven languages.

### Responsibilities of the project champion

The project champion should not be involved in the detail process under any circumstances. It is therefore beneficial for the appointment to be part-time. Their involvement should be in the routine attendance at steering group or board meetings. These should be brief and held at regular intervals. The project manager should prepare and issue the progress/policy reports. A typical supporting role is in problem resolution, for example, a difficulty with the performance of a contractor or subcontractor. The champion would meet the senior executives of the company concerned informally, together with the project manager, to resolve the difficulties and obtain the desired commitments. In the event of difficulties with peers within the organization, or at a higher level, the problems should not be circumvented but faced by bringing them into the open in a suitable meeting. On no account should there be adversarial correspondence. Appeals to a higher authority almost always fail, because this authority is faced with a choice between people or departments of equal status and siding with one produces adverse effects on the commitment of the other. A more suitable approach is to point out the effect of the difficulty on the success of the project. If the problem is likely to recur then a mechanism should be set up to ensure timely communication in the future. Problems at the interfaces between the parties produce severe time and cost pressures. The champion should always be alert to incipient problems, and maintain a good relationship with the project manager. Negative, reactive and defensive attitudes are at the root of project failure. The project champion has a vital role in leading their project to certain success.

## 8.9 Summary

1. There are many people in the organization who need to be influenced in favour of the organization. One key to a successful influencing strategy is to treat all the people involved with a project as volunteers.
2. The first step in developing an influencing strategy is to identify the project's stakeholders. This will include allies and enemies.
3. A key factor in gaining someone's support is to help them understand that rewards from the project are greater than the risks. Rewards may be more than monetary. Rewards and risks may include:
   - Doing something new
   - Learning a new skill
   - Networking and travel
   - Developing a unique product
   - Positive visibility with senior management
   - Negative visibility with senior management
   - No reward for project work
   - A more exciting project may come along.
4. Influencing others is an on-going process, not a one-off step. People to be influenced include:
   - Senior management

 – Customers and end users
 – Department directors.
5. You should also appreciate the value of information, including answers to questions of:
 – *Outcome* What will it do? Will it sell? Who will buy it?
 – *Schedule* When will it be ready?
 – *Resource requirement* How much effort/money will it take/cost?
6. Adoption of a project stakeholder management strategy will formalize the process of identifying stakeholders, evaluating likely behaviour and preparing contingency action plans. This process allows the project team to act on real information and not just on rumour and will operate across changes in manpower to ensure continuity.
7. The role of the project champion is to:
 – Manage the relationship of the project with the organization
 – Coordinate the relationship with the client
 – Maintain focus on the objectives.
8. The champion must:
 – Know how to operate in the organization
 – Have an uncanny knack of knowing which levers to pull
 – Have some knowledge of the technology of the project.
9. The champion must have no role in the detail work of the project.

## References

1. Calvert, S.C., 'Managing Stakeholders', in *The Commercial Project Manager: Managing owners, sponsors, partners, supporters, stakeholders, contractors and consultants*, Turner, J.R. (ed.), McGraw-Hill, 1995.

## Bibliography

1. Graham, R.J., *Project Management as if People Mattered*, Primavera Press, 1990.

# PART THREE
# A CULTURE FOR PROJECT-BASED MANAGEMENT

Part Three looks at creating a culture for project-based management within the organization, and considers several related issues.

In Chapter 9, Lynn Thurloway draws together the threads of previous chapters to show how to create a culture within organizations for a project-based approach to management. She considers the benefits of this approach and then summarizes some of the dilemmas and conflicts, including structure and culture, functions versus projects, selection and allocation of project personnel, and rewards, career development and motivation.

In Chapter 10, Colin Hastings and Wendy Briner consider how to deal with cultural differences when projects and project-based management cross boundaries: national boundaries; organizational boundaries; and professional boundaries. They describe the basis of cultural differences, problems it can create and some of the actions that managers can take to cope with these differences. The actions are more to do with being aware of the differences and building on different people's strengths, than with trying to force everyone into a single straightjacket.

In Chapter 11, Alistair Godbold and Rodney Turner consider ethical project management. This is a cultural issue, as ethics are a matter of philosophical tradition. They identify that there is an increasing awareness of ethical standards. This is a long-term trend (primarily as a result of increasing standards of living), but there has been a marked increase between the 1980s and 1990s. They consider some of the philosophical traditions of ethics. Many ethical problems reduce to a dilemma, either qualitative or quantitative, and some are considered. They then describe how organizations and the people in them can adopt a practical approach to ethics. Ethical differences between cultures often reduce to the balance the culture gives to the rights and duties of individuals and the rights and duties of society. The Prisoner's Dilemma is used to illustrate this, and then both the differences this creates between cultures, and how the balance has evolved through European history are considered.

In Chapter 12, Suzanne Pollock and Rodney Turner consider a particular ethical problem, that of managing the impact of projects on the physical environment. They describe a four-step process to environmental management, involving developing understanding, measuring environmental performance, continuing to develop environmental performance and reviewing progress and deciding next steps.

Finally in Chapter 13, Kristoffer Grude, Rodney Turner and John Wateridge return to diagnostic techniques to help you create an environment for project-based management and to assess the effectiveness of individual projects for delivering change. First they describe a diagnostic technique developed by Kristoffer Grude to help you assess whether your corporate culture and environment supports project-based management and its use to achieve corporate development objectives. They then describe an adaptation of that technique developed by John Wateridge to help you assess individual projects and to establish such projects so as to effectively deliver their objectives.

# 9
# Creating the project culture

Lynn Thurloway

## 9.1 Introduction

The widening use of project management techniques means projects are no longer confined to those areas of industry traditionally perceived to be project oriented, particularly engineering, construction and product development. Today we find project-based management approaches being used in almost every area of industry to manage a variety of projects, especially change projects. However, project management cannot be seen as a panacea, magic solution or philosopher's stone that can be adopted in an *ad hoc* fashion for any situation that seems to require a team-focused approach. To obtain real benefits, organizations need to consider the implications of implementing project-based management, especially as a change management technique, and to ensure they create a culture that supports the approach. We consider the implications of that in this part of the book and end with a diagnostic technique to help you ensure that your corporate culture supports project-based management. In this chapter, we identify some of the requirements for creating a project culture.

## 9.2 Management by projects – a solution or a problem

Project-based management approaches are an effective and beneficial approach to the management of change to achieve corporate development objectives, because they:

- Are strategically flexible, allowing complex problems or change initiatives to be broken into manageable parts
- Offer a clear division between strategic and operational decisions and actions
- Allow managers and their teams to focus on specific issues, taking ownership of both problem and solution

- Offer an opportunity for a multi-functional or multi-disciplinary approach which results in issues being considered from a number of perspectives
- Give project managers clearly defined resources, time-scales and constraints
- Give managers methodologies for problem solving, decision making, planning, budgeting and the control and implementation of strategic, operational or change objectives
- Allow people at any level of the organization to have the opportunity to become involved in decision making and problem solving
- Allow more creative and flexible approaches to be applied to issues, problems and solutions.

Given the potential benefits to be gained from the adoption of project-based management approaches, particularly as business environments become increasingly dynamic and complex, it is not surprising that it has become a popular management technique. However, Hastings[1] suggests that while many organizations now manage by projects and through project teams, few seem to know how to get real performance from them and the vast majority of teams actually under-perform. This implies that managing projects is not just about managing 'hard' management issues, such as cost and quality and achieving goals, objectives and milestones successfully to time, but is also about acknowledging and managing 'soft' issues that result in people acquiring both a personal and team-based motivation to succeed. Failure to gain value from projects is due to a lack of attention to the soft issues, primarily brought about by an ineffective fit between the prevailing cultures, structures and processes and those which support a project-based management approach. The effects of this misfit have a profound impact upon the way the project manager manages and the likelihood of the success of the team.

## 9.3 Dilemmas and conflicts

We identified in Chapters 3 and 4 that projects, especially change projects, tend to exist outside the mainstream activities of the organization. This places pressures and tensions on available resources and results in conflicts between operational and project objectives (shown in Fig. 4.1). Such conflicts are likely to emerge regardless of whether project resources, including people, are integrated into or separated from the main organization. However, it is likely that greater potential for conflict exists when resources are integrated and the boundaries between operations and projects are not clear. Conflict between projects and operations is inevitable. However, it can be managed more effectively if managers and their organizations recognize and address the issues that give rise to such problems and deal with the consequences that emerge. Some of these are discussed below.

## Structure and culture

Chapter 4 suggests that functional, hierarchical structures have been dominant in many organizations and despite downsizing and flattening of hierarchies, accountability and control generally remains centred around status and function. The functional, hierarchical orientation results in the prevalent culture of many organizations being based either on power or role.[2] In this model, power and control are distributed through the organization based on position within the hierarchy or according to functional importance. In the project context, power and control for each project needs to be located with the project manager and project team, especially if flexibility and responsiveness, which are key characteristics of project working, are to be achieved. Therefore, if projects are to operate successfully, the organization needs to adopt a more task-oriented culture. Handy[2] suggests that:

> This culture is extremely adaptable...each group ideally contains within it all the decision making powers required. Individuals find in this culture a high degree of control over their work, judgement by results, easy working relationships within the group with mutual respect based upon capacity rather than age or status.

According to the logic of a task culture, decisions about initial allocation of resources and projects are made by senior managers, but issues related to the organization and running of the project are decided at project level by those directly involved. The advantage of the task culture is that as power sharing becomes devolved the flexibility and responsiveness of the project team to changing situations is enhanced; hence this logic complements the notion of project management. However, Handy[2] notes a key weakness of this model in that when there is competition for resources, the culture often reverts back to role or power cultures as either senior management begin to reclaim operational and strategic control of projects, or project managers begin to compete on a political basis in order to influence the allocation of resources and people. In many organizations, both of these weaknesses are evident, but this is not just due to competition for limited resources, but also because many organizations are unable to make the transition in culture. This is reinforced by structures and processes used throughout the organization. Furthermore, in many organizations attempting to adopt project-based management techniques, senior managers have not been able to make the psychological move from retention of power and decision making to devolving power and decision making downwards, nor have they adopted management styles that encourage such a move to occur.

The experience of many project managers is that they must rely on their personal and political abilities to influence senior managers and others with power and status, in order to obtain resources and get things done. In change projects especially, project managers often spend large amounts of time and energy, which might better be spent managing problems and issues directly related to the project, networking and interfacing with senior managers and others to gain advantageous resource allocations or to reduce the impact of decisions in which they have not been involved but which could adversely affect their project. Much of a project manager's time and energy is spent attempting to influence the environment to gain favourable conditions for the project. You might argue that this is part of stakeholder management. However, in a true project-oriented culture, stakeholder conflict would be constructive in nature; senior managers would visibly support, champion and value the notions of projects, individual project goals and the project team, and conflict that did emerge would be focused on improving overall performance and results. The situation which actually exists in many organizations seems to be dysfunctional and focused upon internal competition. Unless senior management visibly endorse the notion of project management through the sharing of power and decision making with project managers at all stages of the project life-cycle, the fit between project and organizational cultures will remain incongruous and project managers will stay in what is often a politically vulnerable position with limited opportunities to exercise their influence or manage their projects effectively. Ultimately this will result in the overall benefits of the project-management approach becoming diluted.

## Functions versus projects

Project managers have to rely on the cooperation of other managers for staffing their projects. Cooperation is essential regardless of the method of allocation used, as functional managers can influence individual and project performance either covertly or overtly. To engender a climate of cooperation, project managers and functional managers need to consider the key concerns each of them may have regarding their personnel, and not surprisingly, because of the demands placed upon them, these tend to be conflicting in nature. Kanter[3] indicates the sort of concerns line managers may have in relation to project working and these include:

- How do I as functional manager control or manage staff who have been allocated to project teams?

- Why should I release my best staff to work on projects, particularly when delayering and downsizing is placing additional pressures on me, my department and function?
- How do functional managers handle and control extra work that results from projects that are initiated elsewhere in the organization?

On the other hand, issues that project managers may raise include:

- How do I ensure I get those staff who have the most appropriate skills, knowledge, potential or ability released for my project and how can I ensure I keep them?
- How do I reward people who work on my project when I do not have the resources or influence to ensure that they are rewarded appropriately for work they have done on my project?
- How do I get individuals to focus on my project when they are still required to do their functional work or work on other projects?

The prime objective each has is to gain or retain resources best able to help them achieve their goals and objectives. Not surprisingly, this is fertile ground for conflict. Projects, especially change projects, result in the status quo being challenged, which can lead to the development of unclear boundaries and relationships between functions, projects and the wider organization. Managers then tend to resort to protecting their own interests, especially if they are unsure about the overriding priorities of the organization – are they with projects or functions? As we saw in Chapter 8, project managers have to manage stakeholders and this includes functional managers whose interests and objectives may conflict both with other stakeholders and with the overall project objectives. However, line managers have a key advantage over the project manager – they have established and clearly recognized status and power through their position within the dominant hierarchy. For project managers this is rarely the case, and many project managers find themselves placed in a situation which they are unable to manage because they have no clear or universally recognized position or authority. Hence, again they have to resort to their personal abilities to influence the situation or appeal to their project sponsor or champion for help in regaining the situation.

Changing this situation requires senior managers to demonstrate that project management is valued and to raise its profile generally. One way of doing this is to improve the way in which they delegate projects to project managers and give them clearly defined parameters of responsibility and accountability at the earliest stages. Kanter[3] suggests that if projects are to be valued, organizations must encourage managers to manage without using position and status as a crutch. Senior managers need to guide a cultural shift that emphasizes cooperation by encouraging improved communication between departments and projects and making each more accountable. As the emphasis on position and power diminishes, the focus on individual interests (that tend to be of a win/lose nature) become less important and both departments and projects can focus on identifying and promoting opportunities that add value to the activities of the firm. (We will see in Chapters 10 and 11 that the dominant European culture values individual achievement above the organization.) In essence, by removing the crutch of hierarchy, managers are forced to focus on negotiating relationships and find flexible solutions to manage boundaries between projects and departments and combine resources and effort to succeed. In doing this, a synergy between the two can often be found and this will benefit the interests of both parties and the organization as a whole rather than one individual's dominant interests.

## Selection and allocation of project personnel

The way personnel are allocated to projects also reflects the culture and overriding structure of the organization. Traditionally, allocation or selection of personnel has been by role, position and principles of representation.[1] In project management, probably because organizations generally fail to promote a culture that facilitates project management, it is unusual for project managers to choose their project personnel. Senior managers often have their own agendas for selecting particular personnel, which may result in little more than the basic skill needs of the project being fulfilled, and this may not be conducive to overall success. Similarly, line managers usually use their own criteria for resource allocation that is unlikely to reflect the real needs of the project. This may be as simple as whoever is available at the time or who is least likely to be missed. However, for high-profile projects or critical change projects, managers are likely to take the view that the department needs to be represented (perhaps by someone of higher status than the project manager if the project is really high profile or sensitive) to make sure that the department gets a good deal. In such cases it is clear that the project goal is not necessarily the overriding objective and there are hidden agendas such as personal interest, and these can seriously undermine the project's overall success. Hastings[1] argues that selection or allocation of personnel on any other basis than who is likely to be of value to the project is not conducive to the concept of project working. Hence, team members should be selected only on the basis of their experience, potential and likely contribution to the project and team. Thus, as part of the overall raising of the profile of project management, project managers should be encouraged by senior managers to have an input in the decision-making process (whether it is at line level or senior level) regarding allocation of project personnel, not least because this will help ensure that the measures of value used to allocate project members is congruent with the needs and objectives of the project.

### Rewards, career development and motivation

In the era of delayering and downsizing, projects are proposed as a way of developing personnel and offering new challenges. However, in most organizations the focus of reward systems, personal development and career opportunities remains entrenched in the hierarchy, which is incongruous with project working. Unsurprisingly, this can have a profound impact on the motivation of project teams. The most important aspects of this concern the way people are promoted and rewarded within the hierarchy. Traditionally, reward and career processes are clearly designed to be individualistic and are based on the notions of personal advancement and progressive autonomy and status. People advance through the hierarchy on clearly defined career trajectories, and as they move upwards they gain additional job security, salary increases related to status and greater benefits such as larger expense accounts, medical benefits or a more prestigious company car. The essential design feature of this strategy is that managers are motivated through prevailing reward systems to satisfy personal needs for advancement and recognition. Hence, organizations have a propensity to focus on individualistic, performance-based, hierarchically-focused career and reward processes; ones which are difficult to apply in a project environment, where team work, collective autonomy and responsibility prevail. An organization truly committed to project management will review current career and reward systems and adopt strategies that motivate people working in project teams to perform. To do this the concerns of individuals who are recruited to work on projects must be considered. Such concerns include:

- Who determines my rewards and upon what criteria will they be based if the output from this project is part of a team effort and my individual input is less visible?
- How will my career be affected by working on this project rather than within the main hierarchy?
- How will training and development opportunities be affected by working on this project?
- Who will be responsible for the appraisal process and will the work that I do on this project be considered if the project manager is not included in the process?

In other words, individuals who work on projects tend to assess (consciously and subconsciously) the associated risks to their career, and the potential impacts upon rewards from working in a team. In turn, this affects their overall motivation and performance on the project. To address such concerns, project managers and organizations must take responsibility to ensure project team members are motivated to perform to the best of their ability. In Chapter 5, we recalled that Turner[4] believes motivation in a project environment requires a different approach than in a more stable environment and that the emphasis needs to be focused on the higher levels of Maslow's hierarchy of needs. Organizations and project managers need to create a climate in which new motivational techniques can develop in order that project teams feel motivated to perform. The creation of an environment in which motivation for projects can develop requires senior managers to stimulate a cultural shift that defines career development opportunities differently and requires them to implement strategies such as those suggested by Kanter[3] which:

- Emphasize employability, both in the internal and external labour markets, rather than upward progression on a clearly defined career ladder
- Encourage loyalty and commitment through project opportunities not through personal patronage or functional position
- Promote recognition for contributions to project goals and the organization's overall success on both an individual and team level rather than the recognition of efforts on an individual basis
- Encourage people to take responsibility for their own personal learning and development and offer them the opportunities to fulfil their potential
- Allow people to feel they make a difference to the overall success both of projects and the organization.

By employability, Kanter means that individual's responsibilities, skills and competencies are broadened by their increasing exposure to projects and hence their 'value' will increase in the internal and external labour markets. This implies that no longer can jobs be considered for life, but work needs to be seen as a lifelong opportunity. As part of this new orientation, organizations need to adopt systems that encourage functional managers, project managers and individuals to jointly undertake regular formal assessments of skill and competency development in order to ensure that the most appropriate resources are utilized effectively on projects and the best is made of project opportunities for individual learning and development. The adoption of such strategies means senior managers must tolerate a measure of risk in order that people do not feel they are threatened but are challenged to develop and perform. In most organizations the level of risk is minimal due to the selection on most projects of only those personnel who are known to have proven skills and experience.

This results in those who work on projects finding there are few challenges or demands placed upon them and opportunities available to develop their skills and potential are minimal.[5] Thus, if the notions of employability and responsibility for personal development are to be achieved, senior managers must ensure strategies adopted emphasize the values of both the organization and projects that motivate individuals and increase their desire to relish rather than avoid the opportunities and challenges that working on projects can offer, without the threat of retribution.

Project managers also need to adopt different motivation strategies. They need to recognize efforts and contributions made by individuals as well as those of the team. They need to change their focus from controlling to mentoring and supporting, and from managing to leading. They need to learn how to empower their team members in the same way as senior managers have empowered them. They also need to take calculated risks so that those who work on their projects develop their skills, potential and competence. They may do this through effective delegation and the promotion of a sense of contribution and collaboration across the whole project team, in order that team members begin to really work together and everyone feels that they have a part to play.

## 9.4 Summary

1. The adoption of a project-based management approach can offer real benefits and make organizations better able to achieve their corporate development objectives. However, project-based working does not come easily. It requires the creation of a supportive culture.
2. In order to create a flexible and adaptive culture, senior managers need to modify structures and systems and ensure the messages they send to the rest of the organization raise the profile of project management techniques. Managers, whether they be project managers or functional managers, need to change the way in which they work and must:
   - Manage without the crutch of hierarchy
   - Adopt selection strategies based on the experience and potential of team members and the likely value they are likely to add to the project
   - Implement career and reward strategies that encourage people on projects to perform to their full potential
   - Take calculated risks which allow people to develop their skills and work to their full potential.
3. Conflict between projects and other parts of the organization is inevitable and this should be accepted. However, it is important that overall success and effectiveness of project management is not undermined by negative inter-organizational conflict, but is enhanced by constructive

conflict, focused on adding value through the effective use of project management.

4. Project management can offer organizations the opportunity to gain a flexible, responsive approach to managing in a complex and changing business environment. However, this can only be fully realized if organizations and individuals learn to regard project management as a valuable management technique and are willing to adapt and change their structures and processes in order to get the best from it.

## References

1. Hastings, C., *The New Organization: Growing the culture of organizational networking*, McGraw-Hill, 1993.
2. Handy, C.B., *Understanding Organizations*, Penguin, 1985.
3. Kanter, R.M., 'The new managerial work', *Harvard Business Review*, November, 1989.
4. Turner, J.R., *The Handbook of Project-Based Management: Improving the processes for achieving strategic objectives*, McGraw-Hill, 1993.
5. Tampoe, F.M.C., and Thurloway, L., 'Project management: The use and abuse of techniques and teams', *International Journal of Project Management*, **11**(4), November, 1993.

# 10

# Coping with cultural differences

Colin Hastings and Wendy Briner

## 10.1 Introduction

The EU's Eureka programme has lofty ideals. Its purpose is to stimulate companies and research organizations from different member states to form consortiums collaborating on research and development in new technologies. Talking one day to a member of one of these joint research teams, our image of the exchange of ideas, the synergy, the whole being greater than the sum of the parts, was rudely shattered:

> We meet together once at the beginning to carve the work into pieces. We then meet again towards the end to write a report that makes it look like we were all working together. In reality, each institution works totally separately; there are no contacts between people even within the same discipline, there is no desire to exchange ideas or information or to work collectively to find some better solution than either of us could develop alone. In short, we all stayed in our organizational, physical, cultural and professional boxes.

While some will argue that this story is exceptional, we have our doubts. We know that examples of teams that perform exceptionally are the exception rather than the rule. One of the major barriers to performance in these teams lies in the difficulties of managing the interface and communication between disciplines and professions. In one large insurance company, for example, the gulf in world view between actuaries, whose role is to measure and limit risk, compared with that of marketing specialists working on new product development, had to be experienced to be believed. Another major barrier lies in the naiveté of many project team leaders and team members in understanding the decision-making processes and politics of their own organization. People from quantitative technical disciplines in particular experience great frustration when others in the organization do not behave 'logically' or 'rationally'. Add to these professional barriers the increasingly common situation whereby project teams span different locations within the

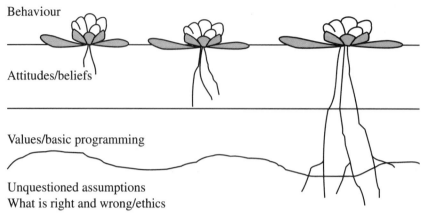

Behaviour

Attitudes/beliefs

Values/basic programming

Unquestioned assumptions
What is right and wrong/ethics

**Figure 10.1** The lily pond

same company, or even different organizations, as in post-acquisition joint ventures or strategic alliances, and it is unsurprising that performance is affected. Different professions with their traditions, different locations with their histories, different organizations with their ways of working and different national cultures and languages add up to a lethal cocktail that can kill cooperation. The project manager working in these complex situations must be tuned into these underlying dimensions of difference. Each difference provides individual project team members and constituent groups with different kinds of mental or cultural programming.

## 10.2 Cultural programming

### Mental models

Europeanization and globalization are producing a proliferation of project teams with members from very different backgrounds. National or ethnic differences may mean a Quebecois working with an English-speaking Canadian, or Chinese or Russians working with the British, where no one has much experience of the others' worlds. One approach we find useful is for the project leader to think of a map of how the world 'ought' to be and to explore how similar this is to the mental maps of others from different environments. The individual's mental map of the world is like the programming of a computer, that is, its operating software. Every application or behaviour is based on the structure of the operating software. The water lily, Fig. 10.1, shows that we all have a complex framework of mental programming connecting our behaviour through our values to our core assumptions; for instance, of what is right and wrong. So a project leader may wonder why Japanese people appear indirect, why their behaviour seems to avoid saying 'no'. This may be misinterpreted by a Briton or American as being unassertive or even misleading, while for a Japanese disagreeing directly with somebody may be seen as rude and personally disrespectful. Hence, project leaders may find that what they experience when they are working with people from other cultures takes them by surprise. The surprises or differences in expected behaviour may be trivial and easily understood. However, some will seem trivial but may be profound. If the profound differences are ignored then this is frequently a source of project disappointment or even failure. One project leader reflected on his experience thus:

> I knew of course that there would be differences working with East Germans since they are not used to our market economy thinking. But I did not realise just how significantly different their ways of thinking would be nor how much time and effort we would need to invest in working together.

Hofstede[1] suggests we have several layers of cultural programming, Fig. 10.2. We learn how to conduct ourselves from our families, education, language, gender and social class. We learn the fundamental rules about how we should treat others and what being a good person is. These views become consolidated among ethnic, regional or national groups. They make sense within their own cultural boundary but can be regarded as strange, illogical, frustrating and sometimes wrong by others. Anthropologists warn that no set of mental models is better or worse than any other. The challenge for project managers, working on a particular project with a unique group of people in an unfamiliar country, is to determine how to get that group to work together well enough as a team to deliver the expectations of the project owner and clients. We have found, through research and discussions with many project managers about what is important to them, that four aspects of mental programming have most impact on project success.

POWER: LEADERSHIP AND MEMBERSHIP

What is the appropriate relationship between those in positions of authority and those not – how equal should the relationship be and what is the right style of interaction? Some cultures strive for little difference. Holland, Denmark, Britain and the USA believe there should be as little difference in status as possible, with few layers of hierarchy. Conflicts should be worked out by discussion and participative approaches to leadership are best. Project management is viewed as a flat structure cutting across functional, hierarchical and geographical barriers. Conversely, in cultures where there

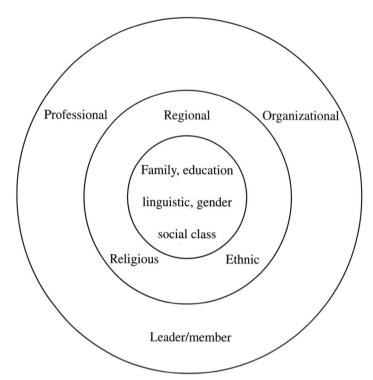

**Figure 10.2**   Levels of cultural programming, as defined by Hofstede[1]

is assumed to be a highly stratified set of relationships with formal rules about who can talk to whom about what, and where the best leader is believed to be a good father or benevolent autocrat, the British or Danish idea of project management is not appreciated. The project management model here is much more structured and autocratic. Understanding the different ideas about leadership helps a project leader to answer the questions: 'How do I influence the customer?' or, 'What are their expectations?' In Arab countries, project leaders say it is important to have a good relationship with one of the senior families. They can help find out who is important and how things link together. Spending time doing this before starting pays off as the project progresses.

INDIVIDUALITY: HOW MUCH?

Managing team members' performance is a cornerstone of project management. This is often a source of confusion in a multi-cultural environment where mental programming is different. In many Western countries, Britain and Germany for example, individuals are expected to accept responsibility for their work and to achieve by using their own abilities. They expect to be rewarded personally for their achievements and to receive feedback on their performance. This way of working is well suited to the task and output focus of project management. This approach to performance management runs into difficulties in more collectively oriented societies. Cashbuild, a South African cash and carry building materials merchant, was run by whites who were the minority of employees. They discovered that their Western individualistic programming was counter-productive in the context of the communal perspective of the black Africans, whose mental programming emphasized:

- My fellow man will help me in time of need therefore I am secure
- It is most important for me to be recognized by my fellow man and my greatest fear is rejection
- I aspire to the improved wellbeing of all of us
- We must discuss things together because we are all affected.

Finding ways of giving feedback indirectly through senior black team members, rewarding collective not individual effort and expecting decisions to be discussed with family members outside the team, were different ways in which the project manager handled problems in this situation.

THE ROLE OF TIME

We all know stories about Latins being free with time and Germans being punctual. Attitudes to time reveal very different mental programming. The average German believes events are controlled through planning and respecting deadlines. Things have to be ordered. Time is something tangible – it is limited and can be wasted and lost. Keeping people waiting is personally insulting, it implies they are not busy and are therefore unimportant. In this environment, a project leader meets few problems stressing the importance of missed deadlines. Plans are carefully thought out and followed. In other parts of the world, the Middle East and Japan, time is seen through much longer lenses. Time flows, it is organic and things come together at appropriate moments. This view does not discount persistence in effort and thriftiness with resources. Emphasis is placed on doing many things at once, particularly getting relationships established. Doing things as they arise, means interruptions which derail forward plans. Deadlines are seen as movable because it is more important to ensure relevant issues are attended to when they occur so that continuity is maintained. Imagine, then, the confusion when a Japanese company attempting to establish a project with an American organization feels that a meeting to sort out how to proceed is urgent. They try to arrange it for two days' time, but are told that senior American executives do not have time in their busy schedules within the next two months! The Japanese believe the Americans are not taking them and the relationship seriously. The Americans think the Japanese do not realize how busy they are running other aspects of their business.

Some cultures like everything spelt out in detail, assuming that unless things are stated they become woolly and a source of disputes. This aspect of multi-cultural working causes most obvious difficulties around contracts. This view is adversarial, concentrating on areas that *may* cause dispute. A different perspective is to focus on the common interest at the centre of most projects. Building sufficient contractual infrastructure to provide shape and a way of working is thought to be important. The conflicts of interest are expected to be worked out as they occur to meet the specific circumstances. The aim is to build and preserve a relationship that will realize the project's purpose. The English project manager, brought up in the adversarial tradition, can expect a pragmatic approach to contracting when working with Swiss or French partners in a project. It does not mean that they are commercially careless or not astute business people.

## Degrees of distance

The water lily diagram suggests that some behaviour may be seen as culturally different but has little impact on project working. How you eat soup or what you eat for lunch or dinner are good to know if you want to fit into another world, but are unlikely to have drastic consequences. More attention needs to be put into multi-cultural projects, but some demand a huge amount. The amount depends on the size of the cultural gap; the psychological distance that separates different parties. Figure 10.3 schematically demonstrates this. New interfaces with project team members from within the same company, but across national and functional boundaries, can be hard going but there will be quite a lot that can be taken as read. Within the same company similar assumptions will prevail about how things should be done. In multinationals there may be a common project methodology or planning approach. The consultants Arthur Andersen work hard at this. This is the relatively easy end of the scale.

The next level of complexity is a project that involves different organizations from different countries, who have no experience of working together. If, for instance, the countries are within Europe there may be among the project team some, albeit touristic, knowledge of the other culture. Clearly a larger and longer investment will have to be made by the project leader,

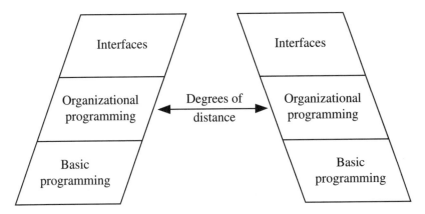

**Figure 10.3**   Levels of cross-cultural crossover

client, project owner and all the project team members to make this work. The widest gap is where the project spans widely differing continents, with little information or experience of the others' mental programming. Then many assumptions will be challenged for all parties involved. There will be many, persistent surprises and frustrations. Project managers working in former Soviet countries experience many cultural shocks of this kind. The infrastructure does not exist, the language is unknown, the former social framework is destroyed and the ways of thinking and relating to each other are unfamiliar. The gap is wide and it will take a long time and much understanding to create viable ways of relating to each other that enable successful projects to be delivered.

**The other key dimensions**

In the same way that national cultures produce different programming and mental models, so, too, do the other main settings or 'cultures' within which managers in particular spend their lives. There are three in particular that can have profound effects on the outlook and programming of individuals.

PROFESSIONS

Every specialism has its own language, jargon and culture. Each has limitations in its 'world view'. Some, such as sales and distribution, have short-term perspectives; others, such as marketing and actuaries, have longer-term ones. The type of education specialists receive conditions them, as does the nature of the subject itself. Professionalism creates tribes with a strong sense of identity, believing that they have the right answers and, correspondingly, a tendency to believe other disciplines do not. Such blinkers between professions which do not understand each other's languages are the cause of considerable misunderstandings and power games. Conversely, a common profession, engineering for instance, can provide something of a common language across national and organizational boundaries. This works for some professions but not others, for example, lawyers operating in quite different legal systems.

ORGANIZATIONS

Every organization has its own culture and way of working; new people joining have to learn the rules. Many United Nations agencies have labyrinthine procedures involved in spending money, even after budgets are approved. Where they work in partnership with commercial organizations, the latter tear their hair out in frustration at the time it takes to get the simplest thing done. Companies with very distinctive cultures, such as Digital and Gore, actually appoint people to coach newcomers in how the company works. Consultants joining Arthur Andersen are sent on a six week induction programme, and a consultant joining McKinsey was handed three typed pages of acronyms which had to be learnt before she could work effectively in the organization. Working in joint ventures across different organizations means that the rules get mixed up or that a project team member from one organization tries to use the set of rules appropriate to their organization to operate in the other and gets very frustrated because it does not seem to work.

LOCATIONS

Despite the telephone, e-mail and other forms of communication, physical separation is still an impediment to project performance. Project teams working apart are increasingly common. One project manager said: 'We have difficulty creating a team identity. However much we plan we still seem to get drift, and we don't know who is who in different locations'. We find different locations, even in one organization, operate in different ways. The key to understanding why this is lies in their different histories, which tend to cast a surprisingly long shadow over the present. One project manager we know solved this in a number of ways. First he insisted on regular meetings between key team members and rotated these between different locations. After each meeting other people from the site who were in some way connected with the project were invited to a buffet lunch and a common database was assembled on the e-mail of all their names, telephone numbers, roles, key skills and experience.

## 10.3 The project leader's role in managing differences

### Strategies for managing cross-boundary project teams

Faced with such a bewildering array of factors, all conspiring to reduce project performance, project managers might be forgiven for wanting to cut and run! However, there are emerging a range of strategies that companies and project managers can employ in order to realize the full synergistic potential of cross-boundary project teams.

PROJECT MANAGER SELECTION

Too often we find wholly unsuitable project managers are dumped into complex situations. No one has taken care to think about which sort of person and experience is best suited to making a success of these complex roles. Before managing such projects, project managers should have had experience working in different organizations, managing a range of disciplines and, ideally, having lived and worked in more than one country, preferably as a member of project teams. Rodney Turner worked with a company in which the head of estimating wanted to try his hand at project management. The first and only project he managed was in Israel. The project was 100 per cent overspent!

AWARENESS OF OWN PROGRAMMING

It is sometimes surprising for project leaders to realize that to work in a multi-cultural environment they need to be aware of their own mental programming. If the project leader is from the company and country owning the project, the automatic assumption is that things will be done 'our' way. One challenge for a project leader is to balance and evolve the demands of the interface between their 'home' organization, the client organization and culture, and team members. Companies who work internationally find that to be successful they have to modify their own thinking and working practices. Cross-cultural working is a two-way street, not colonization.

AWARENESS OF OTHERS' CULTURAL PROGRAMME

Working in multi-cultural environments requires the project leader to appreciate that things will be done, seen and understood differently. Project leaders need to be curious, not shocked, and should demonstrate interest in finding out and understanding different people's world views. They need to respect values leading to behaviours alien to them, but important to the individuals and society to which they belong. Assuming things will be done 'our way' only pushes differences underground so that they become embedded blockages. This easily creates an atmosphere of winners and losers which can prejudice effective delivery.

LEADERSHIP AND MEMBERSHIP OF PROJECT MULTI-CULTURAL TEAMS: WHAT TO DO?

For teams to work effectively, the roles and responsibilities of the leader and team members, both individually and collectively, must always be agreed upon. If the team is composed of people from different cultures, the expectations of leadership and membership differ. Clarifying the degrees of equality, responsibility and accountability expected of the leader and members is fundamental. So team start-up and team building is vital for success. The activities well known in team-building events will be just as important, but extra dimensions need to be added for international teams. There are three dimensions that have to be orchestrated to achieve high performance:

- Ability to discuss and respect established ways of working
- Awareness of own cultural programming
- Awareness of others' cultural programming.

ABILITY TO DISCUSS AND RESPECT ESTABLISHED WAYS OF WORKING

This means building a team culture where cross-cultural issues are openly discussed, so that appropriate ways are found to integrate all needs. In addition to formal team-building sessions, informal contacts between team members, suppliers, clients and other stakeholders establish and nurture networks, and create links that accelerate mutual understanding, curiosity and mutual respect. In low definition cultures, informal relationships and getting to know individuals are considered more important than formal relationships. So an English project manager commissioning a chemical plant in Latin America recognized that he and his family would have to spend a lot of time getting to know local dignitaries, suppliers, politicians and government officials if he was to be able to set up and hand the plant over. He explained that when at home he rarely saw anybody from work. He was keen on his garden and being with his family. However, he realized that his new job would place a whole new set of responsibilities on him and his family in a new culture. Social activities connected with work had to be undertaken. Wilson[2] found in her research that in a joint venture project, frequent contact between team members at different levels and functions of the two organizations helped to build a relationship infrastructure. Once you know individuals, have worked with them and have confidence in them, and can link into others who similarly have confidence in other team members, problems can be raised and differences discussed. Taking time to build this relational network enables a project to be managed as it progresses. Without it the inevitable problems can rapidly become breakdowns or lead to expensive litigation.

ACCELERATE PERSONAL NETWORK DEVELOPMENT

The development of good quality one-to-one personal relationships between people who have shared experiences is one of the most potent ways that a project manager can influence project performance. However, companies in long-term joint ventures can also influence the wider networks through frequent job interchange, personal mobility, lateral career moves, inter-organization conferences, meetings and training courses. The more the webs of relationships between the organizations intertwine the better. This must be done not only at the top, but at all levels of the organizations concerned. IBM call this 'entanglement'.

LANGUAGE

Decide early on a common working language. Provide accelerated language training for all those whose first language is not the chosen language. Work hard on those for whom it is the first language to modify the way they speak. They must think as if it were a foreign language and should talk slowly, enunciate clearly and avoid slang or jargon. Simultaneously, however, find ways to make it easier for those who are learning by translating key documents into several languages and by having a newsletter in more than one language.

CROSS-BORDER COACHES

Identify people across the organization who have an awareness of the dimensions of difference and use them as coaches or mentors to the project team, either on training courses or available to advise less experienced people about how to operate effectively in such environments. Such coaches can be supplemented by more formal cultural briefings about different countries that are increasingly available from specialist organizations.

COMMUNICATIONS INFRASTRUCTURE

New communications technologies are powerful tools for project managers, but ones that frequently fail to live up to their promise. The key lesson is not to fall into the trap of believing that e-mail, electronic and video conferencing, groupware and other technologies get people communicating. The personal relationships and networks need to be built in part first and then the technologies can help dramatically to develop these networks further. Get the basics in place first: good telephones, several fax links and a good directory of who is who, what they do and how they can be contacted. Supplement these with project start-up workshops, where all the key players get to meet each other personally and work together, and you will have rapidly created the basic technical and interpersonal infrastructure you need. Out of this the need and scope for more sophisticated methods will emerge more clearly.

SUPRA-COMPANY PROJECT MANAGEMENT

Deutsche Aerospace is a joint venture between companies in several European countries. They have created a special supra-company project management group that represents all the companies, but 'belongs' to an entity that all can identify with beyond their own locations or cultures. This interesting mechanism has served them well in providing a new sense of identity for the whole team, and has acted as an impartial broker to help iron out some of the many dimensions of difference that inevitably arise in such European consortia.

## 10.4 Summary

1. Individuals have many layers of cultural programming. Four key aspects of mental programming are:
   - Power, leadership and membership;
   - Individuality
   - The role of time
   - Level of definition.
2. As well as cultural and ethnic upbringing, three other influences on mental programming include:
   - Profession
   - Organization
   - Location.
3. The project leader's role in managing differences should address:
   - Project manager selection
   - Awareness of own programming
   - Awareness of others' cultural programming
   - Leadership and membership of multi-cultural teams
   - Respect for established ways of working
   - Personal network development

- Language
- Cross-border coaches
- Communications infrastructure
- Supra-company project management.

## References

1. Hofstede, G., *Cultures and Organizations: Software of the mind*, McGraw-Hill, 1991.
2. Wilson, D., 'A Process Model of Strategic Alliance Formation in Firms in the Information Technology Industry', working paper, MIT, 1989.

## Bibliography

1. Barham, K., and Wills, S., *Management Across Frontiers*, Ashridge Management Research Group and Foundation for Management Education, 1992.
2. Briner, W., Hastings, C., and Geddes, M., *Project Leadership*, 2nd edition, Gower Publishing, 1993.
3. Davison, S., 'Building Pan European Teams', *Eurobusiness*, 28–32, July 1989.
4. Hastings, C., *The New Organization: Growing the culture of organizational networking*, McGraw-Hill, 1993.
5. Koopman, H., *Transcultural Management*, Basil Blackwell, 1991.
6. Mindel, R., *Culture Bridging for Managers Workshop*, Warwick Weston, 1993.
7. Trompenaars, F., *Riding the Waves of Culture*, *The Economist* Books, 1993.
8. Hastings, C., Bixby, P., and Chaudhry-Lawton, R., *Superteams*, Fontana, 1986.

# 11

# Ethical project management

Alistair Godbold and Rodney Turner

## 11.1 Introduction

The 1990s have seen a growing awareness of business ethics, after the materialistic self-interest of the 1980s. This may be due to the public's growing lack of confidence in corporate activity. The public perceives that many of the notorious events of the 1980s and early 1990s, such as Bhopal, the Exxon Valdez and Shetland oil spills, Barlow Clowes, the Guinness and Blue Arrow affairs, were indicative of a paradigm that people do not matter – it is the bottom line that counts. This has now, in the mid-1990s, been replaced by concern that some elements of corporate life are driven by personal greed, giving rise in the UK to interest in the salaries of chairpeople of privatized utilities and standards of behaviour in public life, and leading to the creation of the Nolan Committee investigating the latter and a CBI Committee investigating the salaries of all boards of directors. The standards the public expects from people in public life and positions of authority seem far more stringent than before; although the pervasiveness of the media means people in public life are far more exposed than they used to be.

Another influence on the interest in business ethics is the growing emphasis on quality of life. People are not prepared to be treated as machines; as human resources of the company. However, in some ways the materialistic greed of the 1980s is being replaced by another form of self-indulgence, where personal rights completely dominate over the organization's rights, and people seem to feel no sense of duty to the organization.[1] It now seems that no chairpeople of any company, privatized utility or not, can earn a bonus while the company's staff are being made redundant. It could be said that pious, moral outrage is being expressed, with seemingly little thought for the rights of the shareholders who have invested money in that company and who expect an adequate return. In some cases, old-fashioned envy is being dressed up as ethical and moral outrage.

There is another issue creating ethical dilemmas for businesses. People almost expect modern life to be risk free, whereas in reality it is not, and people in business have to decide whether to make their products more expensive, and less risky, but also less competitive. There is no ethical dilemma if the levels of risk are made quite clear and people know what they are buying. However, there may be the temptation to cut corners, especially since people seem more willing to accept some risks than others, namely those we are familiar with, such as smoking cigarettes or driving cars or partaking in risky sports. Other areas of life we want to be risk free, such as eating processed food or travelling by air or watching sport as a spectator. In some areas we want the risk to be so low that it is not commercially viable for anyone to supply us with that service, and in others we accept ludicrously high levels of risk that could be reduced at very small expense; and therein lies the dilemma.

In many cases, it is quite clear what is right and what is wrong:

– Some things are morally right and some are morally wrong
– Some things are legal and some are illegal.

However, it is where practices are legal, but considered morally wrong, that the issue of ethics, and in particular business ethics, arises. Each of the following are legal, but many people consider each to be unethical:

– For an MP to accept money to ask a question in the House
– For the chairman of a private company to be paid whatever the share-holders will agree
– To use tax loopholes to avoid paying tax
– For calves to be exported to be raised in milk crates.

Many of the ethical decisions we face are of two types:

1. Where, along a fuzzy spectrum between what is clearly right and what is clearly wrong, do we draw a line and say on one side is acceptable behaviour and on the other side unacceptable behaviour? The decision is made more difficult by three further complications:
   – Other people may have different standards to ourselves, and we may make our business unprofitable if we are more stringent than they
   – Different cultures have different standards; what is acceptable to us may be unacceptable to others and vice versa – we need to be aware of that in an international context
   – Good and bad, and right and wrong, are not necessarily the same thing. 'Thou shalt not kill', but the bombings of Dresden and Hiroshima at the end of the Second World War were justified by saying they saved more lives than they cost, and hence were bad but right.

2. Faced with a dilemma in having to choose between two apparently contradictory options, which do we choose? The course of action will often be determined by our cultural heritage.

In this chapter, we describe ethics in business. We consider some of the drivers behind concern for ethics in business. We then explain four standard paradigms for ethical judgement, and describe some of the dilemmas arising out of the two ethical scenarios above (where you draw the line) and look at which of two contradictory options you choose. The former tend to be qualitative, the latter quantitative. A recurring theme is whether you give greater emphasis to the rights of society or the individual. We illustrate this through the Prisoner's Dilemma and show how the balance has varied throughout European philosophical development.

## 11.2 Drivers for ethical behaviour in business

There are several drivers for high standards of expected behaviour in modern business, as follows.

### Pervasiveness of the media

It is difficult to say whether the media creates the moral outrage currently in vogue, or reflects it. During the mid-1990s, the media is waging a crusade against what it sees as unethical behaviour in high places. On the one hand, people in authority seem to deserve it. They preached to the population about standards during the late 1980s and so are now exposed as being hypocritical. There is also an issue about what we expect of people in authority if they are to govern us properly. There is a fuzzy area which at some point crosses the boundary into corrupt behaviour. On the other hand, the media seem to take a far more prurient interest than in previous decades, investigating far more deeply. The UK press were quiet over the affair of Edward VIII with Mrs Simpson, and William Gladstone, Sir Winston Churchill and John F. Kennedy might find it very hard to live up to standards expected today. This media interest is causing people in authority to pay a lot closer attention to their standards of behaviour, and is perhaps contributing to a growing lack of respect for people in authority.

### Lack of respect for authority

It is common to hear modern politicians described as pygmies in comparison to great statespeople of the past. This does not stand up to investigation. Politicians of the 1930s and 1950s are said to have been weak, because many of the good people of their generation were killed in the

First and Second World Wars, respectively. Neville Chamberlain is particularly mentioned. What may be the case is that a far better educated public can make a far more critical assessment of the performance of politicians and when the latter are found to be wanting, the public loses respect. As the public loses respect for the quality of politicians, they expect far higher standards of behaviour from them if they presume to govern. The same seems to apply to our managers, creating new pressures on them. Modern knowledge workers have values in their own lives which go beyond making money and thus are likely to want to work for organizations which have the same values. Difficulty in recruitment is just one of the costs faced by companies which do not invest in social responsibility or whose managers are seen not to act to the highest standards.[2] In times of change, project managers must command respect. Much of their power and authority come from personality and charisma, which will be lost without respect.

### The moral development of society

As standards of living rise, people seem to feel they can afford higher ideals, and hence the moral standards of society rise continuously. Historically, public morality tends to lead legislation. Responsible companies must realize that what was acceptable ten years ago may not be acceptable now and change their practices ahead of public opinion and before legislation is enacted. In Victorian times, children were allowed to work at a young age. The public came to disapprove and legislation was later passed banning it. More recently, ferry companies have stopped exporting live cattle to Europe. Companies still exporting live cattle are being treated as pariahs and legislation is being discussed; but the trade remains legal. Paradoxically, the fallout from the greed of the 1980s reinforced this change in moral stance, even though it creates greater austerity and uncertainty. In the 1990s, higher ideals are one thing people can afford, even while trapped in debt after the excesses of the 1980s. One symptom of this is the interest in the salaries of the directors of privatized utilities, as we discuss in section 11.7.

### A return to puritanical values

This return to puritanical values has also been reflected throughout British history, with periods of self-indulgent excess followed by periods of puritanical morality, even pious self-righteousness; for example:

- From the Elizabethan era to the Stuart era and ultimately the civil war
- From the Regency era to the Victorian era
- From Thatcherism and Reaganomics to Political Correctness.

Not only are people clearly drawing their own lines of what is acceptable behaviour, but they are zealous in imposing their views on other people, other societies and other cultures.[1] Not only are the British forthright in telling other European countries they cannot eat veal meat, we also tell people in the Far East they cannot eat dog meat.

### Greater litigiousness

Finally, greater litigiousness is making people far more cautious about their behaviour. If people are far more willing to sue, especially for negligence, it forces others to be more careful about where they draw the lines of their behaviour, and far more cautious when deciding the balance of a dilemma. Richard Branson's campaign against what he called British Airway's 'dirty tricks' illustrates this on a large scale, but on a smaller scale, negligence suits are growing quite common in all areas. However, in the USA this seems to have gone too far, with some overseas companies wondering whether it is worth doing business there, see Case Study 11.1.

---

## Case Study 11.1 Litigiousness in the USA

A European manufacturer of hearing aids is rumoured to be considering a withdrawal from the US market after being sued for $4 million after a child swallowed a hearing aid. Negligence is claimed because the box did not warn against children swallowing hearing aids! ICI may be sued because the Oklahoma bomb was made from their fertilizer and negligence is claimed because they should have done more to retard the fertilizer.

---

## 11.3 Paradigms of ethical behaviour

We now consider some of the bases of ethical behaviour, and show that some of the heuristic discussions above fit within a wider framework. Table 11.1 illustrates an analytical framework for ethical behaviour. We discuss the three major groupings below. It is important to have some understanding of the paradigms of ethical behaviour, if you are to be able to argue your position:

No competent executive would think of taking the company to the negotiating table without a clear sense of objectives, limits and tactics. And yet some of the same executives lead their companies into the forum of public opinion with nothing more than a grab bag of ethical platitudes[3]

**Table 11.1**  A classification of ethical frameworks

| Major groupings | Sub-groupings | Technical names |
|---|---|---|
| Rule-based | Absolute | – Fundamentalism |
| | | – Golden Rule |
| | | – Categorical Imperative |
| | Conditional | – Prima-Facie Duties |
| | | – Justice Principle |
| | | – Proportionality |
| Consequential | | – Utilitarianism |
| Cultural | | – Relativism |

## Rule-based ethics

Rule-based systems of ethics say that the consequences of actions are not important in deciding what to do, just considerations of fairness and justice.[4] Absolute theories say you should always do something if it is morally right; conditional theories allow the rules to be modified if appropriate.

### ABSOLUTE THEORIES

The main absolute theory is Kant's *Categorical Imperative,* which says that there are certain moral rights and duties people must follow, regardless of the benefits or disbenefits that follow. The theory says that everyone should be treated as a free person, equal to everyone else. The theory is based on three criteria:

1. *Universality*  Reasons for acting must be reasons everyone would act on.
2. *Transitivity*  Do unto others as you would have them do unto you.
3. *Individuality*  Treat every human being as a free, rational person whose existence is to be promoted.

This form of ethics is often considered to be superior to many others, in spite of its weaknesses, which are:

– Universal ideals are not applicable to every situation
– The same action may be ethical in one situation, but not in another ·
– There is no clear balance between conflicting rights of different groups
– It makes no allowance for personal prejudices
– It is Eurocentric, as we shall see.

Consider Case Study 11.2. Would you drive the taxi driver to the hospital in his taxi? According to the absolute theories, it is always wrong to break the law, to drink and drive and to drive without insurance.

## Case Study 11.2 Driving while under the influence.

You have been entertaining a client over dinner. Having had one drink too many, you take a taxi home. While driving you home, the taxi driver suffers a heart attack. You know you are about half a mile from a major hospital, and if you drive the taxi driver there, you may be able to save his life. However, you are probably over the drink-drive limit and you are not insured to drive the taxi. Do you drive the taxi driver to the hospital?

CONDITIONAL THEORIES

This says that in some circumstances the rules need to be broken. Some people consider this to be a variation of utilitarian ethics, which follows. There are two principles of conditional rule-based ethics:

1. An action is right from the ethical point of view, if, and only if, the action would be required by those moral rules which are correct.
2. A moral rule is correct if, and only if, the sum total of utilities produced if everyone were to follow the rule is greater than the sum total of utilities produced if everyone were to follow some alternative rule.

The most common form of rule-based ethics is based on six *Prima-Facie Duties*:

- Fidelity
- Gratitude
- Justice
- Beneficence (the act of doing good)
- Self-improvement;
- Non-maleficence.

The main problem with this approach is determining the appropriate rules, and causing users to focus too narrowly on means rather than ends. Another problem is when duties conflict; what weight and merit should be afforded to them? Consider Case Study 11.2. Would you drive the taxi driver to the hospital? The decision is now balanced. There is an argument in favour, but the decision is by no means clear. Saving the taxi driver's life is a utility which may be outweighed by the act of your driving while under the influence and without insurance. However, there is a risk you will cause an accident, causing someone else to lose their life, and so you must balance the chance that you will save the taxi driver's life (and that he will not get to the hospital in time in some other way) against the risk that you may kill someone else. However, the decision is not as clear as it was above.

## Utilitarian ethics

Utilitarian ethics appears to be an extension of conditional, rule-based ethics. However, it is in reality derived from the ancient Greek philosophy of *hedonism*. This says anything is ethical if it is capable of giving pleasure (*hedone* being the ancient Greek for pleasure). This has evolved to emphasize more rational pleasures and peace of mind. Utilitarian ethics can be defined as saying, 'an action is right from an ethical point of view if and only if the sum total of the utilities produced by the act is greater than the sum total of utilities produced by another act'.[5]

This form of ethics leads to a division of labour which produces the best outcome for society. If people take responsibility for their own actions, society will flourish. There are, however, problems. The first is how do you estimate the plurality of values: happiness; pleasure; health; knowledge; friendship; comfort; pain; harm; when evaluating the consequences of a proposed course of action? Even if you can estimate the utility of an action, it is difficult to add and subtract consequences when comparing one action with another. Finally, there is the concept of justice. If, as an engineer, you observe what you believe to be an unsafe practice, where does your responsibility lie – with your job or with the public? There is also a problem of justice, when the action providing the greatest amount of good violates the rights of a sizeable minority, for example, the citizens of Dresden and Hiroshima in 1945. Utilitarians might argue that the action is not moral because it violates the principle of a fair and equitable distribution of goods, but this contradicts the moral criteria of utilitarianism because it invokes the extra concept of justice. However, in spite of these problems, the approach is a useful decision-making tool. The notion that all decisions can be decomposed into several factors and then built up into a solution appeals to many people. It is an efficient decision-making tool, not only in the process, but also in the output.

## Relativism

This is perhaps the most controversial theory. It has become fashionable since the Second World War, and in its clearest form is based on the existentialist philosophy of Jean Paul Sartre. The argument is that ethics is merely a matter of taste.[6] If one culture or country prefers one set of rules, there is little that can be said or done about it. What people make of themselves is as a result of their own free actions; they create their values dependent on their circumstances. The sentiments can be summarized by the expression, 'When in Rome do as the (good) Romans do'. This type of theory can be used to justify paying bribes in a foreign country in order to gain a contract. US companies are banned by US law from offering bribes anywhere in the world (although an employee of a US company told Rodney Turner that the only reason his company entered into joint ventures with Japanese companies was so as to be able to pass the back handers via them). German companies cannot pass bribes in Germany, but are allowed by German law to give them in countries where it is accepted practice, and they are then deductible against profit. Relativism would also condone low levels of safety in countries with lower standards than ours. There are many arguments against relativism, not least of which is that if it were implemented in its pure form, no state could function and anarchy would reign. This objection even caused Sartre to change the theory slightly. It is not proposed here as a sensible alternative to those above, but is included for the sake of completeness.

## 11.4 Ethical dilemmas

### Qualitative dilemmas: Where do you draw the line?

We consider now dilemmas of where you draw the line. Absolute, rule-based ethics would say that you should draw the line at the extreme of what is unconditionally right. Consider the following cases.

DILEMMA 1: CORPORATE ENTERTAINING

Consider Case Study 11.3. Would you accept the expenses paid invitation to the summer event? Most of us would. Attending functions at a supplier's expense is part of the ritual of summer life in Britain. Most of us would not look upon them as a bribe. We would probably say our decision to buy from that client is not influenced by the invitation, and may try to rationa- lize our acceptance by saying the event offers the opportunity to talk business. We may baulk at the overnight accommodation and may then try to ensure some business is done (fabricate the need) to justify the need for the trip. *What if the event is the summer Olympic Games in an overseas country, say Sydney 2000?* Most of us would now probably refuse. We would view this as too large an expense, and would therefore consider it a bribe and refuse to accept it. There are several reasons why we might do this:

– We may feel there is a chance our decision making will be influenced and we will want to try to avoid that

- More likely, we will want to be seen as being balanced in our decision making and not subject to influence
- Taking bribes may be an offence that could lead to instant dismissal and we will not want to take that risk.

## Case Study 11.3 Invitation to a summer sporting event

You and your partner have been invited by one of your suppliers on an all-expenses paid trip to one of the summer's major sporting events (Wimbledon, Henley, Ascot, Glyndebourne, the British Open). You will be picked up from your home; transported to the event at your supplier's expense; be given free entry tickets and food and refreshments while there; and then taken home afterwards. You may even be given a night's free accommodation in a hotel. Would you accept?

Consider the following questions:

- Would you ever pay a bribe?
- Would you ever accept a bribe?
- Do you collect frequent flier rewards for air fares paid by your employer?
- Has the availability of frequent flier rewards ever meant you have taken a more expensive carrier for a flight paid by your employer?

Most of us would not view Airmiles, or their equivalent, as bribes. However, some public sector employees in the UK are banned from using their Airmiles, even though they are instructed to use the national carrier. They are not even allowed to donate them to charity. Some US government employees are not allowed to accept a biscuit from suppliers. They are allowed to have a cup of coffee or tea, or a minimum lunch with fruit juice, because these are essential sustenance. But biscuits and alcoholic drinks at lunch are luxuries and therefore cannot be accepted. Suppliers often leave out a tray for the government employees to pay for their biscuit. Both this and the laws on bribery that have worldwide application are driven by the American's puritanical heritage.

DILEMMA 2: POLICING THEFT

Consider Case Study 11.4. What would you do? Report the theft? Most of us would opt for the second option, but proceed to the third if that had no effect. *What if the person is the personnel director, your boss's boss, who has been speaking on the course?* Now self-preservation would probably make most of us want to ignore the incident. Can you rationalize this to say it is for the greater good, whereas with a more junior employee it is to the greater good to report the incident? In 1992, Rodney Turner visited Sydney. At the time people were discussing whether Alan Bond would serve time in jail for alleged fraud, involving billions of dollars. At the same time, a youth had been sentenced in Sydney to several years in jail for stealing a few dollars from a telephone booth. There seemed to be no comparison in justice in the minds of the Australian public.

## Case Study 11.4  Theft from the bar in the company training centre

You are manager of your company's training centre. Somebody attending a course has taken a whole bottle of whiskey from the bar in the centre. Do you:

- Ignore it?
- Ask him or her to return it, but take it no further if they do?
- Report the incident to appropriate disciplinary authorities within your company?
- Call in the police?

DILEMMA 3: CONSULTANCY ADVICE

Consider Case Study 11.5. What would you do?

- Offer the wrong advice, which would generate more business for your firm in the short term?
- Offer the correct advice, which may actually lead to more business in the medium term?

## Case Study 11.5  Interviewing a potential commercial director

You are a management consultant and have been asked by the new managing director of a small manufacturing and construction company to interview a candidate for the position of commercial director; the previous director has been moved to special duties. The candidate you have interviewed is weak. If you recommend his appointment, the company will need to continue to use your services to support him, leading to continuing business for your firm. If you recommend rejection, it may be some months before a new commercial director is found and the company is unlikely to use your services until that time. Do you recommend acceptance or rejection of the candidate? Your pay rise is dependent on your ability to 'sell-on'.

## Quantitative dilemmas

Quantitative dilemmas often reduce to a question of how much a human life is worth. After the King's Cross and Clapham rail disasters, London Underground and British Rail started spending money on safety improvements, and found that large improvements could be made for relatively little amounts. However, British Rail reached a point where they were spending £10 million for each additional life saved. The question is whether this is reasonable, and the answer is probably not. British Rail had a sliding scale for the value of a life. The figures that follow are not exact, but they illustrate the concept:

- For someone who has nothing to do with British Rail, their life is worth, say, £2 million. A scaffolder was killed when the scaffolding poles he was carrying swung over a fence and hit an overhead power line. British Rail will spend £2 million to try to save his life.
- The life of a passenger is worth half as much, £1 million. By buying a ticket, they buy some risk.
- For an employee, it is half as much again, £0.5 million. By accepting the salary they accept more risk.
- For vandals, it is half as much again, £0.25 million. You can only spend so much on people who are bent on self-destruction.

Case Study 11.6 illustrates another company dealing with this dilemma. Daly[7] believes this is a misuse of cost benefit analysis, and says that we only accept it because we do not know who the people to be killed are. He says:

Consider that some 50,000 Americans are killed annually by the automobile. Suppose that the specific identities of these people were known in advance. To save 50,000 specific individuals we might lower the speed limit drastically, and return to bicycles for transportation. To save 50,000 unknown, randomly determined individuals we do nothing. Decisions like this are not easy, and have only been made bearable in the past by using the concept of randomness as a moral scapegoat!

It is for this reason that the law is more interested in the criminal than the victim; the criminal is real, the victim is to an extent hypothetical. The eighteenth-century philosopher David Hume took this further.[8] He surmised that the more closely someone is related to us, the more concerned we are about their health and safety. The death of a family member is of more concern than the death of ten strangers living in the same town, and they are of greater concern than 100 people living in another town, 1000 living in another country and 10,000 in another continent. Theories of evolution and human genetics give a rational explanation for this. A greater proportion of our genes are destroyed when a family member dies than when somebody in another continent dies. Our application of utilitarian and conditional ethics will inevitably be shaded by these subconscious considerations.

## Case Study 11.6 The Allwin motor car

There was a make of car, let's call it the Allwin, which suffered a design fault, which meant that in a rear end collision the petrol tank sometimes ignited, often killing the occupants of the car. After each case, the manufacturers were successfully sued. The company looked at moving the tank, at a small cost per car in the production process. However, spread over millions of vehicles being produced, they decided it was cheaper to pay out on the compensation claims. They were criticized for this decision by the courts. They had decided on the value of a human life on purely accounting grounds, without communicating to their customers the risk involved, and without considering the ethical position.

## 11.5 Practical ethics

Faced with these dilemmas, and in these times of ethical scrutiny, it is important for the manager both to act ethically and to be seen to act ethically. The ethical pressures on project managers can be wider than pressures on other managers, because:

− Their scope of control may be wider
− The nature of the environment is more dynamic and culturally diverse
− They are responsible to a number of stakeholders.

There are many ways of promoting ethical behaviour. One way is for the employer to develop a code of conduct or ethics, or for the individual to follow the code for his or her professional society. Some people say that to have a code of ethics is an admission that you might consider behaving unethically. However, the advantages include:

1. The code of ethics will motivate ethical behaviour through peer pressure. A code will hold up a generally recognized set of behavioural expectations, which must be taken account of in decision making.[4]
2. The code of ethics is a more stable guide to right and wrong than the personalities which come and go in a company. They formalize right and wrong.[9]
3. The code provides guidance in ethically ambiguous situations (the moral dilemmas above).
4. The code will not only serve to guide the actions of employees, but also control the power of employers. It provides an excuse for an employee

to make the career limiting stand, 'I am sorry, but the company code forbids me to do that'.

5. The code will specify the social responsibility of a business. This could be used in a project code to help clarify the policy of a project, for example to protect wildlife, keep noise down, etc.
6. The code will help to set a minimum standard of competence for a profession, and give the customers some assurance that a professional meets those standards.
7. A code can help to assure a customer that a profession or supplier will always act in their interest.
8. Codes of ethics help a business or profession get their house in order before government legislates.

In 1992, approximately 71 per cent of companies had their own code of ethics,[10] and in 1989, there were nearly 400 codes of conduct for professional societies.[11] Hence, the majority of people should be able to find some clarification on what is acceptable behaviour in their business area. In the absence of any of the above, then the following ethical test can be useful in determining an ethical course of action:

1. *The effect test* Who, if anyone, does the decision hurt? The point of this test is to be aware of the consequence of the decision on others. There is little doubt that the decision to shut a factory will induce 'pain' on one set of people, as we saw in Chapter 1, but the decision to keep it open will affect another set adversely. The point of this test is to be aware of the consequences of a decision, not to avoid them.
2. *The transparency test* Would I be happy to see my decision or course of action reported in tomorrow's papers? Decisions which have to be kept secret can be justified in a number of ways, but on the whole openness leads to fewer problems in relations with others. If I would rather not have my decision known by others (for example, my mother), then is it worth pausing and asking why?
3. *The fairness test* Would the decision be seen by those affected and those involved as fair? Clearly, some who are affected adversely might complain whatever the situation. However, the degree of thought which goes into a decision and the effectiveness of the communication of the choice will go a long way to see that this test turns out positively.

Your actions can be made more ethical by using the above tests, but you have to want to behave ethically in the first place. This the company or profession can do little about, because most of a person's moral development is influenced outside the workplace through childhood experiences and pressures from other members of society.

## 11.6 The balance between the individual and society

Many ethical decisions are based on a belief in 'Human rights', that is, what we do should not interfere with someone else's rights. Unfortunately, as we have seen with conditional ethics, it is not as simple as that. Often one person's rights conflict with another's, or with the rights of society, and the decision we take depends on the balance we give. For instance, there is a discussion about whether we should carry identity cards in the UK. There is even a proposal that identity cards could carry our DNA imprint; with the information held centrally. The technology exists to hold everyone's DNA imprint against their national insurance number. There is little doubt that identity cards would be beneficial to society, but it is felt that they would be a threat to individual liberty, and so are resisted. Likewise, a central DNA database would help to eliminate many crimes and make others easy to solve, but would be seen as a massive violation of individual rights and freedoms. The balance given to the rights of the individual and society is not the same in all cultures, and so ethical decisions will not be universal. Furthermore, one person's rights impose a duty on another to satisfy those rights, and our ethical behaviour often ought to be driven not so much by the rights of others as by our own duties. In this section we consider the balance between society and individuals, and between rights and duties.

### The Prisoner's Dilemma

A classical ethical conundrum, illustrating the balance between the group and the individual, is the Prisoner's Dilemma, Case Study 11.7. What would be your decision? To optimize your individual position, you should confess. The argument is that in serving ten years or two, both are preferable to being executed. Furthermore, your accomplice will do the same calculation and is therefore also likely to confess. This is a Eurocentric view. It is said in Asian cultures the prisoners will not confess, which will optimize the group position. The best position for the group is for both prisoners to go free. If you can be certain that your accomplice will also try to optimize the group position, then it is best not to confess. Perhaps also in Asian cultures, the shame of living with the knowledge that you have betrayed your friend would be too great, and so it would be better to be executed, rather than serve two years knowing your friend has been executed on your evidence.

## Case Study 11.7 The Prisoner's Dilemma

You have committed a capital offence with an accomplice. You have both been caught, and are held in separate cells. There is no evidence against you except your possible confession, or that of your accomplice. You are asked to confess. You are told that if you confess, but your accomplice does not, then you can turn state witness and escape with a two-year sentence, but your accomplice will be executed. If you both confess, then you both will serve ten years. If you do not confess and your accomplice does, you will be executed. If neither of you confess, then you will both go free. Do you confess?

This tendency to optimize the individual versus the group position, or vice versa, is reflected in business. Contractual arrangements in the construction industry in the West (especially Britain and North America, which inherited the English legal system[12]) tend to be confrontational, as both sides optimize their position at the expense of the other, a win–lose game. This has been replaced in recent years by an approach called *partnering*,[12] which attempts to help both parties to contract to work together for their mutual benefit; a win–win game. Similarly, the construction industry in the UK has traditionally spent very little money on research and development, or on training. The idea being that if a company spends money on R&D, their competitors will then steal their ideas and benefit without spending the money. Likewise, the competitors will poach your trained individuals and benefit without spending the money, again. In Japan, construction companies spend a lot of money on R&D. Their view is that if the industry benefits, they all benefit, thus optimizing the group position. Also, if you are spending money on R&D then you will always stay two years ahead of your competition, rather than lagging two years behind. They have much greater life-long loyalty to the same company in Japan, and so it is easier to spend money on training; but again, if the industry benefits, they all benefit.

### The individual versus the society or group

*Ask not for whom the bell tolls; it tolls for thee* John Donne
*A person is a person through other human beings* African proverb
*We eat from a common bowl of rice, which we all share* Asian proverb

The African and Asian proverbs above illustrate a different approach to the balance between individual and society to that taken in the West. The African proverb says that it is only being a member of a society that gives context to our lives. Without being a member of a society we are not whole or complete. In many African cultures, the group or society dominates. Concepts such as individual ambition, or individual responsibility are almost unknown. The Asian proverb says more about sharing and contributing together. If we all do things from which we all benefit, then we all gain. You might say that the quotation from John Donne also shows a common approach. However, his poem *For whom the bell tolls* was bemoaning individualism. Donne starts by saying that when we hear a bell ringing for someone's death, by asking for whom the bell tolls we imply the loss is not our own. However, he says we are not individual islands, but part of a continent, and when someone dies, part of the continent is eroded. Hence, it is our loss when someone else dies and so the bell tolls for us as well, not just the person who has died. Throughout European history, there have been developments in the balance between the individual and society:[13]

- In ancient Greece, the *Heroic Code*, preached by Homer, Sophocles and Aristotle, said that you should work for harmonization of the organizational goals and individual needs.
- In Renaissance Italy, this had changed, ironically because of the rise of humanism which encouraged individual achievement and ambition. The movement was anti-establishment, anti-church and anti-hierarchical.
- From the Industrial Revolution to the 1950s, the organization submerged the individual. The theories of F.W. Taylor were based on this idea and some successful companies, such as GEC, still follow it.
- By the 1980s, we had returned to the Renaissance approach, with the self-fulfilment of the individual.

## 11.7 Rejoinder

We said, in section 11.2, that there is an increase in the moral awareness of society. This might appear to be inconsistent with the focus on the rights of the individual in Western society, which we have just discussed. However, that depends on whether the increasing moral awareness is truly altruistic, or whether it is equally selfish and self-indulgent as the greed of the 1980s. Rodney Turner believes there is some evidence that the latter is the case and that, for some people at least, their increasing moral awareness arises because:

- It makes them feel good
- It absolves their middle-class angst
- It hides good, old-fashioned, British envy – people are able to hide their envy of others' more fortunate positions behind a moral, self-righteous façade.

Two pieces of evidence to support this are:

- The response to the high salaries of the directors of privatized utilities
- The misuse of emergency services.

**The response to the high salaries of the directors of privatized utilities**

There has been some criticism of the salaries that chairpeople and directors of privatized utilities are paying themselves. There are three groups of people that the directors of a company can take money from to pay themselves a higher salary:

– Their customers
– Their shareholders
– Their employees.

If the stance on the salaries of directors of privatized monopolies was being taken from a moral standpoint, then the arguments would focus on the first of these three groups. However, the arguments often focus on the third group, which may indicate they are a cover for envy.

CUSTOMERS

The chairpeople and directors of a monopoly can pay themselves what they like and pass the cost on to their customers (within the constraints of the regulatory framework in the case of privatized utilities). Clearly this creates an ethical dilemma.

SHAREHOLDERS

The position with respect to shareholders is more contractual. Directors have an obligation to maximize shareholder value over the medium term.[12] Paying themselves higher salaries reduces shareholder value. People say higher salaries should be linked to performance, and self-evidently that is right. If shareholder value is being increased, it is fair to share in that. However, many people view shareholders as nasty, horrid capitalists from the City and therefore are not so concerned about them. The reality is, of course, that the shareholders are pension funds, who hold the shares on behalf of pensioners. By paying themselves high salaries not linked to performance, directors are taking money from pensioners, and that is an ethical dilemma.

EMPLOYEES

However, in a phone-in programme on BBC Radio 4,[14] the arguments with respect to British Gas focused on showroom staff. The argument went that the chairman should not be paying himself a higher salary while making showroom staff redundant, and reducing the salaries of those who are left.

However, this is inconsistent with what was said above. If the duty is to maximize shareholder value, the directors should retrench redundant staff; high pay linked to high performance is linked to redundancies. Hence, the apparently moral positions that people are adopting may actually hide envy and self-interest in not wanting to lose the convenient, local showroom.

### The misuse of emergency services

There is growing misuse of emergency services.[15] People blame the growing inefficiency of the ambulance service on lack of funding by government, and the intransigence of the unions. However, much of the cause is the growing use of the ambulance service for trivial reasons. Much was made of the eleven-year-old girl, Nesima Begum, who died of kidney failure while waiting 55 minutes for an ambulance. It was found later that one of the ambulances that might have gone to her rescue earlier was sent to deal with a woman who had a headache. (Sometimes it is not until the ambulance reaches the destination that the crew find out how serious or trivial the call is.) Johnson[15] reports that ambulances have been called out by people who:

- Wanted help to remove contact lenses
- Had been bitten by a stag beetle
- Had stubbed their toe and broken a nail
- Had run out of cough lozenges
- Got shampoo in their eyes
- Had bought new shoes which were too tight.

When asked why, some of these people said:

- The service is there
- It is free
- It is my *right* to use it.

The focus on individual *rights* is part of the current growing moral awareness. However, one person's rights involve another's duty to satisfy them. To earn their rights, people must:

- Not overindulge their rights, and not pose an undue burden on those whose duty it is to satisfy them, especially not on the taxpayer
- Recognize that they in turn have duties, which many of the 'moralists' seem to ignore.

When people start talking about their duties to society rather than their rights as individuals, and when they start saying that it is ethically wrong for directors of monopolies to pay themselves high salaries because they are taking money from customers and pensioner shareholders, then we can say moral awareness is growing for truly altruistic reasons.

## 11.8 Summary

1. There is a growing interest in ethics. This may be caused by:
   - The pervasiveness of the media
   - A greater sense of egalitarianism and less respect for authority
   - The moral development of society
   - A return to puritanical values
   - The balance between the rights of the individual and the rights of society
   - Greater litigiousness.
2. There are four paradigms of ethical behaviour.
   - Absolute rule-based
   - Conditional rule-based
   - Hedonic
   - Cultural.
3. There are two types of ethical dilemmas:
   - *Qualitative* Where do you draw the line?
   - *Quantitative* How much is a human life worth?
4. It can be useful for an organization to have a code of ethics. In the absence of a code, decisions may be based on one of three tests:
   - *Effect test* Who does it hurt?
   - *Transparency test* Am I proud of my actions, and would I be happy for them to be made public?
   - *Fairness test* Is my action fair?

## References

1. Raphael, F., 'Rightsism', in *Without Walls: Bad ideas of the 20th century*, Channel 4, 1995.
2. Charmichial, S. and Donaldson, J., *Good Business*, Hutchinson Books, 1989.
3. Soloman, R.C. and Hanson, K., *It Makes Good Business Sense*, Athenum, 1985.
4. Bowie, N.E. and Duska, R.F., *Business Ethics*, Prentice Hall, 1990.
5. Velasquez, M.G., *Business ethics: Concepts and cases*, 3rd edition, Prentice Hall, 1992.
6. Donaldson, J., *Business ethics: A European casebook*, Academic Press, 1992.
7. Daly, H.E., 'Economics, ethics and cost-benefit analysis', *Human Systems Management*, **2**, 7–12, 1981.
8. MacIntyre, A. (ed.), *Hume's Ethical Writings,* Collier, 1965.
9. Clutterbuck, D., Dearlove, D. and Snow, D., *Actions speak louder: A management guide to corporate responsibility*, Kogan Page, 1992.
10. Webley, S., 'Business ethics', in *Business News*, City University Business School, May, 1992.

11. Harris, N.G.E., *Professional Codes of Conduct in the UK: A Directory*, Mansell, 1989.
12. Turner, J.R. (ed.), *The Commercial Project Manager: Improving the processes for achieving strategic objectives*, McGraw-Hill, 1995.
13. Symons, J.N., 'A synthesis of leadership and learning in OMD design', *PhD thesis submitted to Brunel University*, Henley Management College, 1994.
14. Ross, N., *Call Nick Ross*, BBC Radio 4, 1995.
15. Johnson, B., 'Why Britain's ambulance service is looking so sick', *Daily Telegraph*, 6 March, 1995.

## Useful address

1. Institute of Business Ethics, 12 Palace Street, London SW1E 5JA, Tel: 0171 931 0495.

# 12

# Managing the environment

Suzanne Pollock and Rodney Turner

## 12.1 Introduction

A particular ethical issue is the managing of the impact of our projects on the environment, and a particular leadership issue is determining that impact, deciding what we are going to do about it, and then convincing the rest of the team it is useful and worth while. The statistics make frightening reading:[1]

- The human race has injected some 50 000 synthetic chemicals into the natural environment
- Current rates of destruction will eliminate the world's remaining tropical forests (where 70 per cent of the earth's biodiversity lives) by the year 2000
- A company car driven 12 000 miles a year can pump six tons of carbon into the atmosphere
- 700 000 people suffered from skin cancer in the USA in 1993 and some 2000 of them died from it.

'Not my problem,' you might say. However, each year in Britain we:

- Produce about 8.4 million tons of packing waste – enough to fill almost 19 000 jumbo jets
- Throw out about two million plastic toner cartridges
- Make 500 billion photocopies – about 930 000 copies every minute
- Throw away enough desks and chairs to furnish the House of Commons a hundred times.

The solutions to these problems may appear to be beyond each of us individually. However, when we pull together we can achieve significant changes. Each of us can do something about how our organization functions, which, when combined, will add up to significant change. In this chapter, we try to show how you can improve environmental performance at work. This need not be daunting. It can involve simple improvements, such as producing less waste paper, reusing plastic cups or switching off lights. It can involve completely rethinking your organization's strategy, so that its direction and success are fundamentally linked to achieving a better balance with the natural environment. You need to ask yourself, 'What can I do? What can my team do? What can my organization do?' and consider how you can:

- Improve the environmental performance of the parts of the organization within your sphere of influence
- Extend your sphere of influence
- Support environmental improvements which are proposed within your organization.

This does require you to adopt a wider perspective, managing outwards and upwards, as shown in Figure 0.1, and to think about the long-term future of your organization. For many, the environment is a cause for concern. In a survey in 1993 by the Institute of Directors, one-third of company chairpeople, chosen from *The Times*' 500 largest companies, said they believed 'environmental responsibility' ranked above growth, performance or balance sheet. There are four steps to improving environmental performance and we consider each one in turn:

*Step 1* Developing understanding
*Step 2* Measuring performance
*Step 3* Continuing to improve performance
*Step 4* Reviewing progress and deciding next steps.

## 12.2 Developing understanding

This can be the most critical stage, since a high level of commitment is required to achieve sustained improvement in environmental performance. In order to help you to develop that commitment in your organization, we consider some of the typical questions which arise when individuals confront the issue of improving environmental performance in their workplace. The responses given here can either be used with your colleagues or as a basis for developing your own responses. The questions commonly asked are:

- Is it necessary?
- What impact does our organization have?
- Can we afford this?

## Is it necessary?

We are not going to list the global threats from increases in population and economic growth. Pollock[1] does enough of that to worry the most timid of people. Just consider what would happen if China, which has one-third of the world's population, and India, which has one-fifth, burned as much fossil fuel per head as the USA, which has one-thirtieth. The main pressures for a more responsible approach to the environment are closer to home, Table 12.1. Remember that we said in the last chapter that the ethical standards of the population run ahead of government legislation and organizations must respond accordingly, and (according to Hume's philosophical tradition and genetic pressures) people are more concerned about the death of a relative than they are by the death of scores of people in a remote country. What people see is that in the 1950s bad smogs in London killed thousands of people a year and the Clean Air Act stopped that. Now, car and industrial exhausts in London kill scores of people. There is a marked increase in deaths from asthma, heart disease and other causes on days of poor air quality, especially those which occur in the cold, still days of early winter (December). Car fumes kill scores of people just in time for Christmas each year. You might say it is not your problem, the government

**Table 12.1**   Relevant legislation

| Reach | Legislation |
| --- | --- |
| UK | Alkali Act |
| | Control of Pollution Act 1974 |
| | Health and Safety at Work Act 1974 |
| | Environmental Protection Act 1990 |
| | Integrated Pollution Control Act 1991 |
| | Water Resources Act 1991 |
| | Control of Industrial Major Accident Hazard Regulations 1984 |
| | Town and Country Planning (Assessment of Environmental Effect) Regulations 1988 |
| | Planning Policy Guidelines |
| | Green Paper on Environmental Liability for Damage caused by Pollution |
| European | Construction Products Directive |
| | Emissions Directive |
| | Environmental Impact Assessment Directive |
| | Hazardous Waste Directive |
| | Integrated Pollution and Protection Directive 1992 |
| | Noise Limits Directive |
| | Single European Act – Polluter Pays Principle |
| International | Environmental Protection Agency |
| | Montreal Protocol |
| | Rio de Janeiro and Berlin Conferences |

| Pressures for environmental change | Low | | | | High |
|---|---|---|---|---|---|
| 1. Government | 1 | 2 | 3 | 4 | 5 |
| 2. Pressure groups | 1 | 2 | 3 | 4 | 5 |
| 3. Public awareness | 1 | 2 | 3 | 4 | 5 |
| 4. Local communities | 1 | 2 | 3 | 4 | 5 |
| 5. Public relations | 1 | 2 | 3 | 4 | 5 |
| 6. Green consumers | 1 | 2 | 3 | 4 | 5 |
| 7. Competitors | 1 | 2 | 3 | 4 | 5 |
| 8. Employees | 1 | 2 | 3 | 4 | 5 |
| 9. Insurers | 1 | 2 | 3 | 4 | 5 |
| 10. Capital markets | 1 | 2 | 3 | 4 | 5 |
| 11. Shareholders | 1 | 2 | 3 | 4 | 5 |
| 12. Uncovering risks | 1 | 2 | 3 | 4 | 5 |
| 13. Crises | 1 | 2 | 3 | 4 | 5 |
| 14. Ethics | 1 | 2 | 3 | 4 | 5 |

**Figure 12.1**  Pressures for change

should sort it out, or that it is not your primary responsibility in your work. The public wants industry to change and that is causing organizations and government to respond. Furthermore, the industries in the firing line grow decade by decade, as Pollock shows.[1] Figure 12.1 includes a diagnostic questionnaire to help you assess the pressures for change on your organization, and Table 12.1 lists some of the legislation within which we must work.

### What impact does our organization have?

Pollock[1] gives several models for determining the impact of your project or organization on the environment. The simplest is the input–output model. Table 12.2 contains a list of possible inputs and outputs, which shows that they go beyond simple raw materials and products. Case Study 12.1 contains an application of this model.

**Table 12.2**  Input–output model of a business

| Inputs | Outputs |
|---|---|
| Raw materials | Products or services |
| People | Waste |
| Water | Sewerage |
| Energy | Emissions |
| – electricity | – smoke |
| – fossil fuel | – greenhouse gases |
| – steam | Noise |

## Case 12.1 South Hams District Council Tourist Industry

South Hams District Council is keenly aware that the tourist industry is a valuable part of the local economy. When the East Gate of the main town burnt down, it was instantly rebuilt. The important balance between inputs and outputs had been severely damaged. Inputs include:

- Long-term holiday-makers and day visitors
- Cars and coaches
- Attractive coastline and moorland
- Picturesque towns and villages
- Sailing and other sports
- Museums and other attractions
- Hotels and restaurants and shops.

Outputs include:

- Contented visitors
- Increased traffic
- Increased litter
- Increased wear on the countryside
- Improved local prosperity
- Improved local services.

### Can we afford this?

What are the costs and benefits of improved environmental performance? The assumption is usually that it will cost money for no return to the business, reflected in questions like:

- How can we worry about this when we might go bust tomorrow?
- Why should I do this when it is not clear I will get formal recognition for my efforts?
- Our business is about making money not 'saving the world'?

The question should really be 'Can you afford not to?' There are of course global issues: greenhouse effect, ozone depletion, polluted oceans, diminishing rain forests, extinction of species and rising sea water levels which should give cause for concern, although there exists contention about some of these. There is the ethical issue about forcing other people to live in our waste; everything from industrial pollution to cigarette smoke. There is the issue of increased deaths from asthma just before Christmas. However, there is considerable evidence and experience to support the fact that a responsible environmental attitude actually saves money and increases profit. Case Studies 12.2 and 12.3 are two such examples. Benefit can come from reduced costs and increased income, arising from:

- Attracting the green consumer
- Attracting investment from ethical investors
- Reducing insurance premiums
- Being an environmentally responsible supplier to others
- Improving staff commitment and satisfaction
- Being better integrated with the local community
- Reducing energy consumption
- Reducing waste disposal costs
- Avoiding fines.

## Case Study 12.2  The Japanese Steel Company

A Japanese steel company found it was not attracting the best engineering graduates, because of the dirty working environment. They decided to change the working environment to a 'white overall environment', that is employees could wear white overalls and they would be clean at the end of the day. Energy consumption *dropped* by 30%.

## Case Study 12.3  3M's 3P Programme

In 1975, the American chemical company, 3M, launched their 3P Programme – 'Pollution Prevention Pays'. The key features were:

- Product reformulation
- Process modification
- Equipment redesign
- Resource recovery.

By 1990, the achievements were:

- Savings in excess of $US 482 million
- Air pollutants cut by 122 000 tonnes
- Water pollutants cut by 16 000 tonnes
- Solid waste cut by 400 000 tonnes
- Waste water cut by 1.6 billion gallons
- Higher efficiency and better quality.

## 12.3 Measuring performance

Measuring your organization's environmental performance is both essential and demanding. It is essential because the organization needs to:

- Know what environmental effects it has
- Know how severe these effects are
- Establish the measurements against which future measurements will be compared.

The measurement of environmental performance is demanding because:

- Careful thought has to be paid to what is measured and how it is measured
- Potentially vast amounts of data could be generated which could not then be acted upon
- It is difficult to compare and rank different impacts
- The underlying issues are complex and their inter-relationships are not necessarily fully understood by the business or scientific communities.

Measuring performance means having a plan, and measuring your performance against that plan. You can do this on two levels:

- On a personal level, that is, your own environmental hygiene
- On an organizational level.

### Personal environmental hygiene

Personal environmental hygiene means doing the simple things which can reduce the inputs to your organization, and hence reduce the outputs in terms of waste. These include:

- Switching off lights
- Reusing plastic cups or using a china cup
- Photocopying only what is necessary and photocopying on both sides of the paper
- Circulating documents rather than sending everyone their own copy
- Recycling where possible.

### The organizational level

Developing the environmental plan at the organizational level means linking it to the way the organization does business; make it part of what you do, not an add-on. If you have a quality policy, link it to that quality policy. It was for this reason that the British Standards organization chose the number BS7750 for their environmental standard, so it would be closely allied with BS5750, the quality standard. After obtaining initial commitment, BS7750 suggests a twelve-step process for developing an environmental management system, EMS:

*Step 1: Initial review* Review the environmental performance of the organization. Construct the input–output model, to determine what is being spent and where.

*Step 2: Strategy* Develop an environmental strategy or policy for the organization. This can be based on the 16-point charter for sustainable development issued by the International Chamber of Commerce, Table 12.3. Over 1200 organizations have signed up to this, including 150 from the Fortune 500.

*Step 3: Organization and personnel* The EMS must be owned by the employees, not imposed on them, and there must be positive attitudes from top to bottom.

*Step 4: Register of regulations* Keep a register of relevant regulations to which you are subject, acts of parliament, government regulations, European directives, international agreements and treaties.

*Step 5: Evaluation and register of effects* Develop and record your input–output model.

*Step 6: Objectives and targets* Set objectives and targets for improvement.

*Step 7: Management programme* Develop a management action plan for how each objective is to be achieved. Action plans should be simple and have a defined timescale. Plan for small, short-term improvements, rather than large, long-term ones. Anything over 18 months will be forgotten. Assign responsibility for the delivery of each plan – good project leadership.

*Step 8: Management manual* Everything so far should be recorded in a manual, on wide circulation.

*Step 9: Operational control* The management action plans must be controlled like any project.

*Step 10: Record* Record what is achieved.

*Step 11: Audits* Audit the effectiveness of your EMS. Audits can be of two types: compliance audits and proactive audits. Compliance audits assess your compliance with regulations. Proactive audits assess your performance against your own standards. They may consider particular activities in the production process, specific environmental issues, the impact of products, the performance of subsidiaries or suppliers and health and safety performance.

*Step 12: Reviews* Review progress annually.

**Table 12.3**   Sixteen-point charter for sustainable development

*Sixteen-point charter for sustainable development*

| | |
|---|---|
| 1. Integrated management | 9. Research |
| 2. Employee education | 10. Precautionary approach |
| 3. Products and services | 11. Contractors and suppliers |
| 4. Facilities and operation | 12. Emergency preparedness |
| 5. Corporate priority | 13. Transfer of technology |
| 6. Process of improvement | 14. Contributing to the common effort |
| 7. Prior assessment | 15. Openness to concerns |
| 8. Customer advice | 16. Compliance and reporting |

## 12.4 Improving environmental performance

BS7750 suggests how we can develop management action plans for environmental improvement as part of the measurement process. However, once started, you need to maintain interest in improving your organization's environmental performance. Motivation needs to be cultivated and maintained. It is the role of the project manager as change agent to maintain enthusiasm for environmental initiatives and to develop progress of the new initiatives. Seven ways to maintain positive attitudes to environmental performance are:

1. Seek senior management support in maintaining positive attitudes. Involve senior managers and expect them to discuss environmental issues at board meetings. Over 50 per cent of companies do so.
2. Hold regular meetings of people within the organization interested in environmental issues. At Henley Management College, the environmental interest group meets every six weeks and has helped reduce costs throughout the College. For instance, significant improvements were made in the kitchens.
3. Network with people in other organizations. There are many groups you can join, see Table 12.4.
4. Run competitions and offer awards. Rank Xerox ran a painting competition for local schools and exhibited the pictures at the entrance to their

**Table 12.4**   Contact telephone numbers of industry groups in the UK

| Organization | Telephone number |
|---|---|
| British Standards Institute | 01908 220 022 |
| CBI Environment Group | 0171 379 7400 |
| Environmental Council | 0171 824 8411 |
| Environmental Data Service Ltd | 0171 278 4745 |
| International Chamber of Commerce | 0171 823 2811 |
| World Research Foundation | 01732 368 333 |

Marlow office. This had a positive effect on the employees, and helped build relationships with the local community.

5. Embark on wider community projects, to help demonstrate commitment to improving the environment. Larger organizations have carried out national initiatives. Shell ran a 'Better Britain Campaign'.

6. Maintain internal communications (newsletters, magazines, company newspapers) to report the achievements of environmental improvement campaigns. This helps motivation, builds positive attitudes and shows that environmental responsibility can give positive benefits.

7. Involve the functions of the organization:
   - Marketing to promote the organization's environmental performance and to adopt schemes such as the EU's Eco-label Scheme
   - Finance to provide financial credibility to the efforts
   - Human resources management to organize training; cascade information through the organization; bring environmental performance into appraisal schemes; and identify and use appropriate levers within the organization to make environmental improvement happen.

## 12.5 Reviewing progress and deciding next steps

Changing organizations, including environmental improvement, is an iterative process. At regular intervals, you need to take stock by asking yourself, '*How are we doing?*' and '*Where are we going to next?*'.

### How are we doing?

The question, '*How are we doing?*' is closely linked to, '*What did we want to do?*'. In answering the question, you can measure yourself against your overall aims, your specific objectives or your tactical achievements. Your aims may have been:

- To act on your concern for the environment
- To progress your career
- To respond to external pressures, see Fig. 12.1.

Measurement against these aims will be longer term and more obtuse, as shown in Fig. 3.2. Measurement against your objectives will be more specific, and if you have given yourself short- to medium-term timescales, 6 to 18 months, you can regularly monitor progress. Tactical measurements may entail:

- Environmental initiatives suggested
- Environmental initiatives achieved

- Staff attending environmental courses
- Staff requesting and receiving environmental information
- Evidence of support of senior management
- Customer satisfaction
- Performance against competitors
- Networking contacts, see Table 12.4.

**Where are we going next?**

It is not unusual for individuals to embark on the road to environmental improvement because they are forced to, as shown in Fig. 12.1. However, there often comes a point where they start to drive themselves, rather than being driven. Then a deeper set of issues come to the fore:

- Why does it have to be like this?
- The world must change, but how?
- Are we masters of our own destiny or creators of our own doom?

(We have a colleague who runs a seminar called 'How to be an environmentalist without being depressed'.) The fact that these questions get asked by an increasing number of people provides hope. Solutions to the need for a sustainable society are suggested.[2,3] Here is what the IUCN (International Union for the Conservation of Nature), UNEP (United Nations Environment Programme) and WWF (World Wildlife Fund) suggest:

- Offer respect and care for life in the community
- Improve the quality of life
- Conserve the earth's vitality and diversity
- Minimize the depletion of renewable resources
- Keep within the earth's carrying capacity
- Change personal attitudes and practices
- Enable communities to care for their own environment
- Provide national frameworks for development and conservation
- Create a global alliance.

Can the individual do anything? The answer is 'yes', a lot! It is a matter of applying oneself, learning the ropes, making contacts, building skills, resisting lies, spreading facts, listening to others as well as speaking out, and trying not to be too boring![4]

## 12.6 Summary

1. Managing the environment is a particular ethical issue facing project managers. The environment is our problem, and we all need to ask:

- What can I do?
- What can my team do?
- What can my organization do?
2. There are four steps to environmental improvement:
   - Developing understanding
   - Measuring performance
   - Continuing to improve performance
   - Reviewing progress and deciding next steps.
3. To develop understanding, the questions commonly asked are:
   - Is it necessary?
   - What impact does our organization have?
   - Can we afford this?
4. The input–output model is a simple technique for determining the impact of an organization on the environment. Many organizations find that there is positive benefit from environmental responsibility. Possible benefits might include:
   - Attracting the green consumer
   - Attracting investment from ethical investors
   - Reducing insurance premiums
   - Being an environmentally responsible supplier to others
   - Improving staff commitment and satisfaction
   - Being better integrated with the local community
   - Reducing energy consumption and waste disposal costs
   - Avoiding fines.
5. Measuring performance involves a classical control cycle:
   - Set a measure
   - Achieve results
   - Compare the results to the measure
   - Take action to overcome variances.
6. BS7750 gives advice on the establishment of an environmental management system. There are 12 steps:
   - Initial review
   - Strategy
   - Organization and personnel
   - Register of regulations
   - Evaluation and register of effects
   - Objectives and targets
   - Management programme
   - Management manual
   - Operational control
   - Record
   - Audits
   - Reviews.

7. Continuous improvement of environmental performance requires:
   - Maintain enthusiasm
   - Progressing new initiatives.
8. Organizations which can provide support include:
   - British Standards Institute
   - CBI Environment Group
   - Environmental Council
   - Environmental Data Service Ltd
   - International Chamber of Commerce
   - World Research Foundation.

## References

1. Pollock, S.E., *Improving Environmental Performance*, Routledge, 1995.
2. IUCN, UNEP and WWF, *Caring for the earth: A strategy for sustainable living*, Earthscan, 1991.
3. Hutchinson, C., *Vitality and Renewal*, Adamantine, 1994.
4. Higgins, R., *Plotting Peace*, Brasseys, 1990.

## Bibliography

1. Brundtland, G.H., *Our Common Future*, Oxford University Press, 1987.
2. Cairncross, F., *Costing the Earth, Economist* Books, 1991.
3. Hutchinson C., Pollock, S.E., Tapper, R., and Taylor, B., *The Handbook of Environmental Management*, Pitman, 1995.
4. Turner, J.R. (ed.), *The Commercial Project Manager: Managing owners, sponsors, partners, supporters, stakeholders, contractors and consultants*, McGraw-Hill, 1995. (See, in particular, Part 4.)

# 13
# Project health checks

Kristoffer Grude, Rodney Turner and John Wateridge

## 13.1 Introduction

In Chapter 2, we introduced several diagnostic techniques to help assess an organization's need for change, its readiness for change and the willingness (compliance) of the people within the organization to change. In the intervening chapters, we have discussed tools, techniques and approaches to help improve the latter two points. If you have established, or are about to establish, projects for implementing change, you may want to determine whether:

- The environment is supportive to projects and project working; that is, can the organization achieve its development objectives through projects?
- The projects established are likely to be successful; that is, will they achieve the development objectives required of them?

We introduce two further diagnostic techniques to help answer these questions; to assess the health of project working within the organization and to assess the health of individual projects. We want to stress that these diagnostics are primarily qualitative. The idea is to identify areas of weakness, but also, and more importantly, to identify differences of opinion within the project team in its widest sense. That is:

- Differences of opinion between the various groupings and factions in the project team, including sponsors, users, designers and managers
- Differences of opinion between the members of these various groupings.

The diagnostic questionnaires ask people to rank their views about various issues on a scale of 1 to 6. We then use simple arithmetic calculations, spreads, variances, means and differences, to highlight where differences of opinion lie, and where weaknesses in the approach to the

| No. | Statement | Score | | | | | | X | S | V | P | D |
|---|---|---|---|---|---|---|---|---|---|---|---|---|
| | *Problem area 1: Foundation and infrastructure for project work* | | | | | | | | | | | |
| 1.1 | It is easy to see the relation between our project plans and overall business plans | 1 | 2 | 3 | 4 | 5 | 6 | | | | 6 | |
| 1.2 | We have established sufficiently clear principles and guidelines for project work | 1 | 2 | 3 | 4 | 5 | 6 | | | | 6 | |
| 1.3 | Our principles and guidelines for project work are understood by all involved parties | 1 | 2 | 3 | 4 | 5 | 6 | | | | 6 | |
| 1.4 | Our principles and guidelines for project work are accepted by all involved parties | 1 | 2 | 3 | 4 | 5 | 6 | | | | 6 | |
| 1.5 | In our projects, the client/user roles and responsibilities are defined before start-up | 1 | 2 | 3 | 4 | 5 | 6 | | | | 6 | |
| 1.6 | In our projects, the project team's roles and responsibilities are defined before start-up | 1 | 2 | 3 | 4 | 5 | 6 | | | | 6 | |
| 1.7 | In our projects, the client/user keeps to agreed prioritizations (tasks/time/resources) | 1 | 2 | 3 | 4 | 5 | 6 | | | | 6 | |
| 1.8 | Our project management is not very good at keeping to agreed prioritizations | 1 | 2 | 3 | 4 | 5 | 6 | | | | 6 | |
| 1.9 | In our projects, line managers contribute loyally to decision processes according to their responsibility | 1 | 2 | 3 | 4 | 5 | 6 | | | | 6 | |
| 1.10 | In our projects, line management keep to agreed time limits for decisions | 1 | 2 | 3 | 4 | 5 | 6 | | | | 6 | |
| 1.11 | In our projects, line management quite often reverse decisions that have been taken | 1 | 2 | 3 | 4 | 5 | 6 | | | | 1 | |
| 1.12 | In our projects actual resources are committed as a part of our planning process without line management being made aware | 1 | 2 | 3 | 4 | 5 | 6 | | | | 6 | |
| 1.13 | Management makes sure that agreed resources for project work is made available at the right time | 1 | 2 | 3 | 4 | 5 | 6 | | | | 6 | |
| 1.14 | Available resources for project work is taken into consideration in our business plans | 1 | 2 | 3 | 4 | 5 | 6 | | | | 6 | |
| 1.15 | Our management plan so that development personnel do not get tied up in maintenance | 1 | 2 | 3 | 4 | 5 | 6 | | | | 6 | |
| 1.16 | Our management plan so personnel are relieved of operational tasks when given project tasks | 1 | 2 | 3 | 4 | 5 | 6 | | | | 6 | |
| 1.17 | We have sufficient adequate tools and methods for planning projects | 1 | 2 | 3 | 4 | 5 | 6 | | | | 6 | |
| 1.18 | We have sufficient and adequate tools and methods for organizing projects | 1 | 2 | 3 | 4 | 5 | 6 | | | | 6 | |
| 1.19 | We have sufficient/adequate tools and methods for reporting and controlling progress | 1 | 2 | 3 | 4 | 5 | 6 | | | | 6 | |

**Figure 13.1**   Projectivity diagnostic

| No. | Statement | Score | X | S | V | P | D |
|---|---|---|---|---|---|---|---|
| | *Problem area 1: Foundation and infrastructure for project work* | | | | | | |
| 1.20 | We have sufficient/adequate tools and methods for reporting and controlling quality | 1  2  3  4  5  6 | | | | 6 | |
| 1.21 | We have sufficient/adequate tools and methods for reporting and controlling time | 1  2  3  4  5  6 | | | | 6 | |
| 1.22 | We have sufficient/adequate tools and methods for reporting and controlling cost | 1  2  3  4  5  6 | | | | 6 | |
| 1.23 | We have clear policies/procedures for prioritizing between projects | 1  2  3  4  5  6 | | | | 6 | |
| 1.24 | We have clear policies/procedures for handling prioritization problems between operational tasks and project tasks | 1  2  3  4  5  6 | | | | 6 | |
| 1.25 | It happens quite often in our projects that the project team and the client/user do not have a common understanding of the deliverables | 1  2  3  4  5  6 | | | | 1 | |
| 1.26 | In our projects, everybody involved has the necessary knowledge of the procedures/methods/tools we use for project management | 1  2  3  4  5  6 | | | | 6 | |
| 1.27 | I have the necessary skills to plan and organize projects | 1  2  3  4  5  6 | | | | 6 | |
| 1.28 | I have the necessary skills to monitor and control projects | 1  2  3  4  5  6 | | | | 6 | |
| 1.29 | I have the necessary skills to handle people's relationships and resolve conflicts | 1  2  3  4  5  6 | | | | 6 | |
| 1.30 | Our project procedures/methods/tools are bureaucratic and tedious | 1  2  3  4  5  6 | | | | 1 | |
| 1.31 | Our project procedures/methods/tools help us obtain commitment from all parties involved | 1  2  3  4  5  6 | | | | 6 | |
| 1.32 | Our project procedures/methods/tools ensure goal direction and effective use of resources | 1  2  3  4  5  6 | | | | 6 | |
| | Sum | | | | | | |
| | Average | | | | | | |

**Figure 13.1** Projectivity diagnostic (cont.)

| No. | Statement | Score | X | S | V | P | D |
|-----|-----------|-------|---|---|---|---|---|
| | *Problem area 2: Planning and estimating* | | | | | | |
| 2.1 | Our overall project plans are understandable and give a good overview/description to all relevant parties, not just the specialists | 1  2  3  4  5  6 | | | | 6 | |
| 2.2 | We make project plans that are too general and generic | 1  2  3  4  5  6 | | | | 1 | |
| 2.3 | We make project plans that are much too detailed and activity oriented | 1  2  3  4  5  6 | | | | 1 | |
| 2.4 | Our plans are tailor-made for the task and focus on what is unique/important for progress | 1  2  3  4  5  6 | | | | 6 | |
| 2.5 | Our project plans have imbedded quality control | 1  2  3  4  5  6 | | | | 6 | |
| 2.6 | We have layered planning, where we focus on results and activities separately | 1  2  3  4  5  6 | | | | 6 | |
| 2.7 | Our plans focus too much on completion date, too little on intermediate results/dates | 1  2  3  4  5  6 | | | | 1 | |
| 2.8 | We often have to change our plans during the project | 1  2  3  4  5  6 | | | | 1 | |
| 2.9 | Our project plans always make it easy to control if intermediate and end results have been achieved | 1  2  3  4  5  6 | | | | 6 | |
| 2.10 | Our project plans ensure that we do things in the right sequence, so that we do not have to do things over again | 1  2  3  4  5  6 | | | | 6 | |
| 2.11 | Our project plans secure effective utilization of resources | 1  2  3  4  5  6 | | | | 6 | |
| 2.12 | In our project plans, we build quality assurance of the process as well as results | 1  2  3  4  5  6 | | | | 6 | |
| 2.13 | We have a planning process that stimulates creativity and finding new solutions | 1  2  3  4  5  6 | | | | 6 | |
| 2.14 | Our planning processes invite involved parties to participate and stimulate communication | 1  2  3  4  5  6 | | | | 6 | |
| 2.15 | All involved parties are 100 per cent committed to our project plans once they are agreed upon | 1  2  3  4  5  6 | | | | 6 | |
| 2.16 | We have formalized estimating procedures to ensure maximum quality and commitment | 1  2  3  4  5  6 | | | | 6 | |
| 2.17 | Our project plans always have a realistic completion date | 1  2  3  4  5  6 | | | | 6 | |

**Figure 13.1**  Projectivity diagnostic (cont.)

| No. | Statement | Score | X | S | V | P | D |
|-----|-----------|-------|---|---|---|---|---|
| | *Problem area 2: Planning and estimating* | | | | | | |
| 2.18 | Our recourse and cost estimates are generally unrealistic | 1  2  3  4  5  6 | | | | 1 | |
| 2.19 | It sometimes happens that we change our time and cost estimates because we don't 'like' them | 1  2  3  4  5  6 | | | | 1 | |
| 2.20 | We often set time and cost estimates too low for 'selling' reasons | 1  2  3  4  5  6 | | | | 1 | |
| 2.21 | In our projects, goals for individual's work are not precise | 1  2  3  4  5  6 | | | | 1 | |
| 2.22 | In project planning, we often overestimate our own and other people's competence and skills | 1  2  3  4  5  6 | | | | 1 | |
| 2.23 | In project planning, we often overestimate our and other people's available time and capacity | 1  2  3  4  5  6 | | | | 1 | |
| 2.24 | With us, everybody can participate in estimating and planning their own work | 1  2  3  4  5  6 | | | | 6 | |
| 2.25 | With us, everybody feels a personal responsibility for their own estimates | 1  2  3  4  5  6 | | | | 6 | |
| 2.26 | In estimating we often do not account for non-productive time (illness, interruptions, etc.) | 1  2  3  4  5  6 | | | | 6 | |
| 2.27 | In project planning, we often 'forget' activities | 1  2  3  4  5  6 | | | | 1 | |
| | Sum | | | | | | |
| | Average | | | | | | |

**Figure 13.1**  Projectivity diagnostic (cont.)

| No. | Statement | Score | | | | | | X | S | V | P | D |
|---|---|---|---|---|---|---|---|---|---|---|---|---|
| | *Problem area 3: Organizing and cooperating* | | | | | | | | | | | |
| 3.1 | In our projects, the right people are always involved in the right activities | 1 | 2 | 3 | 4 | 5 | 6 | | | | 6 | |
| 3.2 | Key people are often not available for the project at the time when planned | 1 | 2 | 3 | 4 | 5 | 6 | | | | 1 | |
| 3.3 | People on the project are often not motivated | 1 | 2 | 3 | 4 | 5 | 6 | | | | 1 | |
| 3.4 | We lack communication procedures/channels within our projects (all involved parties) | 1 | 2 | 3 | 4 | 5 | 6 | | | | 1 | |
| 3.5 | We lack communication procedures and channels between projects | 1 | 2 | 3 | 4 | 5 | 6 | | | | 1 | |
| 3.6 | In our projects, we have agreed and formalized the flow of information before start-up | 1 | 2 | 3 | 4 | 5 | 6 | | | | 6 | |
| 3.7 | We organize our projects so that we secure effective consulting and hearing processes | 1 | 2 | 3 | 4 | 5 | 6 | | | | 6 | |
| 3.8 | We organize our projects so that we secure effective decision-making processes | 1 | 2 | 3 | 4 | 5 | 6 | | | | 6 | |
| 3.9 | Our way of organizing projects ensures maximum flexibility of human resources | 1 | 2 | 3 | 4 | 5 | 6 | | | | 6 | |
| 3.10 | Nobody complains about lack of information in our projects | 1 | 2 | 3 | 4 | 5 | 6 | | | | 6 | |
| 3.11 | In our projects, everybody knows and accepts their own role and responsibility | 1 | 2 | 3 | 4 | 5 | 6 | | | | 6 | |
| 3.12 | Nobody knows what other people are doing on the project | 1 | 2 | 3 | 4 | 5 | 6 | | | | 1 | |
| 3.13 | We very seldom have conflicts within the team that are the result of bad cooperation | 1 | 2 | 3 | 4 | 5 | 6 | | | | 6 | |
| 3.14 | We very seldom have conflicts with our clients/users that are the result of bad cooperation | 1 | 2 | 3 | 4 | 5 | 6 | | | | 6 | |
| 3.15 | Our projects are ineffective because too many people/functions are involved | 1 | 2 | 3 | 4 | 5 | 6 | | | | 1 | |
| 3.16 | In our projects, responsibility for tasks and decisions is always connected directly to individuals, so there is no doubt | 1 | 2 | 3 | 4 | 5 | 6 | | | | 6 | |
| 3.17 | We are organized to use the shortest possible route of communication between two persons | 1 | 2 | 3 | 4 | 5 | 6 | | | | 6 | |
| 3.18 | In our projects, the project organization is more a formality than for real cooperation | 1 | 2 | 3 | 4 | 5 | 6 | | | | 1 | |
| 3.19 | We are organized for resolving conflicts when they arise | 1 | 2 | 3 | 4 | 5 | 6 | | | | 1 | |
| | Sum | | | | | | | | | | | |
| | Average | | | | | | | | | | | |

**Figure 13.1** Projectivity diagnostic (cont.)

| No. | Statement | Score | X | S | V | P | D |
|-----|-----------|-------|---|---|---|---|---|
| | *Problem area 4: Controlling and leading* | | | | | | |
| 4.1 | In our projects, reporting has no purpose because it is never used for anything | 1 2 3 4 5 6 | | | | 1 | |
| 4.2 | In our projects, reporting is used to watch over team members | 1 2 3 4 5 6 | | | | 1 | |
| 4.3 | Reporting is used in our projects to badger team members | 1 2 3 4 5 6 | | | | 1 | |
| 4.4 | Reporting in our projects is used to discuss constructively necessary corrective action | 1 2 3 4 5 6 | | | | 6 | |
| 4.5 | Our project plans are not arranged so that we can report against them for monitoring | 1 2 3 4 5 6 | | | | 1 | |
| 4.6 | In our company, the project managers do not have the necessary authority | 1 2 3 4 5 6 | | | | 1 | |
| 4.7 | Project managers are too concerned with details of the technical content of the project | 1 2 3 4 5 6 | | | | 1 | |
| 4.8 | The project managers are too pedantic | 1 2 3 4 5 6 | | | | 1 | |
| 4.9 | Project managers will always try to cover up the problems to show a successful façade | 1 2 3 4 5 6 | | | | 1 | |
| 4.10 | The project managers spend too little time managing the project | 1 2 3 4 5 6 | | | | 1 | |
| 4.11 | The project managers cannot lead planning processes that result in realistic plans | 1 2 3 4 5 6 | | | | 1 | |
| 4.12 | The project managers are unable to follow up methodically | 1 2 3 4 5 6 | | | | 1 | |
| 4.13 | The project managers are unable to inspire others | 1 2 3 4 5 6 | | | | 1 | |
| 4.14 | In our projects, we have periodical meetings with fixed monitoring procedures that always result in concrete decisions concerning progress | 1 2 3 4 5 6 | | | | 6 | |
| 4.15 | By monitoring our plans we are always able to see the need for corrective measures in time | 1 2 3 4 5 6 | | | | 6 | |
| 4.16 | When we are not able to take corrective action it is always the clients/users' fault | 1 2 3 4 5 6 | | | | 1 | |
| | Sum | | | | | | |
| | Average | | | | | | |

**Figure 13.1** Projectivity diagnostic (cont.)

| Problem area 5: Project execution and delivering results | | | | | | | |
|---|---|---|---|---|---|---|---|
| No. | Statement | Score | X | S | V | P | D |
| 5.1 | Due to our way of working and use of methods we are good at getting people we are not familiar with working together | 1  2  3  4  5  6 | | | | 1 | |
| 5.2 | In our projects, we use complicated methods too often | 1  2  3  4  5  6 | | | | 1 | |
| 5.3 | In our organization, everybody has their own way of doing things | 1  2  3  4  5  6 | | | | 1 | |
| 5.4 | Our projects are often subject to uncontrolled changes of scope, objectives and goals | 1  2  3  4  5  6 | | | | 1 | |
| 5.5 | Our projects lack formal start-ups | 1  2  3  4  5  6 | | | | 1 | |
| 5.6 | Our projects lack formal close-outs | 1  2  3  4  5  6 | | | | 1 | |
| 5.7 | Lack of documentation is a frequent problem | 1  2  3  4  5  6 | | | | 1 | |
| 5.8 | Insufficient quality control is a problem | 1  2  3  4  5  6 | | | | 1 | |
| 5.9 | We often deliver an inferior quality result | 1  2  3  4  5  6 | | | | 1 | |
| 5.10 | Our clients/users often report that they are pleased with the way we conduct our work | 1  2  3  4  5  6 | | | | 6 | |
| 5.11 | We often deliver a superior quality result | 1  2  3  4  5  6 | | | | 6 | |
| 5.12 | Our clients/users often report that they are pleased with the results we deliver | 1  2  3  4  5  6 | | | | 6 | |
| | Sum | | | | | | |
| | Average | | | | | | |

**Figure 13.1**    Projectivity diagnostic (cont.)

project or project working within the organization lie. However, these calculations are designed to focus attention, not calculate some answer, like the number 42, which will determine whether or not your project will be successful. Having undertaken the diagnostic exercise, you will want to spend as much time working on determining why differences of opinion exist and then to eliminate them, as you will spend trying to reduce the impact of areas of weakness.

In section 13.2 we describe the *projectivity diagnostic* (Fig. 13.1), which will help you assess the health of projects and project working within your organization. In section 13.3, we present the *success/failure diagnostic*, which will help you assess the health of individual projects, and to determine whether an individual project has been established in such a way as to increase the chance of success. The projectivity diagnostic may be conducted at any time to assess the health of project working. It may also be used in the start-up stages of an individual project to induct people joining a project team, who have not previously worked on projects, into project-based ways of working. The success/failure diagnostic will be used shortly after the start of a project to determine if the project has been set up in such a way as to ensure success. It needs to be conducted late enough that the project has become established, but not so late that corrective action cannot be effective.

## 13.2 Projectivity diagnostic

In Section 4.2, we introduced the concept of *projectivity* to represent an organization's ability to achieve its development objectives through project work. Organizations with low projectivity are unable to deliver projects effectively, and therefore consistently fail to achieve their development objectives. High projectivity is partly dependent on the relationship between all the people involved in development work, particularly the relationship between the project managers delivering change and the operations managers who have to operate the facility produced in the long term, shown in Fig. 4.1. The projectivity diagnostic is designed to help you identify how well projects are established, planned, organized, executed and controlled in your organization and, more importantly, whether there is a common agreement on these questions by all the people involved in work on your project, on both sides of the projects/operations divide. This diagnostic is designed to help you:

– Understand the culture and climate of project work in your organization
– Focus on problem areas that need to be dealt with
– Identify where improvements can be made to project working in your organization.

There are no right or wrong answers to the questions. For some of you it will be a worry if the responses are not what you expect. For instance, if the majority of people say they cannot clearly see the link between organizational strategy and projects, or if they think there are no established, clear principles and guidelines for project work, then that will be a cause for concern. However, this diagnostic is primarily designed to help you identify areas of agreement and disagreement in your project team (and we mean the project team in its widest sense).

### Using the questionnaire

There are 106 questions, grouped into five main problem areas. These are areas identified by Kristoffer Grude as those where projects consistently fail:[1]

– Foundation and infrastructure for project work

- Planning and estimating
- Organizing and co-operating
- Controlling and leading
- Executing and obtaining results.

However, when you give people the questionnaire to complete, you may not want to leave the questions grouped, but rather give them a sequential list, in order not to influence their thinking. The questionnaire asks people to rate each question on a scale of 1 to 6, where 1 = false and 6 = true. However, the questions are designed so that sometimes 1 indicates poor performance, and sometimes 6. This is so that people do not get into a routine of ticking every answer 4 to 5, but actually have to think about what the question is asking them. We recommend that you give the questionnaire to a wide variety of people within the organization:

- Senior managers representing sponsors, champions and customers
- Peer groups representing professional colleagues, resource providers, users and other stakeholders
- Project workers, representing designers and implementers
- Project managers.

**Analysing the results**

The results can be analysed in several ways, as follows:

WITHIN GROUPS

When analysing the results within groups, you will want to see whether the group:

- agrees on the organization's performance in all areas
- thinks that the organization's performance falls short in any areas.

These can be broken down, as follows:

1. *Agreement* In looking to see whether the group agrees on the answers to questions, you will be looking to the spread of answers. We have allowed space for you to record two measures of spread:
   - The spread, S; the difference between the highest and lowest score for the group against that answer
   - The variance, V; calculated as $V = \sum (x - X)^2 / N$,
        where: x is the individual score
               N is the number of people in the group
               X is the mean score for that question, $X = \sum x / N$.

Recording the answers in a spreadsheet, such as Excel or Lotus 123, will enable you to calculate the mean, spread and variance of the scores easily. We suggest you do not include the X, S and V columns on the questionnaires that you give to the people completing them; they are there to help you analyse the responses. Where there is a high spread, 3 or greater, at least some members of the team disagree about the response to that question. Where there is also a high variance, 2 or greater, there is fundamental disagreement among team members about the answer to the question. (A high spread but low variance indicates that only one or two members of the team disagree with the majority opinion.) The reason for any disagreement is worth exploring, question by question, and can be made part of the team-building process. We have kept the mathematics simple, because we are interested in qualitative comparisons, not quantitative results or statistics. This is a qualitative exercise; the numbers are just a way of helping to focus attention. You do not need to worry about such things as confidence limits, because they are not relevant here.

2. *Performance* You can analyse the results to see where they indicate poor performance. We have indicated the polarity, P, of each question, to show which end of the scale in our view indicates good performance (1 or 6). (Again we suggest you do not include this column on the questionnaires you give to the project team for completion.) You can compare the average answer to each question, X, to this polarity and calculate the difference, D, to determine where the team think the organization falls short in performance. A difference of 2 or 3 will indicate below average performance, and 4 to 5 poor performance. The reason why the team think the performance is below average or poor will be more interesting than the fact that they do, and exploring the reason can again be part of the team-building process.

3. *Problem areas* By adding the differences, D, over each of the five problem areas and dividing by the number of questions, you can determine which of the five problem areas the group considers are weaknesses of the management of projects within the organization. Now, because you expect some questions to indicate acceptable performance, an average difference of 2 or 3 over the problem area will indicate poor performance, and an average difference of 4 or 5 will indicate very poor performance.

BETWEEN GROUPS

You can repeat the comparisons between groups. Primarily, you will inspect the mean answers, X, question by question to see whether one of the groups differs from the other groups. Differences are quite likely between managers, team members, users and so on. Exploring the reasons for differences is more important than the existence of the differences. Similarly, you can inspect the overall results on the problems areas to see whether one or other of the groups views one of the problem areas as more of a threat than do the other groups. (Obviously, if all of the groups view one of the questions or one of the problem areas as a threat, then that will be addressed in the comparisons within groups. Here we are only looking for differences between groups.)

## 13.3 Success/failure diagnostic

In the early days of project management, the success of projects was said to be judged by whether they were:

- On time
- To cost
- To quality.

The first two of these were easily measured, and the first almost became the primary criteria for success of projects. When people talked about what they meant by quality, or how it should be achieved, they tended to fudge the issue. They talked about achieving performance or meeting specification as alternatives, without really qualifying what they meant by those either. As far as choosing project management methodologies to help achieve these criteria, then much of the time the only methodology proposed was critical path analysis. A recent survey showed that during the 1970s, 80 per cent of the papers on project management published in academic journals dealt with critical path analysis[2] (and many of the European National Associations have the letters 'NET' in their shortened acronym names, being a pun on network analysis and a network of people).

As for managing the second criterion, cost, people sometimes suggest the use of earned value analysis, based on the C/SCSC methodology (see for instance Turner[3]). And quality? Its management received no mention until books appearing in the 1980s and 1990s.[3,4,5] In the fifth edition of Locke's book[6] (which was the main text on project management in the UK for 25 years, from its first appearance in 1968 until 1993), quality is mentioned only twice in the index, and on both pages it says its management is important but nothing more. During the 1980s, people began to say that before you can choose appropriate project management methodologies, you need to decide what the key success factors are.[7,8,9] Pinto and Slevin[7,8] and Baker et al.[9] each had a list of top ten success factors. They agree on just the first three:

- Project mission
- Adequate planning and control methods
- Competence of the project team.

However, they do not agree beyond that. Looking at these three success factors, they can be reduced to:

*Step 1* Identify your success criteria and stick to them
*Step 2* Choose appropriate project management methodologies to deliver them
*Step 3* Select a project team with the skills to implement them.

Wateridge[10,11] looked again at the issue of project success and failure and derived the project health check that follows from first principles. He said that you should identify your success criteria, and hence select appropriate success factors, and then, and only then, select your project management methodologies. Wateridge started by trying to identify whether there is any difference between the success criteria used by people working on successful and unsuccessful information systems projects. He spoke to a range of people across many projects, and classified them as sponsors, users, designers and managers. He found the startling result that on successful projects people agreed about the success criteria, and the same criteria were mentioned across a range of projects; whereas on unsuccessful projects people disagreed (*there is nought common about common sense*).

- On successful projects, people said that the project was successful if it made a profit for the owner or sponsor
- On unsuccessful projects, sponsors said that they wanted to make a profit; users wanted the functionality they first/last thought of, with all the bells and whistles; designers wanted to deliver a sophisticated solution with sophisticated functionality; and managers wanted to complete the project within time and cost.

Perhaps with people in disagreement on unsuccessful projects, not only is the chance of success reduced, you also cannot satisfy everybody and so some will judge the project successful while others judge the same project unsuccessful. However, what contributes to the owner's profit? It is a function of:

- *Functionality* The solution must have the right functionality to deliver an income stream

| No. | Statement | Score | | | | | | X | S | V | P | D |
|---|---|---|---|---|---|---|---|---|---|---|---|---|
| | Part 1: Success criteria | | | | | | | | | | | |
| 1.1 | The success criteria for the project are defined | 1 | 2 | 3 | 4 | 5 | 6 | | | | 6 | |
| 1.2 | The success criteria for the project are agreed upon | 1 | 2 | 3 | 4 | 5 | 6 | | | | 6 | |
| 1.3 | I believe the success criteria are appropriate | 1 | 2 | 3 | 4 | 5 | 6 | | | | 6 | |
| 1.4 | The project should achieve quality constraints | 1 | 2 | 3 | 4 | 5 | 6 | | | | 6 | |
| 1.5 | The project should be a commercial success | 1 | 2 | 3 | 4 | 5 | 6 | | | | 6 | |
| 1.6 | The users should be happy | 1 | 2 | 3 | 4 | 5 | 6 | | | | 6 | |
| 1.7 | The sponsors should be happy | 1 | 2 | 3 | 4 | 5 | 6 | | | | 6 | |
| 1.8 | The project team should be happy | 1 | 2 | 3 | 4 | 5 | 6 | | | | 6 | |
| 1.9 | The project meets its stated objectives | 1 | 2 | 3 | 4 | 5 | 6 | | | | 6 | |
| 1.10 | The system should achieve its purpose | 1 | 2 | 3 | 4 | 5 | 6 | | | | 6 | |
| 1.11 | The project should be delivered on time | 1 | 2 | 3 | 4 | 5 | 6 | | | | 6 | |
| 1.12 | The project should be delivered within budget | 1 | 2 | 3 | 4 | 5 | 6 | | | | 6 | |
| 1.13 | The project should contribute to the organization's overall business strategy | 1 | 2 | 3 | 4 | 5 | 6 | | | | 6 | |
| 1.14 | There is a clear relationship between the project and business plans and strategies | 1 | 2 | 3 | 4 | 5 | 6 | | | | 6 | |
| 1.15 | The project team do not appreciate the important success criteria | 1 | 2 | 3 | 4 | 5 | 6 | | | | 1 | |
| 1.16 | I am confident the project will be a success | 1 | 2 | 3 | 4 | 5 | 6 | | | | 6 | |
| 1.17 | The project goals are clear to me | 1 | 2 | 3 | 4 | 5 | 6 | | | | 6 | |
| 1.18 | The project goals have been explained to the team | 1 | 2 | 3 | 4 | 5 | 6 | | | | 6 | |
| 1.19 | I can explain the benefits of the project | 1 | 2 | 3 | 4 | 5 | 6 | | | | 6 | |
| 1.20 | The project has an unrealistic completion date | 1 | 2 | 3 | 4 | 5 | 6 | | | | 1 | |
| | Sum | | | | | | | | | | | |
| | Average | | | | | | | | | | | |

**Figure 13.2**   Success/failure diagnostic

| No. | Statement | Score | X | S | V | P | D |
|---|---|---|---|---|---|---|---|
| | *Part 2: Success factors* | | | | | | |
| 2.1 | The estimates for the project are realistic | 1  2  3  4  5  6 | | | | 6 | |
| 2.2 | Project estimates are generally over-optimistic | 1  2  3  4  5  6 | | | | 1 | |
| 2.3 | Estimates were developed in consultation with the person allocated to the task | 1  2  3  4  5  6 | | | | 6 | |
| 2.4 | The project has been planned strategically | 1  2  3  4  5  6 | | | | 6 | |
| 2.5 | The project plans are understandable to all | 1  2  3  4  5  6 | | | | 6 | |
| 2.6 | The project plans are often changed | 1  2  3  4  5  6 | | | | 1 | |
| 2.7 | Our plans focus too much on the completion date and not on intermediate results/dates | 1  2  3  4  5  6 | | | | 1 | |
| 2.8 | The project plan effectively utilizes resources | 1  2  3  4  5  6 | | | | 6 | |
| 2.9 | I am happy with the plans and estimates | 1  2  3  4  5  6 | | | | 6 | |
| 2.10 | The project participants are motivated well to achieve the project objectives | 1  2  3  4  5  6 | | | | 6 | |
| 2.11 | Responsibilities are not well delegated | 1  2  3  4  5  6 | | | | 1 | |
| 2.12 | The clients and users know their roles and responsibilities | 1  2  3  4  5  6 | | | | 6 | |
| 2.13 | I am happy with the leadership shown by senior management | 1  2  3  4  5  6 | | | | 6 | |
| 2.14 | I am happy with the leadership shown by project management | 1  2  3  4  5  6 | | | | 6 | |
| 2.15 | Communication and consultation channels have been effectively set up | 1  2  3  4  5  6 | | | | 6 | |
| 2.16 | There is poor communication between the project participants | 1  2  3  4  5  6 | | | | 1 | |
| 2.17 | The users are involved effectively | 1  2  3  4  5  6 | | | | 6 | |
| 2.18 | Communication channels are poor | 1  2  3  4  5  6 | | | | 1 | |
| 2.19 | The project managers do not fully report project status to sponsors/users' project teams | 1  2  3  4  5  6 | | | | 1 | |
| 2.20 | Corrective measures are always taken in time when the project encounters problems | 1  2  3  4  5  6 | | | | 6 | |
| 2.21 | All roles and responsibilities are well-defined | 1  2  3  4  5  6 | | | | 6 | |
| 2.22 | All parties are fully committed to the plan | 1  2  3  4  5  6 | | | | 6 | |
| 2.23 | Resources are available at the right time | 1  2  3  4  5  6 | | | | 6 | |
| 2.24 | Procedures for handling priorities are adequate | 1  2  3  4  5  6 | | | | 6 | |
| 2.25 | Quality assurance is not a major aspect of the project | 1  2  3  4  5  6 | | | | 1 | |
| | Sum | | | | | | |
| | Average | | | | | | |

**Figure 13.2**  Success/failure diagnostic (cont.)

| Part 3: Tools, techniques and methodologies | | | | | | |
|---|---|---|---|---|---|---|
| No. | Statement | Score | X | S | V | P | D |
| 3.1 | The tools, techniques and methods available for planning the project are adequate | 1  2  3  4  5  6 | | | | 6 | |
| 3.2 | The tools, techniques and methods available for controlling the project are adequate | 1  2  3  4  5  6 | | | | 6 | |
| 3.3 | The tools, techniques and methods available for organizing the project are adequate | 1  2  3  4  5  6 | | | | 6 | |
| 3.4 | I agree that the tools, techniques and methods used are appropriate | 1  2  3  4  5  6 | | | | 6 | |
| 3.5 | The development tools and methods are sufficient for the project | 1  2  3  4  5  6 | | | | 6 | |
| 3.6 | The management tools and methods are sufficient for the project | 1  2  3  4  5  6 | | | | 6 | |
| 3.7 | The development tools and methods are poorly applied on the project | 1  2  3  4  5  6 | | | | 1 | |
| 3.8 | The management tools and methods are poorly applied on the project | 1  2  3  4  5  6 | | | | 1 | |
| 3.9 | The chosen methodologies stifle creativity during the project | 1  2  3  4  5  6 | | | | 1 | |
| 3.10 | There are established methods which are to be used | 1  2  3  4  5  6 | | | | 6 | |
| 3.11 | These established methods are being used on this project | 1  2  3  4  5  6 | | | | 6 | |
| 3.12 | I believe these methods are appropriate for the project | 1  2  3  4  5  6 | | | | 6 | |
| 3.13 | There are computer-based tools available for this project | 1  2  3  4  5  6 | | | | | |
| 3.14 | Computer-based tools are being used effectively | 1  2  3  4  5  6 | | | | 6 | |
| 3.15 | The project uses methods for assessing and managing risks | 1  2  3  4  5  6 | | | | 6 | |
| | Sum | | | | | | |
| | Average | | | | | | |

**Figure 13.2**   Success/failure diagnostic (cont.)

| No. | Statement | Score | X | S | V | P | D |
|-----|-----------|-------|---|---|---|---|---|
| | *Part 4: Skills* | | | | | | |
| 4.1 | There are the necessary skills available to plan the project | 1  2  3  4  5  6 | | | | 6 | |
| 4.2 | There are the necessary skills available to organize the project | 1  2  3  4  5  6 | | | | 6 | |
| 4.3 | There are the necessary skills available to control the project | 1  2  3  4  5  6 | | | | 6 | |
| 4.4 | There are the necessary skills available to develop the system | 1  2  3  4  5  6 | | | | 6 | |
| 4.5 | Project management are unable to handle fully the human relations aspects | 1  2  3  4  5  6 | | | | 1 | |
| 4.6 | Conflicts are resolved easily and satisfactorily | 1  2  3  4  5  6 | | | | 6 | |
| 4.7 | The project plan overestimates the skills and competences of the team | 1  2  3  4  5  6 | | | | 1 | |
| 4.8 | Project management is astute in dealing with the politics of the project | 1  2  3  4  5  6 | | | | 6 | |
| 4.9 | Project management is unable to inspire others | 1  2  3  4  5  6 | | | | 1 | |
| 4.10 | Project management is good at getting the project team working together | 1  2  3  4  5  6 | | | | 6 | |
| | Sum | | | | | | |
| | Average | | | | | | |

**Figure 13.2** Success/failure diagnostic (cont.)

| | Part 5: Execution | | | | | | | | | | | | |
|---|---|---|---|---|---|---|---|---|---|---|---|---|---|
| No. | Statement | Score | | | | | | X | S | V | P | D |
| 5.1 | A life-cycle approach is being applied | 1 | 2 | 3 | 4 | 5 | 6 | | | | 6 | |
| 5.2 | I agree with the life-cycle used | 1 | 2 | 3 | 4 | 5 | 6 | | | | 6 | |
| 5.3 | An effective start-up meeting was held for this project | 1 | 2 | 3 | 4 | 5 | 6 | | | | 6 | |
| 5.4 | The right people are allocated to the project | 1 | 2 | 3 | 4 | 5 | 6 | | | | 6 | |
| 5.5 | Project team members are carrying out appropriate activities | 1 | 2 | 3 | 4 | 5 | 6 | | | | 6 | |
| 5.6 | Resources for the project are selected well | 1 | 2 | ·3 | 4 | 5 | 6 | | | | 6 | |
| 5.7 | There are no problem areas during the project | 1 | 2 | 3 | 4 | 5 | 6 | | | | 6 | |
| 5.8 | I do not foresee any problem areas on the project | 1 | 2 | 3 | 4 | 5 | 6 | | | | 6 | |
| 5.9 | The management of the project is excellent | 1 | 2 | 3 | 4 | 5 | 6 | | | | 6 | |
| 5.10 | The project team has appropriate members at appropriate times | 1 | 2 | 3 | 4 | 5 | 6 | | | | 6 | |
| 5.11 | The project risks were assessed at the outset of the project | 1 | 2 | 3 | 4 | 5 | 6 | | | | 6 | |
| 5.12 | I believe that the assessments of risks are appropriate | 1 | 2 | 3 | 4 | 5 | 6 | | | | 6 | |
| 5.13 | The project risks are not being managed well | 1 | 2 | 3 | 4 | 5 | 6 | | | | 1 | |
| 5.14 | The deliverables are fully identified | 1 | 2 | 3 | 4 | 5 | 6 | | | | 6 | |
| 5.15 | The deliverables are quality assured constantly | 1 | 2 | 3 | 4 | 5 | 6 | | | | 6 | |
| | Sum | | | | | | | | | | | |
| | Average | | | | | | | | | | | |

**Figure 13.2**  Success/failure diagnostic (cont.)

**Table 13.3** Success factors delivering success criteria

| Factors | Commercial success | Meets user requirement | Meets budget | Happy users | Achieves purpose | Meets timescales | Happy sponsor | Meets quality | Happy team |
|---|---|---|---|---|---|---|---|---|---|
| Leadership | P | | | S | | | S | | P |
| Motivation | P | | | S | | | | | P |
| Planning | P | S | P | S | S | P | S | S | S |
| Development method | P | S | P | | | | | P | |
| Monitoring | P | | P | | | P | | | S |
| Management method | | | | | | | | | P |
| Delegation | | | | S | | | | | P |
| Communication | | P | | P | | | P | | |
| Clear objectives | S | P | | | P | | | S | |
| User involvement | S | P | | P | P | | P | P | |
| Management support | P | | P | | | P | P | | |

*Notes*  P = primary success factor
         S = secondary success factor

– *Time* It must be delivered at a time when the revenue gives an appropriate pay-back and net present value
– *Cost* Likewise.

Hence, the criteria chosen by people on unsuccessful projects are important, but only for their contribution to the owner's profit. It is the skill of the project manager to get agreement to the one unifying criterion, rather than have everyone disagreeing over which of the other, secondary, criteria are more important. The consultants McKinsey showed that the three secondary criteria are probably ranked in importance as shown above, at least on product development projects. [12] There is a very high gearing between functionality and income. There is no such thing as an 80 per cent solution; 80 per cent of the functionality gives none of the benefit. There is also no such thing as a 150 per cent solution. Too much functionality can also kill the project. There is a positive gearing between time and profit; small delays can cause a large loss in profit, as market share is lost, but less so than with functionality. Overspend can also cause a loss in profit, obviously, but the percentage loss in profit is often less than the percentage overspend, so the affect is the least marked. If this is the case, and functionality is the key success factor, then configuration management[3] should be the primary methodology used.

However, we do not want to commit the mistake of the 1970s and say one methodology should be used always, above all others. Hence, the health check contained in Fig. 13.2 (Success/failure diagnostic) first asks you to consider what the success criteria for the project should be. It then asks you what success factors you have chosen, what methodologies you have selected and whether the team have the right skills. Finally, it asks you whether the project is being executed properly. There are 85 questions in all. The health check can be used to do the intra- and inter-group comparisons as described above. That in itself will provide interesting conclusions about whether the project team members are pulling together or pulling apart. However, you can also use it to do consistency checks between the various sections of the questionnaire. Are you using consistent factors and consistent methodologies for your success criteria? You can make this analysis for yourself. However, Table 13.1 provides guidance on which success factors help to achieve which success criteria.

## 13.4 Summary

1. The projectivity audit can be used to determine whether the environment supports project-based management.
2. The project audit can be used to determine whether an individual project has been set up in such a way so as to ensure a successful outcome.

## References

1. Andersen, E.S., Grude, K.V., Haug, T. and Turner, J.R., *Goal Directed Project Management*, Kogan Page, 1987.
2. Gareis, R. (ed.), *Proceedings of the Project Management Research Workshop*, University of Economics and Business Administration, Vienna, December, 1994.
3. Turner, J.R., *The Handbook of Project-based Management: Improving the processes for achieving strategic objectives*, McGraw-Hill, 1993.
4. Cleland, D.I. and King W.R. (eds), *The Project Management Handbook*, 2nd edition, Van Nostrand Reinhold, 1988.
5. Dinsmore, P.C. (ed.), *The American Management Association's Project Management Handbook*, Amacom, 1993.
6. Locke, D., *Project Management*, 5th edition, Gower, 1992.
7. Pinto, J.K. and Slevin, D.P., 'Critical success factors in project implementation', *IEEE Transactions on Engineering Management*, **EM34**(1), 22–27, February 1987.
8. Pinto, J.K. and Slevin, D.P., 'Critical success factors across the project lifecycle', *Project Management Journal*, **19**(3), June, 1988.
9. Baker, B.N., Murphy, D.C. and Fisher, D., 'Factors affecting project success', in *The Project Management Handbook*, 2nd edition, Cleland, D.I. and King W.R. (eds), Van Nostrand Reinhold, 1988.
10. Wateridge, J.F., 'Delivering successful information systems development projects. Eight key elements from success criteria to review via appropriate management methodologies and teams', PhD Thesis, Henley Management College, 1995.
11. Wateridge, J.F., 'IT projects: A basis for success', *International Journal of Project Management*, **13**(3), June, 1995.
12. Dumaine, B., 'How managers can succeed through speed', *Fortune*, 1988.

# PART FOUR
# CASE STUDIES

Part Four presents two case studies on major change projects undertaken by large organizations to illustrate the application (or lack of application) of the principles in this book.

In Chapter 14, Wendy Briner, Tony Grundy, Frank Tyrrell and Rodney Turner describe changes in two insurance companies in the early 1990s. They explain the competitive environment in the insurance industry in the early 1990s, against a background of boom in the early 1980s, deregulation in the mid-1980s and recession in the early 1990s. Tony Grundy then describes his experience in helping to manage change in the Life Administration Division of the Prudential. He describes how they managed the change, and draws lessons from their experience which reinforce some of the messages in Chapter 3. Wendy Briner and Frank Tyrrell then describe their experiences at Norwich Union. They describe strategic changes at the head office and the experience of establishing a northern office in Sheffield, why this was done and how it was managed.

In Chapter 15, Kristoffer Grude describes strategic change in the Norwegian Defences, and the downsizing and rationalization following the end of the Cold War. In particular, he describes what followed the proposal to close an army base that provided a significant part of the employment in a central Norwegian town, how the army originally went about it, and how that was changed following a review by consultants.

# 14

# Case studies from the insurance services industry

Wendy Briner, Tony Grundy, Frank Tyrrell and Rodney Turner

## 14.1 Introduction

In this chapter, we describe two change programmes in the insurance sector in the early 1990s, a time when the financial services sector was a growth area for the application of project management. In Chapter 3, we said it was difficult to find case studies from that sector because writers in project management have tended to focus on its application in heavy engineering. We hope this chapter will help rectify the situation. The two programmes described are those implemented by the Prudential and Norwich Union. In the next section, we describe the competitive pressures facing the insurance market in the early 1990s, brought about by external changes. We then describe the programme of projects undertaken by the Life Administration Division of the Prudential, and explain how they were managed. In the final section, we explore two specific projects undertaken at Norwich Union.

## 14.2 Changes in the insurance market in the early 1990s

The late 1980s were a time of turbulence for the insurance industry. The early 1980s had been a time of boom in the financial services sector. There was an increase in the size of the market, with new premium income increasing by some 50 per cent. However, by 1990 the industry was beginning to come under serious pressure. Historically, the insurance industry has been accustomed to fluctuations in growth of premiums, changes in investment performance and variable claim rates. However, the changes facing the industry in 1990 were profound. The industry was subjected to several market influences, each of which on its own would have had substantial impact on the industry, but the resilience of the players would have been sufficient not to cause more than temporary concern. Their joint impact, however, was enough to destabilize the industry and cause individual insurance companies to rethink their strategy. The influences included:

- Deregulation
- The 1992 harmonization of the market in Europe
- Rapid growth of the pensions business during 1986–1988
- Increasing demands of customer service
- Falling stock market
- High claims.

## Market influences

### DEREGULATION

The 1988 Financial Services Act had several effects. Its prime purpose was to increase competition, so that the financial services industry then changed from having clear divisions between suppliers (banks, building societies, insurance companies), to a broader market, with financial services offered by a wide range of suppliers. This increase in the number of suppliers also led to an increase in the number of products available. Many suppliers ventured into services that were not home territory, such as insurance companies buying estate agencies with sometimes disastrous results. (When it was floated on the stock market, the Trustee Savings Bank used the money raised to diversify into many new sectors, some of which proved loss making. Abbey National, on the other hand, took a much more cautious approach, their ethos being to 'keep to the knitting', and this proved to have been prudent with the onset of the recession in the early 1990s.) Increasing the number of suppliers in the financial services sector has led to competitive pressures in terms of price, products and customer service levels. The 1990 annual report from the Norwich Union expressed the view: 'Parts of our industry are seemingly determined to compete for business at absurdly low and uneconomic prices'.

Deregulation meant that agents had to be tied to the insurance company directly, selling only their products, or they had to be independent financial agents (IFAs), able to offer an advisory service to customers. The Life Assurance and Units Trust Regulatory Organization (LAUTRO) was set up to monitor and control the independence and standards of agents and insurance companies. Conforming to these externally set and monitored standards created the need for internal revisions of policies and practices.

1992 COMMON MARKET

The free market introduced at the end of 1992 was seen both as an opportunity to expand the market for UK insurance products, and as a threat because other European insurers would gain access to the UK market. Joint ventures and alliances between companies in European countries have increased.

RAPID GROWTH OF PENSIONS BUSINESS 1986–1988

This was a bonanza period in the growth of demand for private and corporate pensions. Advantageous tax opportunities and an optimistic economic climate made this a very buoyant sector. This good news was somewhat tempered by the stresses and strains that were put on inadequate or ageing administrative systems. Both manual and automated systems were overloaded with the attendant problems and backlogs accumulated. Questions began to be asked about the efficiency and costs of administration.

CUSTOMER SERVICE

The 1980s were the days when the customer became king – at least in the eyes of the service industries. Following the Japanese and Americans, British industry began to see its activities from the customer's perspective. Customer choice became a reality, particularly where there was strong competition for similar products. Selling standard products no matter how unsuitable they were for the customers became an attitude of the past. The increasingly competitive financial services industry found itself having to view its customers seriously and view their operations from the customer's perspective. They became market driven rather than product driven.

FALLING STOCK MARKET

Black Monday, in October 1987, put an end to the optimistic period in the City of London. The stock market crash significantly reduced the value of investments. For life insurance reserves, this was seen to be the worst year in two centuries. As the recession set in, investment performance continued to drop. Companies who had invested funds in the property boom began to see this decline quickly, as property did not sell and prices dropped. Significant losses were made in general insurance which meant that companies were squeezed from both sides – investment losses and claims losses – and so they were less resilient; unable to compensate in one area by gains in another.

HIGH CLAIMS

Unfortunately, this period turned out to be one in which claims were unusually high. There were two major storms in the UK causing damage to property, coupled with floods and other natural disasters. The continuing increase in crime against motor vehicles steadily raised claims on motor insurance. This all took place against a background of increasing claims internationally, with major claims and record losses in Lloyds of London.

CASE STUDIES

Against this background, we consider how two insurance companies responded. We describe:

– The change programme at Prudential's Life Administration Division
– Strategic change in the Norwich Union
– Norwich Union's attempt to establish a Sheffield office.

## 14.3 Change programme at the Prudential's Life Administration Division

The first case study comes from the Prudential, in particular the business processing centre of the life insurance business, located in the Home Services Division. However, before we consider the project management processes, we first need to consider the context of the project.

### Background to the Prudential case

The Prudential has always been famous for the 'Man from the Pru', who called into UK households on a regular basis. Through its direct salesforce, the Prudential services a large share of the UK life insurance market through its Home Services Division. The administrative workload is serviced by the Life Administration Division in Reading. In the late 1980s and early 1990s, a major change was undertaken to make the Life Administration Division a more responsive, effective and lower cost organization. This involved transforming a somewhat traditional and introspective department of 2000 people into a flatter, fitter and faster organization. This was a major change project. The 2000 staff in Life Administration were employed in a complex, hierarchical structure. The objectives of the change programme were:

– To turn Life Administration from an average performing administrative centre into one excelling in delivering service quality, yet providing it at low cost, and so making it the 'engine room of the Prudential'

- To retain key elements of the culture which make Life Administration an 'attractive place to work'
- To effect this change while ensuring continuity of operations.

To reinforce the magnitude of this change process, it is worth considering the size of the Life Administration machine. The department services 15 million policies, handles 18 million items of mail annually and receives 1.2 million telephone calls each year. Prior to the change, this service was provided through a complex set of systems and administrative processes, and many tiers of management.

### Initial definition of the change projects

From February 1988 to April 1991, several change projects were begun:

- To devise a mission for Life Administration which could provide a vision for the other change projects
- To conduct a detailed market research exercise to learn more about perceptions of Life Administration
- To launch a major quality programme, aimed at creating a measurable change in the quality of the organization's outputs and processes
- To establish measures of performance, in order to give more bite to the business planning process; the performance measures included quality measures.

### Reshaping project definition

After initial launch, the change programmes were reshaped through a combination of improvement projects and workshops. An external consultant helped to devise a programme of projects, as follows:

1. Extensive discussions were held with Tom Boardman, the then head of Life Administration (as key stakeholder), to focus the programme. This determined the learning and behavioural changes required, and identified key strategic change issues and areas where specific action would be necessary.
2. Interviews were held with the management team, including both 'new blood' and 'old blood'.
3. Two-day workshops on managing change were held; run twice for 12 managers each time. All of the top management attended one of the two workshops.
4. Four improvement projects were devised for managers to work on as learning vehicles:

- Customer care
- Productivity
- Rewards and recognition
- Information systems, IS and strategy.

These incorporated similar issues to those which had already been addressed by the Business Unit Planning Head, and provided useful ammunition for learning and change workshops. (This was a good example of internal and external change agents working in close partnership.) The problem to be solved by each project was identified by the Head of Life Administration, with some help from external consultants. Each of the four learning projects involved group work, in workshops held periodically over a two-month period and each attended by six managers.

5. Finally, a two-day conference was held for all the management team, consisting of over 21 managers. During these two days, the output from each learning project was presented and debated. The conference was attended by Tom Boardman's superior, a service director of Prudential Home Service.

In mobilizing change, it is essential to link change initiatives and improvement projects explicitly, rather than hope linkages are self-evident. This enables change to be time-compressed. Otherwise, initiatives may just meander towards their goals. During the Life Administration change workshops, it was remarkable how much the speed of implementation of improvement projects could be accelerated by making them a hot-house for organizational learning. For instance, during the second two-day workshop, a new change project emerged from the analysis. A syndicate group had been given the task of analysing issues associated with the changing role of the first-line supervisor. From the top team's perspective, this area of change had been recognized, but had neither been seen as being of high impact nor extremely difficult to implement. The syndicate performed a force field analysis, identifying enabling and constraining forces. The external consultant was able to compare the output from the syndicate with a more adverse diagram drawn up for a more difficult change (generated by a similar exercise held on a change project at British Rail). Several of the managers were physically shaken as they came out of their syndicate rooms – clearly an insight into the challenge facing the organization had emerged. The rest of the management team were able, using force field analysis, to share the syndicate's vision of the change and to confirm that this appeared to be both vitally important yet uncertain.

The force field analysis also helped to confirm the management levers needed to move the change forward. These included defining the objective more tightly, and deriving a strategy for change which built ownership rather than isolating key stakeholders. By 9.30 am on the Monday following the second change workshop (held on Thursday and Friday of the previous week), Tom Boardman had set up a new change project based on this syndicate's output, called the Structure Project. This was to be managed by an experienced change manager, seconded from his line role on a full-time basis. This manager was still operating as a full-time project manager, still with principal responsibility for implementing the Structure Project, 18 months later. Other key insights also emerged, which led to improvement projects. For instance, although Life Administration had set up a project management process by late 1990, the linkage and dependence between related improvement projects were implicit rather than explicit. A second key task of the manager of the Structure Project was to map these inter-dependencies, to identify any overlaps and, where necessary, to reconfigure projects. Surprisingly, this took several weeks to accomplish; highlighting how important it is to identify interdependencies between change projects from the outset.

Three out of the four key improvement projects listed above were uncontentious. The content of the IS strategy project caused some discussion, and it is worth examining this to understand the underlying issues. This project focused on a change already in progress. This had a major impact on Life Administration, and there was a significant degree of commitment to a particular action. The syndicate group studying it highlighted that there were significant short- and medium-term problems in achieving the change milestones envisaged. However, these milestones were critical in improving operational performance. It was necessary to face the considerable difficulty in implementing change, both in organizational structure and supporting management style. Some of these changes may have been prompted, in part, by the learning project programme, and some by continuing development by the top team; change strategies are often the result of the intermingling of ideas.

### The Structure Project

The Structure Project was central to the change strategy of Life Administration and led to some major changes. Some of these are listed below:

1. The Life Administration structure was to be refocused to be more outward facing. At a senior management level, one manager was made responsible for liaison with outside locations and one with internal services. Both managers were from the original management team.
2. The number of senior and middle managers was reduced considerably, from about 25 to 12. This involved some redeployment of people to

other parts of the Prudential, which was preplanned, but still left existing managers competing for a smaller number of jobs.

3. There were also some major changes at the level of first-line managers, with about 100 people from the old structure competing for about 70 jobs in the new structure. This change was conducted in parallel with a rigorous recruitment and selection process, which included psychometric testing and counselling of all candidates. The new roles were more managerial than supervisory or technocratic.

4. At the clerical level, staff were required to become multi-skilled, so that they could work without having frequent contact with their supervisors to check what they were doing.

## Key lessons

From this example we see that in managing change through projects, there are several keys to success:

1. Define a clear and explicit strategy for the change, to which the improvement projects can easily be linked. This strategy needs to spell out what the organization is moving from and where it is moving to. It also needs to define the main thrusts of the change (quality, simplification, employee involvement, new technology, etc.), which will provide the key elements of the change.

2. Define strategic objectives for each change project, and show how these interrelate. Manage the interdependencies involved.

3. Define the key issues involved:
   − At the strategic level
   − For each of the main thrusts of change
   − Project-by-project.

4. Use workshops to share the outputs from change projects, and to test options and plans.

5. Use cross-functional teams to collect and analyse data, and to generate and test options.

6. Build ownership for the change projects by soliciting input from a variety of sources.

7. Manage stakeholders explicitly at each stage of the improvement project.

8. Ensure all outputs from projects are defined, and that these mesh with assumed inputs to other improvement projects.

9. Allow for the possibility of emergent projects crystallizing (like the Structure Project), rather than resisting change in project definition at all costs.

10. Analyse and evaluate the difficulty of change projects in terms of:

- Scope and complexity
- Duration
- 'Iceberg issues' (especially behavioural resistance)
- Fluid outcomes.

## 14.4 Strategic change at the Norwich Union

In 1990–1991, Norwich Union also faced the pressures for change outlined in section 14.2. However, they also faced additional pressures arising from their unique history.

### Origins

Norwich Union's roots go back to 1797, when Thomas Bignold set up a mutual association providing insurance against fire damage. The story goes that when moving from Kent to Norwich, he had been unable to insure himself against the theft of his personal possessions by highwaymen. This frustration stimulated his entrepreneurial nature, and some years later he set up a fire society, followed by a life society in 1808. Thomas Bignold was a man of wealth and philanthropic principles. His company was set up on a system of mutual guarantee. He wanted to: 'prepare and educate the public towards security and relief of suffering by mutual guarantee'.

### Norwich Union during 1990–1991

Since then, Norwich Union has had an unbroken track record; expanding steadily without major setback. Its 1991 annual accounts showed £20 billion of assets under management, and £4 billion of premium income. It is one of the largest life insurers in the UK. The mutual structure continues; Norwich Union Group is owned by its policy-holders, so there are no shareholders to satisfy. Policy-holders benefit directly through the bonuses they earn from their with-profits policies. There are few worries about share price fluctuations or hostile take-overs. Over the years, Norwich Union has become something of an institution in Norwich; the symbol of the Cathedral became the logo. It is an old, traditional, respectable and wealthy part of the fabric of Norwich, with a prominent, historical headquarters building in the centre of town. The weight of tradition is heavy in a city that is out of London, off the country's main arterial routes and dominated by agriculture. It is said that the people of Norwich have strong attachments and do not move readily away. Expanding demands for jobs in 1988 caused Norwich Union to recruit 1400 people, a large percentage of which were local school-leavers with four or more GCSEs.

Demographic trends showing declining numbers of school-leavers raised several issues:

- Would they continue to be able to find sufficient people in the Norwich area?
- Would they be able to maintain their recruitment standards?
- Norwich Union was seen as the 'last resort' by many school-leavers.

In 1991, one in ten of the Norwich workforce was employed by Norwich Union; 9000 people in all, based in 32 sites across the town. The local council and Norwich Union were concerned about the limits to growth of accommodation. Norwich Union centred its operations in Norwich. All that was outside Norwich were nationwide sales branches and a specialist unit in Sheffield.

**Company culture**

With the centralization of people and activity in Norwich, the company was demonstrating many of the problems associated with a functional, hierarchical organization, as outlined in Chapter 4. This manifested itself in a monolithic organization where no individual mattered, or felt it necessary to take a personal interest in anything. Backlogs of work built up, and the buck was passed from one department over the wall to another. Turnaround times were long and tracking the progress of a claim was labyrinthine. Work was oriented along product lines and not customer oriented. Customers ringing to discuss a query were often bounced around the organization until they chanced upon the right person. There was no single point of contact (see Case Study 14.1). There were many separate departments within the headquarters. Functionally, these departments were rather introverted, thinking and administering within their own world. Hierarchically, there were many levels, between management and staff and between layers of management. There were four levels of dining room, the times of sitting were fixed and the routine of who sat at what table and who ate with whom were often conformed to by convention.

---

## Case Study 14.1 No single point of customer contact

Rodney Turner has two policies with Norwich Union, an endowment mortgage and a personal pension. When he moved house in 1993, he had to write twice to Norwich Union to inform them of his new address, once for each policy. They have a separate customer database for each policy. For some time after he moved he continued to receive junk mail from Norwich Union (and other insurance companies), which was sent to his old address. They had obviously copied his address into a marketing database sometime before the move and had not updated that database when told of his new address.

On the other hand, creating a single integrated customer database is no mean feat. British Telecom did it in the 1980s. It took six to eight years and cost about £2 billion. Implementing the single point of customer contact was included in the change project, and substantially added to the complexity.

---

Independent Financial Advisers (IFAs) often complained about lengthy turnaround times and compared Norwich Union unfavourably to its competitors. Other insurance companies were able to deliver quotations within two days; Norwich Union often took ten. Furthermore, Norwich Union had a reputation for promising to do things and then not delivering. Reliability was becoming an issue. During the pensions explosion, Norwich Union did particularly well in writing new business. However, as a consequence the computer systems and administrative procedures came under heavy strain. Even more delays and inaccuracies crept in.

Many of these symptoms are typical of a company dominating employment in a town off the main arterial routes. As the main employer, there is little competition for good staff. People spend their whole lives working for the one organization, so the organization does not bring in new blood who bring with them new ways of working. The organization recruits people young and trains them in established ways of working, so old habits are perpetuated. They have no benchmark against which to judge their performance, because the employees have no external experience. Rodney Turner observed the same symptoms, but worse, at Vickers Shipbuilders in Barrow-in-Furness, in the middle 1980s. Vickers employed virtually the entire working population of Barrow, so the company ethos dominated the town. It was not until privatization in 1986 that the company felt any pressure to change, but when the change came it was far-reaching and effective.

### Norwich Union's financial performance

Norwich Union prospered during the boom, but by 1990 things were less rosy. Despite a fall in the investment market, Norwich Union performed well with 10 per cent after-tax bonuses distributed to with-profits policy-holders. However, Life Investment Reserves fell from £5.2 billion in 1989 to £2.6 billion in 1990, thereby recording the worst year in its 193-year history. High demands on claims through motor insurance, due to rising accident and crime rates, were compounded by the Piper Alpha disaster, and heavy flood and storm damage.

**Changes during 1990–1991**

In 1990, the chief general manager retired and a new group chief executive, Alan Bridgewater, was appointed. In October 1991, Alan Bridgewater launched a new mission statement and list of core values as follows:

The Group Mission is to develop Norwich Union as a leading provider of insurance and related services, principally within the European Community.

Our priority is to satisfy present and future customers through value for money, fair dealing, and high quality service

Our seven core values are:

1. Customer focus
2. Customer responsiveness
3. Dependability
4. Openness
5. Team work
6. Concern
7. Integrity.

However, managers were becoming concerned about the size of the company in Norwich. They were listening to the 'small is beautiful' message and were becoming aware that customer service issues were denting the company's image. With the recruitment pressure dominating, the general manager for Life and Pensions decided, supported by many senior managers, to move 1000 jobs in administration out of Norwich to a new regional office in Sheffield. The idea was to move as many people as wanted to go from Norwich to the decentralized office in Sheffield. The main aims, beside taking the pressure off Norwich, were:

– To move closer to customers, particularly IFAs, thereby becoming more responsive
– To recruit people from an economically more depressed area, stimulating a change in culture
– To establish the first of six independent business units as part of a policy of decentralization (in the event the recession meant that Sheffield was the only decentralized office opened)
– To use the same computer system on a decentralized basis, but also to clear up procedures and start with no backlog.

## 14.5 The establishment of a Sheffield office

**Life and Pensions Administration in Norwich Union**

About 3000 of the 9000 people employed by Norwich Union worked for Life and Pensions. The organization was a product-based, bureaucratic

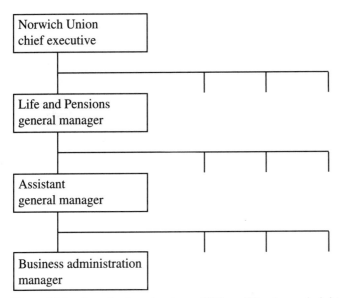

**Figure 14.1**   Organization structure of Life and Pensions administration in Norwich Union

structure, Fig. 14.1. Work was passed to Norwich by the branches, where it was sorted, mostly alphabetically, for distribution to administrative teams. A clerk received a flow of work and entered the data into a terminal, carrying out sometimes quite complex calculations. The main efficiency measure was how long work stayed in an in-tray. With about a million life policies, there was no sense of relationship between work done and a customer, nor any sense of priority of personal responsibility. When things were difficult, or information missing, work was passed on to the next department. Therefore, much of the work was delayed and frequently inaccurate. The corollary to this was that if an independent financial adviser or sales office tried to chase up a policy, it was virtually impossible to find out where it was or what had been done to it. Norwich Union had a reputation among its IFAs of not fulfilling its promises and giving a poor service in comparison to some of its competitors. The systems recording data were driven by two large Amdahl computers. Programming and support were provided by a computer centre. Products were being upgraded, or new products introduced, quite quickly, yet some of the systems were somewhat inflexible and were thus unable to keep up with the need for capacity support.

**The Sheffield office**

A feeling developed among senior managers that something had to change. The recruitment problem was seen as a particular pressure. The view was that about 1000 jobs should leave Norwich. Initial discussions about which functions should leave met with resistance; no solution seemed ideal. The debate lasted several months. Eventually, the idea was floated by the general manager of Life and Pensions that all functions associated with a particular geographical region should be moved out of Norwich. Senior management were happy with the solution and decided to proceed. A project was established with the main aim of: 'Creating a North East Region in Sheffield of business administration of all Norwich Union services in the region, in such a way that service levels are not compromised during the move'.

The project had the secondary aims of:

– Moving jobs out of Norwich
– Getting closer to IFAs and sales branches.

Initially, the idea was to relocate some people from Norwich and to employ new people in Sheffield. A project team was established consisting of several business administration managers. Overall control was given to one of the assistant general managers. Their initial approach was to scope the project and develop initial time estimates. The first estimate was for a completion date of April 1992. The general manager of Life and Pensions said that the project had to be finished by July 1991, even if just one person had been moved by then.

## Establishing the project

As the project was established, the team found they had to address several of the issues discussed in this book:

– What impact would the project have on the organization, given that it was a strategic change project? (Chapters 1 and 2)
– What planning and control systems would be adopted? (Chapter 3)
– What project organization would be adopted? (Chapter 4)
– What project team culture would be adopted? (Chapter 5)
– How should the project be sponsored? (Chapter 8)
– What were the risks?
– How should the project be established; what would be the first actions?

IMPACT

The desired impact of the project was to:

– Create a new working culture within Norwich Union
– Reduce employment pressure in Norwich

- Improve the level of service received by IFAs and sales offices
- Improve profitability by reducing error
- Improve sales
- Establish a new model for the organization, both in terms of new regional offices and new ways of working.

This was to be achieved without disruption of service to the customers; they should see just an improving service, not a hiatus of falling and then rising service. There should also be no difference in the method of corresponding with the Sheffield office compared to head office in Norwich. The business administration manager (North East Region), BAM(NE), who was the overall project manager had his own covert objectives:

- To disentangle himself from the crushing weight of Norwich
- To offer a far better service to his region, thereby getting himself noticed for promotion.

The project sponsor, the general manager of UK Life and Pensions, GM(UKLP), also had covert objectives:

- To move 100 staff out of Norwich
- To create cultural change in the organization.

Fortunately, both sets of covert objectives reinforced the overt objectives. Meanwhile, the administration staff just thought they were management games and would not affect them.

PLANNING AND CONTROL

A project control philosophy document was prepared, specifying how the project was to be planned and controlled. The plan was to be monitored against high-level, milestone plans. The plans were maintained on Project Manager Workbench, PMW, by a central project office. The project control philosophy document also specified quite closely the style of project control meetings to be held by project team leaders, and the reports to be produced. These meetings were to be held monthly, in both Norwich and Sheffield. Variances against plan were to be reported immediately to the overall project manager, the BAM(NE). The authors believe that the project control process was rather rigidly specified, allowing little variation to account for differences across the project. It rather reflected the bureaucratic, command and control structure of the parent organization that the project was trying to break. It is an interesting thought about whether the project should reflect the underlying culture, because that is the environment people are used to working in and are comfortable with, or whether it should reflect the culture you are trying to achieve.

PROJECT ORGANIZATION

The project organization was a small core project team, consisting of the overall project manager, BAM(NE), and the team leaders, who were other interested managers. Everyone else was to be involved on the basis of a coordinated matrix. Clear and strong sponsorship was provided as is discussed below, and there were strong links to managers of departments and groups providing services.

TEAM CULTURE

The work of the project team was to be mould-breaking, demanding and innovative. There would be considerable risk, and high resistance by people involved. This required a strong 'can-do' culture in the project team, with no place for pessimism or even diffidence.

SPONSORSHIP

The project required strong sponsorship at a strategic level, and this was provided by the GM(UKLP). The sponsor set clear success criteria, with several effects:

- People had a clear target
- There was less chance for argument, dissent or misinterpretation
- People were less able to sabotage the project with their covert objectives.

RISKS

The risks of the project were thought to be:

- A lack of volunteers for the move from Norwich
- The project becoming isolated from the rest of the organization, and so not contributing to overall cultural change within Norwich Union
- The quality of the solution losing out to time pressures to implement it.

In the event, the main risk was unforeseen – the recession of 1990–1992.

FIRST ACTIONS

The team's first actions were:

1. To hire a consultant to advise on the management of a strategic change project, and to help devise the strategic solution to the pressures for change.
2. To hold a series of awaydays, to:
   - Undertake a SWOT analysis
   - Scope and agree the project
   - Develop an outline plan
   - Plan work packages.
3. To recruit a personnel specialist, skilled in redundancy, redeployment and mobility.
4. Identify and contact the stakeholders (Chapter 8).

POSTSCRIPT

The project was successfully implemented, on time, cost and quality. The problem was that the recession reduced the pressure on staff numbers in Norwich, thus removing the main driver for the project. As result of the recession, Norwich Union centralized its operations, consolidating them back into Norwich. No other regional offices were opened, whereas six had been intended. The project's contribution was to initiate cultural change within Norwich Union; it was the beginning of the beginning.

# 15

# The Norwegian Defences: A case study in restructuring and downsizing

Kristoffer Grude

## 15.1 Introduction

The Norwegian Defence is based on a professional officer corps and general conscription of the rank and file. Norway is a long, stretched country, densely populated, with a long coast to defend and bordering Russia in the far north. Although the main defence is located in the north, the different garrisons and units are widely distributed throughout the country. The presence of the defence is therefore of material importance to many a small community in Norway. Over a period of 10 years, the Norwegian Defence is to be restructured to make it responsive as both a war and peace organization. This will have major consequences for the structure of the defence, the personnel and societies locally and nationally. The main vision is to restructure the defence as a more technology-based organization. This means a considerable reduction in personnel and units, in order to finance the investment in equipment and technology. Personnel is to be reduced by 3200 in five years, and twice that over the ten-year period. In the same period, the defence budget, in absolute terms, will be reduced. At the time of writing, the general impression is that this is a difficult task being well handled. A considerable amount of effort has been put into establishing the organizational and managerial prerequisites for managing the change, including the setting of guidelines for the process and the development of an information strategy accompanying this. The following principles and policies have been stated for the initiative:

1. The restructuring and downsizing should take into account job security of the individual. The main means of reducing personnel should be natural wastage and coincidental departure from the organization. However, measures encouraging mobility and voluntary severance are to be evaluated.
2. Cooperation and understanding are required on all levels of the organization and will be facilitated.
3. A clear division of responsibility between the Ministry of Defence and the Chief of Defence and his staff is essential. (In Norway, the military leadership is not part of the Ministry of Defence.)
4. Responsibility for the carrying out of necessary measures will be decentralized within the line organization.
5. Results-oriented management and control will be adopted within all levels of the organization.

Since the war, the Norwegian Defence has experienced stable growth in its budgets and the organization has adjusted to this. Within the organization, there is obviously major resistance to the downsizing plans. Similarly, there is major resistance within local societies affected, and considerable political lobbying is to be expected.

In this chapter, we consider the response when an army garrison was closed in a small town in the middle of Norway (called here Thorsheim). We describe how the closing was handled and the local response. We consider positive and negative factors of the approach taken by the Norwegian Defence to the closure. We then consider what lessons there are to be learnt; drawing general conclusions about the downsizing and restructuring process adopted by the Norwegian Defence and recommending five keys to future success. We then consider factors influencing the achievement of that success and obstacles in the way. We finish with a ten-point action plan.

## 15.2 The case

Thorsheim (the name is fictitious) is a small town in the middle of Norway, which has been a pillar of society for 150 years. The proposal to close the local army garrison (the first in a long list) resulted in a series of conflicts involving military leaders, politicians and local businessmen. This led the Ministry of Defence to doubt the defence's ability and willingness to carry out parliament's intentions; whether the necessary strategies and means were in place; and whether the right cooperative climate existed for carrying out a successful restructuring and downsizing operation. Consequently, they wanted assistance from external consultants to evaluate the situation and to advise on how to improve it, so that future similar exercises could be better handled. In particular, they wanted to ensure that necessary decisions were taken and carried out, avoiding conflicts of interest arising, in part, from the army officers' attachment to the local communities in which they were garrisoned. Problems encountered in Thorsheim were to be avoided in future closures by determining what went well and what went badly in that case and drawing conclusions for the future. This was done by:

1. Reading documentation concerning the restructuring of the defence in general and the specific case in question. This documentation amounted to 630 000 words, leaving the impression that most matters had been surveyed and recorded. The challenge was in turning all this knowledge into management competence, focus and action.
2. Interviewing political leaders locally and centrally, heads of the military and defence, army chiefs locally and centrally, trade union and local civilian employees of the army base.

### Problems encountered in Thorsheim

The investigation showed that many problems had been encountered in the closing of the Thorsheim base, which could have been avoided by a more structured approach to the handling of the affects of the change on the local population:

1. The process should have been initiated by a joint statement from the Minister and Chief of Defence. Instead, it was initiated by local army staff, resulting in lack of visible support from the top. Defence management had not issued the necessary policies and guidelines for managing the change, and those that existed were not satisfactorily incorporated into the organization.
2. Although there was a plan for the physical restructuring and down-sizing of the defences, naming specific units to be cut back, there was no masterplan for the change process; nor for the defence as a whole; nor specifically for the army (of which the Thorsheim garrison was a part). Thus there was no overall strategy within which it could be placed. As we shall see, this allowed mirage proposals which raised the hopes of the local population, only to then dash them again. Further-more, there was no management information system for planning and reporting, so financial, organizational and human consequences could not be monitored. What information that was issued was uniform (country-wide) and not tailor-made for target groups, or specifically relating to the needs of Thorsheim. This added to the communication problems.

3. Means for handling redundant employees were not in place. A support organization should have been established at the start. Perhaps there was to be no compulsory redundancy, but that only related to army personnel. The local support staff were not needed and were therefore redundant. The trade unions were neither informed, nor invited to participate in discussions. Lack of openness caused frustration and anger. Management and unions together were not able to handle the reactions and questions from people at risk.

4. The Ministry and the central and local defence chiefs had no common strategy for handling politicians, media and pressure groups. This created uncertainty and uncoordinated actions and contacts with stakeholders. The time from planning directive to action was hopelessly long, enabling different pressure groups to organize effective counteraction. The military leaders did not think in political terms in their dealings with parliament, local politicians, unions or media, and were incapable of deviating from a strict military plan. There was much political horse-trading (why Thorsheim before Wotansheim or Frigasheim) and suggesting of promises (maybe we can use Thorsheim for environmental forces and avoid closing the whole base), clouding the situation and creating unrealistic expectations.

5. Neither the Ministry nor the military leaders planned for the handling of the turbulence, due to a lack of understanding of the process and human behaviour. They expected people to follow orders.

### The way forward: drivers for and barriers to change

In planning the way forward for Thorsheim, the consultants identified much that was positive, thereby reinforcing the change taking place. However, there were also constraints upon and blockages to the change.

DRIVERS FOR CHANGE

There were many positive factors driving the change. The problems with closing Thorsheim were then a matter of the past. Local support and collaboration teams had been especially well received. The army's planning foundation and platform for cooperation were positively received by all involved parties. The unions had been involved and become positive team players. The local society had come to realize the impact of the presence of the defence on the local economy and seen that it was not particularly large, nor all positive. The promise of environmental forces was withdrawn, which enabled the local population to get on with planning for life without the military. Initiatives such as early pensioning and support for reschooling and education were put in place.

There was good local military management of the operation. In ·general, the defence has well-educated and competent leaders; although they lack the culture and competence for this kind of operation. The experience of Thorsheim was well documented and became a valuable input to future processes.


BARRIERS TO CHANGE

On the other hand, there were still considerable barriers to change in Thorsheim.

The culture of the defences was not supportive of management by projects. In addition, there was a lack of management information relating to the general programming of the restructuring activities (project management was lacking) and a lack of formalized financial control. From top to bottom, the defences was characterized by a 'briefing culture'. All progress reports were 'made for the occasion', by different people, and therefore lacked continuity, making it difficult to get an overview of the development. There was also a lack of formalized management control meetings, with Ministry and Defence managers attending, where decisions could be jointly made and progress monitored, making it difficult to create a feeling of joint ownership for decisions. A more purposeful, fixed and periodic management information reporting structure was required. In addition to these specific problems, there were some of the more classic symptoms of an operations management culture. The restructuring process did not have equal priority alongside daily operations for the Chief of Defence; the projectivity problem. That led to his losing identification with the management process. The leaders, overall, were remote, with the process being staff driven. 'Parade ground' management does not work well with these development processes. There was also a lack of continuity in top management positions, with rapid job rotations, leading to a loss of ownership and, worse, an attrition of valuable competence and experience.

The project definition and planning was itself also weak. This started with the Ministry and Defence managers having a lack of clear strategy and focus. The actual life-cycle stages of the project were unclear; for instance, it was not clear when planned activities were laying the foundation for the taking of a decision, or when they related to the implementation of a decision. There were comprehensive general plans, but these were almost too comprehensive. They were not based around a clear breakdown structure, and so were not very visible and did not provide a clear sense of mission for the project.

There were also continuing problems with the project stakeholders, involving differences of opinion between the interested parties about the need, means and consequences of the changes. Local politicians were still antagonistic towards the military command, but that may have reflected an historical tension between military and civilian society. There were also unsatisfactory guidelines for the use of central support organizations by individuals affected by the project.

## 15.3 Recommendations for future implementation

Following their investigation, the consultants drew some general conclusions about the overall approach to the downsizing programme, and made five recommendations for the future success of individual projects. They completed their report with a ten-point action plan for the immediate refocusing of the programme.

**General conclusions**

The general conclusions drawn by the consultants about the overall downsizing and restructuring programme, based on their investigation into the closing of the Thorsheim base, were as follows:

1. Norwegian Defence had produced a large number of reports concerning the restructuring programme, and most ideas had been put on the table in one way or another. Many good reports had been produced without the ideas being implemented. A major challenge for the organization was to exploit the valuable experience built up over time by working a coordinated way. There is a joke about a consultant being someone who borrows your watch to tell you the time. We see that here. The information the consultants used to make their report was all held internally. They brought no new information in. Many of the ideas in their recommendations were already held internally – although they had considerable previous experience of organizational development projects so were able to bring some new perspectives. There are probably several reasons why the Norwegian Defence needed consultants to read their own reports to them, including:

   - People internally were too busy with routine operational duties to take time to read the reports thoroughly and implement the recommendations
   - The information was held in different places and there were internal barriers (Chinese walls) to its internal communication
   - With their previous experience, the consultants were better able to interpret the information to form usable recommendations.

There was, of course, a risk that the consultants' report would go the same way. It was therefore important:

- That the consultants' recommendations were clear and simple and easy to read (reflected in the bullet point nature of this chapter)
- That the consultants would stay to help the client implement their recommendations (known as process consulting); this would obviously cost more money, but the value would not be obtained until after implementation.

2. Most tools, techniques and guidelines were in place. What was needed was their overall consolidation as support tools for projects. The planning procedures and documentation that had been developed were comprehensive and structured, but were more focused on technical activity planning. They took no account of the context within which the work was done, nor of the changes to people systems and organization within that context. The documents focused on technical activities and not the change process. The military and political leaders were not able to take account of the human dimension and the reactions of people as they were used to orders being followed. However, in spite of the good plans, monitoring of the process and the achieved results, especially at the top, was casual and poorly structured.

3. The people involved seemed to have confidence in the competence of the military officers and their willingness to carry out the actions decided. Overall, progress was more constrained by the culture of the organization than the competence of the people in it. Top management did not sponsor or champion the process in a visible or consistent way. There was no vision. The process was staff driven and delegated to non-commissioned officers – what was labelled 'parade ground management'. Someone commented: 'They don't seem to understand that this is not just any military operation, but the disruption of the lives of a great many people, military and civilian'.

4. From parliament, where decisions were taken, to the operational level, where action was taken, the chain of command was long and not suitable for a change process of this kind. Although detail plans were good, the overall strategy had not been communicated down this chain of command to the people involved at the bottom, in particular what the new defence structure meant as a peace organization; why a change was necessary; and what the rationale was behind the downsizing and resultant closures.

**Five recommended keys to future success**

As a result of these conclusions, the consultants recommended five keys to future success, as follows.

STEP 1

Create a clear and visible division of management responsibility at the top (Ministry versus Chief of Defence), with defined management meetings and communication lines with fixed reporting. This is essential if the process is to be managed effectively, and a team feeling and joint ownership to decisions are to be developed. In particular:

- The Ministry should develop and communicate strategy, not plan details (interestingly, that is what they would do in a war, leaving the front-line officers to plan the battles)
- Political and military management must be involved with and take ownership of the process and the means
- People demand to know who is responsible for disrupting their lives, and want them to publicly take responsibility.

STEP 2

Create a sustainable vision of the peace organization for Norwegian Defence, in both quantitative and qualitative terms, that can be communicated to the organization and externally to other stakeholders:

- People need to know what the new organization will look like, and why, if they are to understand and accept why certain measures are needed to get there (and why they are to lose their livelihoods)
- The vision must be accompanied by an overall plan, with clear delegation to the military leaders of responsibility and authority and the means to carry out the plan.

STEP 3

Create a visible plan and implementation process involving all stakeholders at the start of each project:

- This must comprise cultural and human aspects, as well as structural aspects, and secure timely and consistent information internally and externally
- It is also important that the process includes a thorough analysis of alternative solutions and their consequence.

STEP 4

Create a plan for qualitative and quantitative reporting of the process and the results:

– This will provide overall continuity and consistency of the reporting process, unlike the 'made for the occasion' reports they had used previously; made for the occasion reports reflect personal prejudices of the moment, rather than giving a true picture of what is happening.

STEP 5

Create a project organization to supplement and support the line organization, for all services on all levels, which will provide stability and continuity, and survive individual shutdowns:

– The organization is to facilitate internal and external cooperation, to take care of the rights and duties of individuals and to provide experience to the parties involved
– The project organization must have clear guidelines for use of the means to handle redundancy on all levels, so that quick reaction can be given to individual problems without going up and down the line organization – that is, the people at the coalface must be empowered to take decisions
– There is a long way from the top to the bottom of the line organization and hence there is a need to delegate authority and to empower individuals lower down.

**Ten-point, short-term action plan**

In order to make immediate progress, the consultants also recommended a ten-point, short-term, action plan:

1. Develop a detailed peace organization, specifying concrete job and competence needs for military and civilian personnel, for the whole of the Norwegian Defences, based on an agreed future war structure, and comprising definitions of personnel levels, running costs and finance requirements.
2. Develop coordinated plans for all services, and obtain all necessary decisions in parliament about the closure of sites and the reduction and moving of personnel.
3. Establish a project organization with necessary authority to secure speed in handling individual problems, and make sure it is based on stable and continuous management.
4. Discuss all measures with the unions and obtain agreement and involvement.
5. Establish a separate organization, a relocation service, with the necessary means to handle redundant personnel in the way of channelling civilian

job offers and other opportunities to them. Continuously transfer redundant personnel to this organization.

6. Implement as soon as possible, an accounting and financial control system to monitor the reduction of personnel, and other running costs, and investment connected with individual projects.
7. Implement a progress monitoring system for realizing the new defence organization and the relocation service.
8. Carry out a training programme in the management of change.
9. Establish a bonus system for cutting costs other than personnel.
10. Establish a plan and resources to actively improve information, communication and coordination between affected local municipalities and differing government bodies.

# Subject index

# Source index

# Project index